THE TOWN THAT VANISHED

THE TOWN THAT VANISHED

Ian Robinson

Published by Worktown Publishing

A CIP catalogue record for this book is available from the British Library.

ISBN 978-1-9996883-0-1

Book layout by Clare Brayshaw

Prepared and printed by:

York Publishing Services Ltd
64 Hallfield Road
Layerthorpe
York YO31 7ZQ

Tel: 01904 431213

Website: www.yps-publishing.co.uk

"For mum whose hand print will always be on my heart"

CONTENTS

PREFACE

U nusually perhaps for a first time author, I got the idea for this book at a funeral. In August 2009, my mother, Joyce Cain, died after a seven year battle with cancer. Whilst preparing a few words to say at her funeral, I was struck by how uneventful, modest and undistinguished her life seemed. Yet at the same time, I became aware of the fact that her life story was quite extraordinary.

Born in 1938 in the Lancashire mill town of Bolton, my mother was typical of her generation. With few educational opportunities and restricted by her social class, she might have been expected to live the whole of her life amongst the cobbled streets, cotton mills and smoky chimneys of her native town. She didn't. Neither did thousands of her contemporaries. Within fifty years, working class Boltonians swapped grimy terraced houses for green suburbs, potato pies for pizza, Blackpool for Benidorm, corner shops for curry houses and tin baths in front of coal fires for takeaways in front of televisions. Arguably, no generation has seen the world they were born into change so rapidly within a lifetime.

This book is about that transformation. To tell the story of how and why it happened I was gifted a unique starting point. Purely by coincidence, the year that my mother was born, Bolton was being spied on. This radical project was an offshoot of Mass Observation, a socially concerned movement which aimed to create a better understanding of life in Britain. To help them find out how ordinary people lived, its founders wanted to make a detailed study of a typical industrial town. They chose Bolton to do it, all those involved living and working secretly in an ordinary house in order to find out what it was like to live in one of Britain's biggest industrial towns – a town they called "Worktown". Due to their efforts, thousands of reports, surveys, newspaper cuttings and photographs were collected resulting in an unprecedented archive of material which is not only an extraordinary resource for anyone interested in Bolton, but also anyone who wants to know what life was like in any of Britain's industrial towns in the mid twentieth century.

Until recently however, little was known about this project even amongst native Boltonians. Indeed whilst preparing this book, more often than not I found most people had never heard of it; all the more surprising as many of those who professed to have no knowledge of the Worktown investigation have lived in the town all their lives. This may partly be explained by the fact that most of the books about Bolton planned by Mass Observation were never published. Only two ever made it into print: *The Pub and the People* first published in 1943 and *Britain Revisited* published in 1961, both focusing primarily on the work undertaken in Bolton. I hope therefore that this book will introduce the Worktown project to people who have little or no knowledge of it.

In doing so, I am of course indebted to others who have already trodden this path, the most recent being David Hall whose excellent *Worktown* book provides a comprehensive story of the project and the people who conducted it. Prior to its publication, *Worktowners at Blackpool* by Gary Cross and *Mass Observation at the Movies* by Jeffrey Richards and Dorothy Sheridan examined specific aspects of the Worktown investigation. In 1981, *Worktown People*, a book featuring a selection of photographs taken by Humphrey Spender, the project's principle photographer, introduced his extraordinary, haunting pictures of Bolton to a new generation. Latterly, permanent and temporary exhibitions in the town's museum as well as an excellent website have in their different ways helped to increase awareness of what took place seventy years ago whilst the term Worktown – Bolton's pseudonym – has begun to gain wider currency amongst poetry groups and local history societies as well as appearing in the title of a series of anthologies of contemporary writers as part of the ongoing *Live from Worktown* arts project.

For those already familiar with the subject, this book differs from previous ones because the Worktown investigation is used primarily as a frame of reference for exploring why industrial towns like Bolton disappeared. Therefore, it may be seen partly as a history of Bolton, partly what Bolton has become. For those reasons, I have also used other sources, most commonly the *Bolton Evening News*, the town's main newspaper, published histories about Bolton, photographs old and new, television documentaries, archive film on YouTube and even ITV's long running soap opera, *Coronation Street*, because its template were the kinds of terraced streets found in Worktown. In addition, internet forums, social media, personal memoirs, family histories – other peoples and my own – are also included in spite of the shortcomings of human memory and the tendency to see the past through the warm mist of nostalgia. I have used these other sources to draw a wider picture of life in Bolton when it was an industrial town and more importantly perhaps, because they support and occasionally contradict the conclusions drawn about it by Mass Observation.

Of course central to this book are the sometimes poignant, occasionally puzzling, often hilarious, but always compelling Worktown reports preserved at the University of Sussex. The town they describe was of such brutish dimensions and industrial power, to the Observers and the observed, it must have seemed that it would continue indefinitely. Its permanence however proved an illusion for the Bolton they witnessed then has all but vanished. As a native Boltonian, for that reason especially, it was a joy to pore over the thousands of reports about pubs, shops, streets and mills that I remembered so well. Whilst doing so, I was continually astounded by the contrast between the "then" and the "now". Outside the archive centre, young students ate lentil dhal, perused laptop computers and tapped away at iPhones while yards away I read about factories and football, pubs and preachers, and the all too evident desperation and poverty of 1930s Bolton. Although Worktown as recorded in the documents may seem to belong to a completely different age, astonishingly some people reading this book could be the subject of a report or maybe even feature in one of the photographs taken during the project.

Had she lived longer, my mother might have been one of them. Born in Halliwell a short walk from Bolton town centre, as a child she was a Rose Queen, she left school at fifteen, was married in her teens and had three children before her twenty-second birthday. The place of her birth, as well as the kind of life she led, made her by definition, a "Worktowner". So were my maternal grandparents. But unlike them, my mother moved houses several times, drove a car, ate regularly in restaurants, flew to holiday destinations, used the internet and enjoyed the sunset years of her life, in the southern Spanish idyll of Nerja, a whole world away from the long demolished Villiers Street where she grew up. Because it was my mother's life that inspired me to write for the first time, this book is dedicated with gratitude to her memory, making it above all else a labour of love.

INTRODUCTION
THE "SAVAGES" OF BOLTON

"The whole object of travel is not to set foot on foreign land, it is at last to set foot on one's own country as a foreign land."

G.K. Chesterton

A view of Bolton taken from the roof of Mere Hall.
Humphrey Spender

Bolton, 1937. Drab, grimy, cheerless, industrial. Intimidating. Red bricks, blue slates, brown cobbles; all blackened by soot. Grey skies, most days. Damp air, every day. One hundred and eighty thousand people; mainly mill workers. Fifty thousand terraced houses, two rooms downstairs and the same upstairs – no bathrooms inside, lavatories outside. Churches, plenty of them. Pubs, even more of them. Cinemas all over the place. Shops everywhere. One football team, one newspaper, one wash day, one industry, one holiday destination. One way of life.

Just on the western edge of Bolton, Davenport Street. With two rows of houses, a few gas lamps and a carpet of cobbles, it was no different to dozens of others that surrounded it. In the spring of 1937, new occupants moved into the house numbered 85, strangers to the neighbourhood and to the town they had chosen to live in. Although they spoke with unfamiliar accents, dressed well and were university educated, they tried to blend in, to be anonymous. If the other residents of the street did notice anything odd about their new neighbours, it was only that they disappeared into Bolton every day clutching notebooks and pencils. Keeping quiet about what they were up to was necessary and probably safer because they were only living in the grubby house in order to spy on the people around them. In keeping with the secrecy shrouding the project, the strangers gave Bolton a more anonymous name. They called it "Worktown".

The Worktown project had one purpose: to put the lives of the people who lived in a northern industrial town under a microscope. For over two years, wherever Boltonians went – the pub, the theatre, the football match, in fact anywhere they gathered in public – they were silently observed. All the while, those conducting the experiment were determined to be "unobserved, observers" to better discover what ordinary people said, the food they ate, where they worshipped, how they spent their money, which political parties they supported and also what they did when they went on holiday. No other comparable British town has had such a detailed, vivid picture drawn of how people once lived in it at a particular point in time. Bolton then, was a major manufacturing hub defined by its cotton mills, huge smoking chimneys, rows of terraced houses, cobbled streets and its working class communities. Seventy years later, it isn't. This book explains why.

The unique frame of reference the Worktown study provides resulted from the widespread ignorance about Britain's industrial heartlands in the 1930s. Despite Bolton's economic importance, its position as one of the country's biggest towns and the staggering scale of its textile industry, the way of life of its inhabitants was a virtual mystery to anyone living in other parts of the country. This state of affairs was not peculiar to Bolton as at that time hardly anything was known about Britain's working class people in general. However, Bolton was singled out to be the subject of a detailed study partly because there were huge numbers of industrial workers concentrated in one place; partly because several strands of social science came together at the same time, and – not least – Bolton became Worktown purely by coincidence.

The imperatives to find out about Bolton were a product of one of the most turbulent, divisive decades in British history. In the 1930s, with the worldwide economic slump affecting Britain's industrial heartlands, a growing number of middle class intellectuals became increasingly alarmed by the social problems being experienced by working class people. For them, it was indefensible to know so little about those who were after all their fellow Englishmen. This interest found expression in the documentary movement which aimed to redress the imbalance between the social classes by drawing attention to the widespread poverty which was regarded as just part and parcel of life in Britain's manufacturing districts. This resulted in a number of books that aimed to widen awareness of the daily struggles many working class people faced. Walter Greenwood's influential novel *Love on the Dole*, published in 1933, weaved its plot around the problems of unemployment in Salford just outside Manchester. About the same time, the author and playwright, J.B. Priestley, travelled across the whole country to write his classic account *English Journey* which included a considerable focus on the troubled industrial north. Most famously, George Orwell's encounters with the ghastly poverty found in Lancashire's mining communities resulted in his unforgettable book, *The Road to Wigan Pier*, first published in 1937.

Perhaps least well known amongst those investigating day-to-day life in the 1930s was a mercurial, young anthropologist called Tom Harrisson. Although born in Argentina, Harrisson was actually educated in England, first attending Harrow public school before studying at Cambridge University. Harrisson was an impulsive, capricious and energetic man who achieved considerable fame when still relatively young partly because when he studied primitive peoples, he chose to go and live amongst them. In 1932,

3

whilst living with tribes of head-hunters and cannibals in the Far Pacific, Harrisson was startled to find that the tribesmen had heard of Bolton because of the international operations of the Unilever soap manufacturing company; a company with its origins in the town. More significantly as it turned out, Harrisson was shocked to discover that the tribesmen on the other side of the world knew as much about Bolton as he did.

On returning to England, Harrisson contemplated looking at Britain's people with fresh eyes, the same way he had looked at the natives of the New Hebrides. Furthermore, he questioned why he and his fellow anthropologists found it necessary to travel to other continents to study primitive societies when so little was known about their own. But perhaps most important of all, Harrisson became convinced that the methods he had employed in the Far Pacific could be just as useful to study a different "tribe", the urban working class, who he thought were in some ways the "savages" of Britain. Given Britain's immense manufacturing base at the time, Harrison could have chosen any of its many industrial towns to do it, but he chose Bolton he later claimed, only because of its association with the Unilever concern.[1] Consequently, in the autumn of 1936, Harrisson travelled north for the first time to investigate Bolton's industrial "tribe" disguising his motives by working in one of the town's many cotton mills.

At the same time, other academics were thinking about similar socially minded projects. In early 1937, Charles Madge, a poet and journalist, wrote a letter for the *New Statesman* periodical exploring the role of myth and superstition in national life. Purely by coincidence, on the same page, a poem about cannibals written by Harrisson had also been published. Realising they shared similar interests, the two men met in London. Shortly after, a further letter appeared in the same periodical signed by Madge, Harrisson and another middle class academic, the documentary filmmaker, Humphrey Jennings. It formally announced the creation of a new national movement which would be called Mass Observation. Its founders claimed it would be dedicated to simply observing how people behaved as a means to better understand Britain's increasingly complex society.[2] To this end, they called for volunteers to become "Observers" and suggested a range of topics for investigation. Some were serious, such as anti –Semitism and people's behaviour at war memorials; others were more prosaic including the social significance of bathroom behaviour, beards, armpits and eyebrows![3]

The leaders of Mass Observation quickly established two main centres of operation with very different ways of working. The first in Blackheath led by Madge, used panels of volunteers from all walks of life to answer questions directly; the origins of the methodology widely used today in market research. The second in Bolton would be led by Harrison and involved watching people without them knowing they were being watched; an approach championed by Harrisson because he believed only secret surveillance would truly reveal how they lived. Besides the tenuous connection to Unilever, Bolton with its vast ocean of dirty houses, pubs and corner shops skulking under a pall of noxious soot was a natural target for Mass Observation because it offered an unrivalled insight into the working class gathered *en masse*; the very people about whom least was known.

When the project began, virtually all of Bolton's unskilled and semi-skilled workers – those who would be at the heart of the investigation – were in some ways involved in textile production, the industry which dominated Bolton's social, economic and political life. Indeed, taking any given working class family in 1930s Bolton, there was a very strong chance that both parents worked in a cotton mill and moreover, their own children would be expected to do the same in turn. Tom Harrisson wrote on seeing Bolton that its "power over nature is centred on cotton... The mills dominate landscape, life and atmosphere."[4] Harrisson was far from overstating the importance of textiles to Bolton at the time. Just as Sheffield was defined by steel making; St. Helen's, glass; Liverpool, its docks; Tyneside, shipbuilding; South Yorkshire, its coal mines; Bolton's character, pride and identity was embodied in its cotton mills.

In the spring of 1937, Harrisson came back to Bolton to begin organising his teams of Observers, all of whom would be joining him as volunteers. From this point on, Harrisson's project became known as the Worktown investigation; a generic name for Bolton because although it had many unique characteristics, it was thought to be a representative example of other similar industrial towns found throughout the country. Just as the town was given a pseudonym by the Observers, the people who lived in it were called "Worktowners" but in spite of the names and the clandestine methods used to gather information, there was never any real effort to disguise the project's links to Bolton.

Tom Harrisson explained the central principles that governed the way the Observers were expected to behave when making their reports:

> … observe, be quiet yourself. For our first two years in Worktown we did not make a *direct* interview with anybody. At least three-quarters of the work was concentrated in *describing* what observers could *see* and hear without doing anything to alter the situation (or the conversation). In this way we were able to penetrate into most corners of Worktown life….[5]

And the reports that were made demonstrate they did. Although Harrisson was variously described as arrogant, egocentric and a "bit of a bully" by the Observers who worked for him, he succeeded in getting them to record with no shortage of enthusiasm how Worktowners once held their teacups, what hand they used when playing games of dominoes, the way people lit their cigarettes, and rather more strangely, what they talked about in public lavatories.[6] Through this random, scattergun approach, Harrisson was striving "to see England as he had seen Malekula; to ask the same questions: how the dead are disposed of, how marriages are celebrated, how indeed the complex social structure of England works."[7]

It was an important time to try and find out, because in the 1930s Britain's social structure was creaking at the seams. All across Europe, totalitarian governments were threatening the fragile international peace. Closer to home, the Abdication crisis in 1936 had shaken the faith of the British people in the established order while the scars left by depression were still red raw in the manufacturing districts whose inhabitants had become all too used to degrading unemployment and poverty. Bolton had plenty of both which only increased the imperative for Mass Observation to find out what ordinary people were really thinking during such difficult times.

Whilst doing so, despite their best efforts to remain anonymous, the Observers working in Bolton were occasionally identified by their unfamiliar accents, erudition and even their motor cars; something few Worktowners owned or were ever likely to own. When they were identified, relations between the Observers and the observed were sometimes frosty. Apart from the obvious threat it posed to their privacy, there was some resentment towards what appeared to be southern dandies flouncing around amidst people who were enduring hard lives of which the strangers knew nothing. There was also some unease about the secrecy which shrouded the project. One Labour MP shared the misgivings saying "If I catch anyone mass-observing me there's going to be trouble"; an outburst which neatly summarised the mistrust of the mostly well-meaning people beavering away in Davenport Street.[8]

Undeterred by accusations that they were nothing more than nosy busybodies or worse still, untrustworthy, sinister spies, the Observers continued to make their reports of everyday life in Bolton. A substantial number of them – the "overheards" – are simply records of the conversations of Worktowners about all sorts of mundane, everyday topics. Their very ordinariness is what makes them so fascinating as they provide a rare glimpse of how working class people lived, their daily concerns, the things that mattered to them, and their relationships with one another and their home town in what was still an industrialised Britain. A conversation in a pub in 1938 gives a flavour of the kind of social interactions being recorded: "'Is he wed?' 'Ay' 'Then I mentioned his wife. She's carryin.' The tall one told them how 'our kid' had been injured at work by a 'ot steam pipe' which 'shot up in the fuckin' air and fell on 'is head. Up to then he never had a day off.'"[9]

Neither did the Observers, for similar reports eventually numbered in their thousands. Little wonder when there were up to sixty Observers at peak times, all coming and going from Davenport Street, each feverishly writing reports in return for minimal board and lodgings. Soon, the bug-ridden house became cluttered up with boxes overflowing with their reports as well as letters, newspaper cuttings, pamphlets and any other paraphernalia which it was thought might provide some kind of insight into life in Worktown. Although the subjects covered in the documents were unfocused and idiosyncratic – even the Observers sometimes doubted the usefulness of what they were doing – the result is a vivid, evocative and detailed picture of life in Bolton just before the Second World War.

To supplement the growing mountain of written documentation, Tom Harrisson also invited several artists – most notably William Coldstream and Julian Trevalyan – to join him to produce a more subjective response to Worktown. This initiative resulted in a number of paintings and collages of Bolton which are considered to be of international importance mainly due to their unerring emphasis on the lives of ordinary, working people.

At the same time as the artists were making a visual record of Worktown, Harrisson also encouraged Humphrey Spender, a talented young photographer, to join the project in Bolton to take photographs in secret. Spender was another product of the upper middle class who later admitted that he had been both "repulsed and fascinated" by Bolton's working class people in equal measure. Unsurprisingly, on first arriving in the town, Spender claimed to find the Worktowners "quite frightening" but nevertheless, he furtively photographed them, risking the outrage of people he had been brought up to fear.[10]

What makes Spender's photographs so unusual and arresting was his insistence on only photographing people *who did not know* they were being photographed. As a result he produced an extraordinarily intimate portrait of working class people and their daily life; a group it should be stressed that had previously been dismissed as being of little interest to anyone else. With the passage of time, his Worktown photographs have assumed an even greater importance as Spender produced a visual record of a way of life and a town which disappeared within the lifetimes of the people he photographed.

The story of their disappearance is at the heart of this book. Whilst discussing various aspects of worktown, there are several themes that inevitably recur from chapter to chapter. In the mid years of the twentieth century, Bolton was a more homogenous town, home to a substantial urban working class that shared a particular way of life, one that was still largely a product of the Victorian age. Most adult Worktowners tended to adopt the same values, had similar religious beliefs, and usually held one of two political convictions (either Conservative or Labour) because the vast majority of them had been born in Bolton, usually began work when they were teenagers, expected to marry at a relatively young age, were generally family orientated, enjoyed and sought out communal solidarity with other local people, wore similar clothes, ate the same type of food, worked in the cotton industry, and earned roughly the same amount of money.

Their children however – those who became young adults after the Second World War ended –began to break with this established way of life. Of chief importance in this extraordinary rupture with the previous generation was the hitherto unimaginable growth in home ownership, a more diverse job market, the seemingly unstoppable momentum of car ownership, the growth of a consumer society which resulted from rising prosperity, and of course the influence of television. All these would profoundly transform the way working class people lived and worked and greatly affected the visual appearance of Bolton as well.

At the same time, immigration into Britain which was at first concentrated in the old manufacturing districts began to affect which parts of Bolton people lived in, employment opportunities, places of worship and even the most popular places to eat. Over a relatively short period however, the labour intensive factory work the first immigrants came to do disappeared for the immigrants and indigenous Boltonians alike. This loss was at first mitigated by a widening of educational opportunity which over time led to a greater social mobility for many of those who had been born into what were originally working class families. As a result the old indicators of the middle class – salaries, bank accounts, pensions, cars, telephones, university education, foreign travel and of course home ownership – became quite normal for many contemporary Boltonians who it is fair to say gradually joined the ranks of the middle class, leaving their roots in Worktown far behind. Another theme explored in this book.

The Worktown project eventually petered out when the Second World War began. As the war progressed, the work in Bolton was abandoned and Mass Observation became more closely allied with government objectives on the home front – a fundamental shift in emphasis. After the hostilities ceased, the Bolton investigation was never fully revived most likely because Tom Harrisson simply lost interest in it. He did however return to Bolton briefly at the end of the 1950s which resulted in the publication of *Britain Revisited* – one of only a handful of Mass Observation's planned books that actually made it into print. Harrisson's last book about Worktown explored in what ways if any Bolton had changed since the original investigation; again another important reference point used throughout this book to explore what has happened to the town since.

One of the most striking things Harrisson discovered on returning to Bolton was how little the town had changed in the intervening years. The stability, continuity and "unchange" (Harrisson's rather odd word) that characterised Bolton in the mid years of the twentieth century helps explain why there are still significant numbers of relatively young Boltonians who vividly remember Worktown and its way of life – part of the story in this book because although the original Worktown investigation chronicled Bolton in the late 1930s, for thousands at present only contemplating late middle age, in appearance, function and social culture, Worktown was also the town they grew up in during the 1960s and 1970s. Moreover, it was this generation that experienced what were arguably Worktown's best years due to the fact that in the aftermath of the Second World War, working class people made substantial social and economic progress because there was some redistribution of wealth, a long period of full employment and the reassurance of social security for all following the founding of the welfare state.

In the early 1980s, Humphrey Spender briefly returned to Bolton; to all intents and purposes, the last meaningful contribution to the original Worktown investigation. Spender's final visit to the town was the subject of *Return Journey*, a documentary television programme featuring the photographs he had taken in Bolton. Whereas his 1930s photographs show a purposeful, powerful, vital, industrial town, *Return Journey* shows Spender striding past disused mills and lifeless streets on his way to visit Davenport Street again. When Spender arrived at the house he had lived in forty years before, like the rest of the surrounding streets, it was boarded up and awaiting demolition. Evidently by then – physically, economically and culturally – Worktown was rapidly disappearing.

The speed of its disappearance in the last quarter of a century renders the Worktown investigation even more important. Whatever motives first brought Tom Harrisson to Davenport Street – whether intellectual curiosity, an interest in the politics of the Left or, equally possible, a touch of Oxford dilettantism – his investigation produced an archive of some 40,000 documents and over 800 photographs. They are of unparalleled importance because they show Bolton at a pivotal point in its history for had they but known it, Harrisson's teams of Observers were witnessing the slow fading of the light in a departing time. As the number of the original Worktowners inevitably dwindles with each passing year, the documents collected in Davenport Street become increasingly more poignant because individually and collectively, they bear witness to innumerable ordinary lives spent amongst the mills and chimneys, the terraced houses and the gas lamps of a once proud northern mill town.

For the generations who knew Bolton when it was still Worktown, lived in it and loved it, this is the story of how and why *their* town vanished.

THE BOLTON ODEON

"Primus inter pares: noun a first amongst equals; the senior or representative member of a group."

Cinema goers on the steps of Bolton Odeon.
Humphrey Spender

As Tom Harrisson was settling down in Davenport Street, one of Bolton's most fondly remembered buildings was nearing completion. Costing an estimated £60,000 to build, the Bolton Odeon was about to become the latest addition to over 200 cinemas already owned by Oscar Deutsch, a Jewish Hungarian immigrant's son from Birmingham. Although he named his cinemas after ancient theatrical arenas, Deutsch's publicists claimed with customary hyperbole that the word ODEON stood for "Oscar Deutsch Entertains Our Nation." As Deutsch's new Odeon began to tower above Bolton's bus station, the people living in one of the country's gloomiest towns started to see for themselves that whenever Oscar entertained, it was only in buildings of breath-taking style and panache.

The unique appearance of the Odeon cinemas was an important part of their enduring appeal. They were designed by the Weedon Partnership, English architects who were commissioned to create a distinct, contemporary image for Deutsch's cinema chain. In the heart of Bolton, W. Calder Robson, one of Weedon's youngest architects did that and more delivering a radical, dramatic building that shone like a beacon in the shadow of the town hall clock.

Being large enough to occupy the whole parcel of land sandwiched between Black Horse Street and Back Spring Gardens, Bolton's Odeon seemed to soar above the pavement, its enormous pale frontage only relieved by six windows which thrust upwards from a streamlined canopy. Beneath the canopy, curved walls of shimmering black tiles framed the six steps that led up to the doors. With an ocean of cream, green and black tiles, the Odeon's facade provided a startling contrast to the soot-drenched buildings that surrounded it. If its futuristic appearance wasn't exhilarating enough, neon up-lighting bathed the whole cinema in a soft pastel glow at night with only the word Odeon picked out in red fluorescent letters.

In keeping with Deutsch's vision for his chain, the Bolton Odeon was as ultra-modern inside as it was outside with its patrons treated to an ambience that embarrassed the town's other cinemas. The foyer came complete with geometric patterns on the floor, potted plants scattered all around and a streamlined box office which looked like an American tram car. Several curvilinear settees adorned the space complemented by large circular light fittings which hovered like flying saucers above the patrons queuing at the box office.

After buying their tickets, a luxurious auditorium awaited whereupon the film goers' attention was immediately drawn to an enormous screen glowing under the expanse of the proscenium arch. On either side of the screen, honeycombed walls flowed towards this focal point creating "a sweeping ellipse" which drew the eye to the stage beneath the screen. In comparison with many earlier cinemas, the interior decoration in the auditorium was exquisitely restrained, the lower walls finished in a burr walnut, whilst above them the panels were fluted and painted in pale gold.

Fittingly for one of the country's biggest towns, the Bolton Odeon on completion became the largest cinema in Deutsch's chain and also one of the biggest in the whole country. Its foremost position didn't last long however, as Bradford got an even bigger Odeon within a year which in turn was dwarfed by yet another which opened in Blackpool in 1939. Nevertheless, Bolton's Odeon could still accommodate some 2534 cinemagoers with an impressive 936 seats in the balcony (or "circle") alone. Unusually for a cinema at the time, all the seats were identical in terms of their size and comfort. Furthermore, each of the Odeon's customers could expect the same standard of seat regardless of the price of admission; an innovation that gave its owners the opportunity to boast to their patrons that "only the actual position of the seat governed the price".

Such attention to detail was a feature of the whole cinema. The much admired seats and carpet were both finished in red; the eventual choice of colour if the Odeon's breathless publicity brochure is to be believed only being made after "many hours … devoted to the careful study of the colour scheme." Adding to the sophistication, the lighting deployed throughout the cinema was concealed; an attractive detail so characteristic of the period that extended to the soon-to-be-opened cafe as well.[1]

Leslie Halliwell, born in Bolton in 1929 and later a well-respected film critic and compiler of the *Filmgoers Companion* wrote about the impact on his younger self of seeing the Odeon for the first time:

My first impression, after I got my breath back, was of rounded corners everywhere, without a right-angle in sight. The immensity of the red velour curtains; the curiously concealed lighting; the great golden honeycomb grills on each side of the screen; the green octagonal clocks in which the letters THE ODEON took the place of numerals; all these played their part in the magnificence of that massive decorated space.[2]

He continued:

> … the design was in fact simple to the point of austerity. There was nothing that could catch dust. The foyers and corridors were laid with rubber tiling in green and black abstract designs with just a touch of red; and even the toilets had a smooth severity which counterpointed the general grandeur. Henceforth Bolton's older halls with their plaster canopies and decorated pillars would seem tawdry indeed.[3]

To further increase the enjoyment of patrons, live music was played between films on a huge Compton organ that rose elegantly from a pit below the screen. In a voguish nod to the glamour of the period, this magnificent beast was framed on each side by a console of illuminated, reeded glass which changed colours as it was played. In keeping with the prestige associated with Deutsch's cinemas, the first musician privileged to play the organ in Bolton's Odeon as it ascended to the stage was Mr Harry Croft of the Grand Theatre in London.

On completion, the Odeon became Bolton's premier cinema. It was however, just one of an impressive array of "picture palaces" already operating in Worktown. In 1938, Mass Observation recorded that there were forty-seven cinemas within a five-mile radius of the boundaries of Bolton.[4] Such numbers were common in towns and cities all across the country – the result of the growth of an industry that in its early days at least, catered mainly for a working class clientele. Cinema's growth spurt in the early years of the twentieth century meant by 1916, there were some 5000 purpose-built picture houses in Britain busily entertaining audiences with silent films before the initial novelty of watching moving images began to give way to the development of a new art form.[5]

Between the wars, technological innovations like sound, first used in *The Jazz Singer* in 1927, and later films made in colour, did much to broaden the appeal of films and consequently the number of people wanting to see them. The growing audiences of the 1930s – arguably cinema's golden age – led to the building of ever bigger and grander cinemas. To fill them, 600–700 films were released in Britain each year. During the same decade, there were close to a billion admissions to British cinemas taken as a whole; an extraordinary figure confirming that cinema was the country's most popular paid for leisure activity in the years before the Second World War.[6] With cinema of such importance to working class people, not surprisingly the people of Bolton – an overwhelmingly working class town in the 1930s – embraced cinema eagerly and its development in the town might be seen as a microcosm of cinema-going in the industrial north.

Bolton's cinema story began after a local man, Fenton Cross, brought "living pictures" to the Temperance Hall (later renamed The Rialto) on St George's Road; to all intents and purposes the town's first cinema. By 1914, the *Kinematograph Yearbook* recorded that there were eight cinemas in Bolton.[7] As cinema gathered momentum in the interwar period virtually every town, suburb and major new housing development in the country gained one or two cinemas and Bolton was no exception with the number of its cinemas growing year-on-year. As bigger audiences and rising customer expectations influenced cinema design, some older cinemas in British towns were modernised or virtually rebuilt whilst a number of the more outmoded and surplus cinemas from the first wave of cinema building disappeared altogether; a pattern seen in Bolton with its earliest cinemas, the Beehive on Bark Street, the Paragon on Bradshawgate, the Ideal on Silverwell Lane and the Princess on Churchgate all going out of business before the end of the 1920s.

Despite losing some of its cinemas, Bolton was still an enticing prospect for cinema lovers. Indeed Halliwell wrote in the 1930s that "it seemed … sometimes apart from its excellent shopping facilities, the town centre served no purpose except to hold them all together."[8] When the Worktown investigation began, there were over twenty cinemas within Bolton's boundaries proper. There was a distinct hierarchy amongst them determined by their relative comfort, the seating capacity they could offer, variables in the price of admission and if urban myth is to be believed, any bugs or even rats said to live in some of them.

The most prestigious cinemas were the "first run" cinemas which as the name suggests, got to show the latest films when they were distributed to provincial cinemas after being premiered in the country's major cities. After their first run, films generally returned about four weeks later for a "second run" usually as part of a double feature in the next tier of the town's cinemas. This left the third, fourth and even fifth run cinemas to screen films that had already been shown several times. Obviously this reduced the price the lesser cinemas could charge for a ticket as interest waned in films which had already been screened in the town several times.

Worktown's principle first run cinema – before the arrival of the Odeon – was the Capitol on Churchgate; a relatively large cinema with an impressive 1642 seats. The other first run cinemas were the Hippodrome on Deansgate, a grand Edwardian edifice with 1086 seats; the Queens with nearly fifteen hundred seats, at one time considered the town's plushest cinema handily located by the train station; the previously noted Rialto, advertising itself as "the cinema where you might meet your friends" with plenty of room for them apparently as it boasted some 1147 seats; and lastly, also on Churchgate, the Theatre Royal with seventeen hundred seats which as its name implies began life as a variety theatre before the arrival of cinema caused a slump in audiences necessitating its conversion to a cinema in the 1920s. With its size and prestige, the Odeon was a first run cinema from the beginning as was the similarly imposing Lido cinema on Bradshawgate which also opened in the same year as the Odeon.

All the first run cinemas could be found in, or at least very close to the town centre. Perhaps surprisingly given the recent clamour for a new cinema to be built in the heart of Bolton, many of Worktown's cinemas were not. The allure of the silver screen extended as far as Crompton Way where the Crompton Cinema, advertising itself as "The Superb Cinema", offered filmgoers a "large free car park" as early as 1937. Despite seating for twelve hundred patrons and the amenities, it always lacked the Odeon's style having a somewhat "disappointing, unimaginative foyer" according to Halliwell even though both cinemas were built at roughly the same time. Another large cinema, the Majestic, with 1913 seats was located on St. Helen's Road whilst the much smaller Belle Cinema with just 580 seats (reduced to 470 seats in 1937) could be found at the bottom of Belmont Road. These three cinemas were well over a mile or more from the centre of Bolton.

Closer to the town centre but not in it as such were several sizeable cinemas located on the main roads into and out of Bolton. Deane Road, a major route leading away to the west had two cinemas, the Regent with 944 seats and the Windsor (originally the Plaza) which was a Methodist chapel before its pews were replaced with over 600 seats. Heading further southwest into Daubhill, the Majestic cinema could seat some sixteen hundred patrons. To the north of the town centre, the much shorter St. George's Road alone boasted two cinemas; the previously noted Rialto and the New Royal Cinema with its 761 seats housed incongruously in a mock black and white half-timbered building (currently HW musical instrument shop) – both cinemas just yards from Mass Observation's Bolton headquarters.

In addition, there were also several cinemas that remained profitable even without the considerable advantages of town centre locations or frontages on main roads. These unexceptional picture houses included the Empire on Howard Street with just 472 seats and a rather down-at-heel appearance which unsurprisingly showed films on their fifth run in the town, the Ritz on Fletcher Street with some 750 seats, the Carlton on Mount Street with a thousand seats (always called "the Mount" by local people) and the Gem, a fourth run cinema with 1050 seats located on Shepherd's Cross Street. This group of cinemas were unflatteringly called "fleapits" or "bug huts" by local people although alleged insects aside, they still retain the affection of Boltonians old enough to remember them.

Other cinemas also demonstrate the wide variety of film-watching experience in Worktown. The Embassy on Deansgate with 600 seats – advertised itself variously as "The modern cinema" and more enticingly "Bolton's armchair cinema" at a time when not all Worktowners had a decent one to sit on at home; the Palace, just off Bury Road was another converted chapel which became a medium-sized cinema with over 1000 seats; the slightly larger but "oddly dark and sinister" Palladium with 1238 seats on Bridge Street, and one of the largest in Bolton, the 2380 capacity Regal located on Spa Road which rather neatly began life as a roller skating rink (The Olympic) and ended as a roller skating rink (The Nevada) with a period as a cinema sandwiched in between. Altogether, at the time of the Worktown investigation, Bolton's cinemas could seat an astonishing 25,000 filmgoers at once.

Big or small, glamorous or unsophisticated, cinemas always advertised their programmes on the front page of the *Bolton Evening News*, the town's principle newspaper. At the time of the Worktown study, it was an important regional publication boasting a circulation of some 70,000; just under half the town's population.[9] Indeed Tillotson's Directory of 1932 claimed that it was delivered to an extraordinary nine out of ten homes. Unsurprisingly, all Bolton's cinemas used the newspaper to advertise their programmes as well as the experience they offered in comparison with their rivals. "You must see it at the cinema where 'sound' is 'sound'!" proclaimed the Lido's owners in the 1930s whilst the Gem's owners boasted that it was "Comfortably appointed: efficiently conducted, seating capacity 1100" (no wonder the bugs liked it). Bolton's hierarchy of cinemas is apparent in the newspaper advertisements with the first run cinemas having the biggest and boldest; the third and fourth run cinema's advertisements as might be expected being smaller and less obvious on the page. Perhaps their owners need not have been overly concerned by the imbalance; Mass Observation discovered that by far and away people choosing a particular film to watch were most influenced by onscreen trailers and posters rather than anything in the newspaper.[10]

Besides the advertisements for films, cinema was so important in Worktown that the *Bolton Evening News* devoted plenty of column inches to it each day. Articles featuring film stars appeared alongside reviews of the latest films in the "Filmland Gossip" and "The Week on the Screen" columns. With cinema-going so predominant, Tom Harrisson established the Cinema Research Unit as part of the Mass Observation team. Despite the rather grand title, the unit seemed to consist of only one Observer, John Morton Jones, about whom little is known. Despite the limited resources devoted to its study, Tom Harrisson claimed that "from the beginning film was of the highest interest to us. We were film minded..."[11]

With the secrecy surrounding the Worktown project, strangely enough, more direct methods were employed to investigate the role of cinema in the town. In March 1938, Mass Observation carried out a survey to explore the cinema going habits of the Worktowners. To this end, questionnaires were left in the foyers of three cinemas – a very different approach to gathering information which may reflect the influence of Charles Madge. However it came about, the questionnaires are all the more unusual because they record the names, ages and addresses of the cinemagoers who took the time and trouble to respond, a rare detail not usually found in other Observer's reports where most of the people recorded remain anonymous apart from a brief description of sex, age and occasionally their clothes.

The three cinemas chosen for the survey reflect the hierarchy that once existed. The Odeon was obviously the most upmarket of the three, next the Crompton was more of a midrange cinema with a twice-weekly change of programme, and lastly, the unprepossessing Palladium which was the most downmarket of the three. Over 500 people responded to the Mass Observation survey, probably enticed to do so by two first prizes of £1 and several free cinema tickets for the most articulate responses. The questionnaires reveal the frequency of cinema visits, the reasons for going and also the appeal of different genres of films to various age groups and different social classes in Worktown.

With so many profitable cinemas in Bolton, it is hardly a surprise that Mass Observation discovered many Worktowners often visited the cinema three times a week. "You ask how many times a month I do go. Well, it's once a week I go to the Odeon and if there is any Picture that I enjoyed so much, go again later in the week. You see, you give [sic] a change of news. I go to other cinemas and the total is 12 or 16 times in the month" responded Beatrice Hart who lived on Manchester Road. Other completed questionnaires demonstrate that the frequency of cinema visits varied from just once a month to a quite extraordinary twenty-four times a month. With such an ingrained cinema going habit, no wonder Mr Hull, the manager of the Embassy Cinema, boasted to Martin Jones that he didn't make a loss in any week of the year. He also told Jones that at peak times like Boxing Day and the New Year week he did "exceptional business" before adding "Week in week out, I get 6000 people or more who come here regularly twice a week. They won't only go once, but two and even three times to a good musical."[12] Attracting such audiences at the Embassy must have been no mean feat as being near the River Croal, it was always rumoured to be infested with rats.

With an insatiable demand for films, the town's cinemas changed their programmes every three or four days which ensured there was always a wide selection of films showing at any one time. Sometimes whole programmes were simply swapped between two cinemas located in different parts of the town; a practice colloquially known as "bicycling" although taking the reels of films across the town by bicycle – the origin of the term – had disappeared before the 1930s. Of course, the quality and overall appeal of programmes varied tremendously. This was especially true of the low budget British films of the time which somewhat humiliatingly, were often only included in a programme to satisfy a quota imposed to protect the British film industry.

Almost by definition, cinema going in Worktown was a predominantly working class activity but the difference in the price of admission did to some extent indicate the social class any given cinema attracted or aspired to attract. With tickets priced as low as 3d (just over one pence) at the Carlton, to as much as 1/6d (seven and a half pence) at the first run cinemas, it is fair to assume that some cinemas were always perceived to be more upmarket than others – a difference highlighted by the Mass Observation questionnaire. It was noted that the written replies from the Odeon generally had a greater fluency of literacy suggesting it attracted a higher proportion of middle and upper working class patrons. Indeed the number who put pen to paper from the Odeon was significantly more than the number of responses from the other two cinemas put together.

In terms of the decor, maintenance, outward appearance and just the overall experience of watching films in them, there was a huge variation in the appeal of different cinemas. Some had a reputation for poor projectors which broke down regularly whilst others were noted for poor sound reproduction. Oddly enough, a good view of the screen – a prerequisite for enjoying any film it would be reasonable to suppose – was by no means guaranteed. The Majestic had at one time been a skating rink so the seats were all on the level forcing the owners to place the screen in an unnaturally high position. The discomfort caused by looking up was compounded further by the fact that the screen was located on the longer side of the rectangle so those sitting at the extremities of each row of seats had an even poorer view caused by the awkward viewing angle.[13]

The Regal had also been a skating rink but at least the seats in the stalls were raked after its conversion. However, the auditorium was so huge that a good proportion of the audience struggled to see properly because the back rows of seats were such a long way away from the screen. There was no discernible advantage to be gained from sitting in its notoriously rickety balcony either as, rather oddly, it was positioned on the long side of the oblong building so those sitting in it were actually side onto the screen.[14]

Other Worktown cinemas promised more from the outside than they delivered inside. As already noted, the Royal was housed in a building with a fine mock-Tudor facade but Halliwell recalled that "the interior was very seedy indeed." Conversely, the Theatre Royal was better inside than outside as it had a rather tawdry frontage made worse by the advertising of its programmes on sandwich boards plonked on the pavement outside. Just up the road, the Embassy offered its patrons the option of "lover's couches" – double seats in the rear of the stalls each wide enough for two people although presumably the rats might have dampened any adolescent ardour. On the other hand, the front rows of the Belle had neither lover's couches nor individual seats as uniquely the rows nearest the screen consisted of backless wooden forms riveted to the floor with patrons charged a penny to sit on them: a legacy of the earliest cinemas where similar seats could be paid for with washed jam jars.

Whatever difference in the quality of the amenities, "going to't pictures" was relatively inexpensive – an important part of its appeal. In addition, the number of cinemas meant there was enough choice to satisfy even the most diverse tastes usually within a bus, tram ride, or short walk of most peoples' houses. Although cinemas were both cheap and accessible, by far the most important reason they thrived was that films provided an all-too-brief escape from the drab reality of life in Worktown. A manager of one cinema told an Observer "They're working all day, and they come here at night dressed up like dandies. They think they're on top of the Earth, you've got to make them think they are." Unfortunately, the efforts of those dressing up for a night at the cinema were not always fully appreciated. One eighteen-year-old responding to Mass Observation's survey commented: "Also a word of praise for modern cinemas – their luxurious interiors increase one's enjoyment of the show but must we have … lady patrons in front of us wearing eccentric head gear?"[15]

The disengagement from the real world that was so important in films was explored in some detail by Mass Observation. When asked if they saw people like themselves on the screens, well over 300 said "no" including two women who wrote tellingly "No, thank goodness."[16] Little wonder then that films from Hollywood were the dominant force in cinema's golden age. Mass Observation found there was a strong preference for American films which were generally thought to be slicker and more polished than British films that didn't offer the same glamour and escapism; the two prerequisites it would seem for enjoying a film at the time.[17] Nor apparently were there sufficient male heartthrobs to drool over in British films. One fourteen-year-old old girl wrote: "Must our British films be so entirely lacking in handsome heroes? Surely among millions of men we could find just one Robert Taylor."[18]

The preference for American films strongly suggests that the Worktowners sitting in the darkened auditoriums above all else wanted to escape the drab realities of urban life by seeing different, more fabulous worlds. This explains why the musical extravaganzas of Busby Berkeley, the swashbuckling adventures of Errol Flynn, the magical dance sequences of Astaire and Rogers and the sweeping, panoramic landscapes in epics such as *Gone with the Wind* were always guaranteed to attract huge audiences. For as long as the films lasted the Worktowners could forget that afterwards they would journey home past the smoky chimneys, railway viaducts and forbidding mills of their daily experience. One response to Mass Observation's survey succinctly captures the inherent escapism of cinema: "The critics might say I am easily pleased, but to think that for a few coppers, one can enter the world of make believe and leave behind all the worries and cares, well I say long live the films."[19]

Time and again, Mass Observation found a desire to "escape the cares of the world and everyday life" as one respondent put it was paramount to the cinemagoer's experience. James Hope of Duke Street wrote "Royalty, Aristocracy, beautiful people and beautiful things help us to compare the other side of life"; a rather poignant response, as "beautiful" was a word that could never be used to describe the terraced houses of Duke Street just around the corner from Davenport Street. One respondent commented: "Life is drab, life is full of worries, let's have a hearty laugh" whilst another, echoed the same sentiments: "Let us by all means have entertainment of a light character so that after a monotonous day's work everyone can be made to feel happier and brighter." The response of one forty-three-year-old man perhaps says all that needs saying about this aspect of cinema's appeal: "Good films help one to forget the workaday world."[20]

Despite the escapism, it is important to remember that cinema did appeal in other ways as well. The supporting programme was an important source of visual news in the pre-television age as one respondent confirmed when she wrote: "Whatever picture is being shown I always look forward with interest to the news each week. It's the only way of keeping in touch … (with) what is happening every day."

Notwithstanding the other worldliness of many films, some were thought to have educational value especially if they had had an historical theme. One of the Crompton cinema's patrons wrote: "The working classes who are the bulk of your patrons haven't the time to read or delve into historical books. Hence the cinema is indispensible." In another remarkably articulate response a Worktowner argued that: "Films in general are too divorced from reality and thus cinema instead of educating and uplifting the ordinary life of working people has degenerated into a mere mode of escape from man's day-to-day life. In a word it is pure 'dope' for the workers deliberately encouraging a lack of deep thinking."[21]

There were two notable exceptions to the escapist fare served up by Hollywood's studios. Films starring Rochdale-born Gracie Fields and Wigan's George Formby were immensely popular in the 1930s. *Sing As We Go*, directed by Stanley Holloway and starring Gracie Fields – a film about cotton workers partly shot on location in Bolton – was the most popular film screened in Bolton in 1934 closely followed by *Love, Life and Laughter*, another film starring Fields. Such was Fields' popularity, unusually for any film coming to the town for the first time *Sing As We Go* billed as "Bolton's own film", actually opened in two cinemas simultaneously; in this instance, the Queens and the Rialto.[22] George Formby's films, also being rooted in a northern working class world, enjoyed a similar popularity. Mass Observation however did find that not everyone enjoyed their happy-go-lucky antics, one Worktowner commenting: "I resent as a Lancashire man the portrayals of Stanley Holloway and in a lesser degree of Gracie Fields as north country people. North country people are not the 'Gobbins' as typified by Stanley Holloway. I would like to see more films of real Lancashire and Yorkshire people and not films of them as somebody in London thinks they are."[23]

As well as Martin Jones's research on cinemas, Humphrey Spender also recorded this important part of Worktown's cultural history. Given cinema's importance, somewhat surprisingly there is only one photograph specifically featuring film going in the whole body of work he produced while in the town. Perhaps inevitably, Spender photographed the Odeon although very little of it can be seen in the picture for as usual it is the people leaving the cinema who are the focus of Spender's attention.

Spender's photograph of the Odeon was taken just a month after it opened. As befitted the status of one of Oscar Deutsch's cinemas, the Odeon had opened amidst a blaze of publicity on Saturday 21 August 1937. The film that night was *Dark Journey* starring Vivien Leigh and Conrad Veidt. This largely forgotten First World War spy yarn was accompanied by the Gaumont British News; *More Kittens*, a colour cartoon film and a "short colour musical", *Sun-Kissed Stars at Palm Springs*. Unfortunately, the supporting films were the only splashes of colour on the screen on the opening night, for the main feature and the news were both in black and white. To ensure the Odeon ran like clockwork from the outset, its first manager, Mr Abercrombie, was supported by an Assistant Manager, a Chief Projectionist, five other projectionists; twelve cleaning and maintenance staff, four doormen, two pageboys, twelve usherettes, four cashiers and four salesgirls; all of them full-time employees.

For those fortunate enough to be attending, gilt-edged, specially printed programmes were placed on their seats, in which the Odeon's owners grandiloquently claimed: "The coming of the Odeon is an epoch in the entertainment life of Bolton. It is a distinct and unique addition to the amenities of the town."[24] It proved a generous addition too for all the proceeds from the opening night along with further donations from the attendees were given to local charities. To welcome this latest addition to Bolton's family of cinemas, Mayor Alderman Russell was invited to perform the opening ceremony. To add to the grandeur, the Band of the Battalion of the Royal Scots were engaged to provide a stirring welcome for a host of special guests including Oscar Deutsch and his wife who were "expected to attend" according to an excited local press. Less conspicuously, Tom Harrisson also went to the opening night making secret observations which included noting the green uniforms of the cinema officials and the scarlet uniforms of the soldiers on the steps.[25] As the band struck up, few – if indeed any of those enjoying the occasion – could have known that they were already witnessing the beginning of the end of Worktown's cinemas.

At precisely the same time the Odeon started showing films, the portents of its subsequent decline were becoming apparent. In the autumn of 1938, Proffit's, a Bolton based electrical goods store, whilst advertising their radios, were reassuring any potential customers that *even if* television should ever reach the North of England, it would not negate the need for radio. Proffitt's owners promised their prospective customers that "if television does come within reach of Bolton during the next eighteen months you will still need it (a radio). Nevertheless if you wish, we will cheerfully take the set back, and allow all that you paid on it, off a new television receiver. Fair?"[26]

Fair indeed, for even as Boltonians were pondering Proffit's offer, 2000 homes in London were already receiving the first flickering pictures being beamed from Alexandra Palace, the early centre of British television broadcasting. Although at first programmes were only broadcast for up to four hours a day, it was an ominous sign for the nation's cinema owners.

However, Germany's invasion of Poland on 1 September 1939, put an abrupt stop to the fledgling BBC television service when, in the interests of national security, broadcasting was brought to a sudden stop in the middle of a Disney cartoon. When Britain declared war on Germany just two days later, the nation's cinemas were immediately closed. Unlike television – which did not resume until the war was over – cinemas were quickly reopened across the country as they were deemed to be an essential aid to morale on the home front. In an admirable display of patriotism, some cinema owners put up signs advertising that members of the armed forces would be admitted free of charge, but as cinema-going retained its pre-war popularity despite the dangers and privations of total war, they were often as not replaced by another more business-like notice: "Free List entirely suspended for the current attraction".[27]

Bolton's film lovers making their way through the blackouts to the town's cinemas were assured that "programmes will continue. Unless... enemy planes are directly overhead." On 9 January 1941, German planes were directly overhead and the Bolton Odeon was nearly put out of business for good when two bombs dropped on either side of it. Incredibly, the projectionist heeded the advice of the Ministry of Defence and kept calm and carried on with none of the audience choosing to leave the cinema.[28] Whether this was evidence of the legendary Blitz spirit or equally possible as Leslie Halliwell thought that "stupidly audiences instinctively believed in the absolute impregnability of the Odeon", the film *The Ghost Breakers* continued to its conclusion, despite one fatal casualty and a fire in the town's sugar store a few yards away.

When the war ended, television broadcasts resumed. On 7 June 1946, the same Mickey Mouse cartoon Hitler's European ambitions had interrupted was symbolically broadcast again. Equally symbolic, the cartoon re-started at the exact moment it had abruptly stopped. A legend persists that as the cartoon finally finished after a seven-year hiatus, Jasmine Bligh announced in the style favoured by presenters of the era, "Sorry for the interruption of our programme service. Our next presentation is…" like nothing had happened. Although it is difficult to substantiate the truth of this story, it is nevertheless endearingly British.

Whatever the reality, in those first few years after the war, television's impact on the nation's social life remained negligible. Indeed in the immediate post-war months, cinemas were almost always packed due as much to the enduring popularity of films as the fact that cinema was at least one commodity that wasn't "on the ration". Indeed in 1946, British attendances peaked with an extraordinary all-time record of 1635 million admissions to the country's cinemas.[29]

Despite these record figures, television's influence was gathering momentum as the novelty of just being able to watch moving pictures at home gave way to a new medium of mass communication. Between June 1948 and March 1949, the number of television licenses in Britain doubled: from 50,000 to 100,000 mainly because television sets were becoming cheaper to buy.[30] Notwithstanding their increasing affordability, in 1948, only 4.3 per cent of the adult population had access to a television set; all in the south of England as programmes could only be received in an expanding but severely limited radius of fifty miles from Alexandra Palace. Because of the limitations, by 1950, there were still only 357,000 television licenses throughout the whole of Britain.[31] Although television sets were still far from the norm in the overwhelming majority of the nation's houses, as the new decade dawned, the onslaught of the most pervasive form of mass entertainment in history began in earnest.

In the early 1950s, even for those people fortunate enough to own televisions, there was only one channel to watch: BBC. Moreover, on most weekdays, it only broadcast from 3 p.m. to 6 p.m. before a blank screen followed for the next two hours to enable mothers to get small children to bed – a break known as "the toddler's truce". This was followed by another couple of hours of programmes before broadcasts finished at 10.30 p.m. or sometimes 10.45 p.m. on special occasions. In its infancy, television was seen as very much a rich man's plaything and it appeared unlikely that it would usurp radio let alone the cinema as the most popular form of mass entertainment. However there were two turning points which significantly broadened television's appeal. The first, Queen Elizabeth II's Coronation on 2 June 1953, affected the number of people wanting to own television sets, the second, the launch of commercial television three years later had a dramatic impact on the kinds of programmes people could watch if they got one.

Despite considerable opposition from the Palace and the Church to televising the Coronation live due to fears about wires, technicians and engineers interrupting the most solemn of state occasions, the broadcast eventually went ahead with Richard Dimbleby narrating from a soundproofed box suspended from the ceiling. Peter Lewis in his history of the 1950s argues that "Thanks to his faultless performance for an audience of twenty million this was the day when television came of age in Britain. After all it had a better view than even the most exalted participant." A year before the Coronation, when most of the country was already within reach of the television transmitters, there were still only two million sets, mostly grouped around the main cities.[32] Due, in no small part, to the popularity of the historic broadcast, televisions now became something people aspired to and equally importantly, could actually afford.

When they got their television sets however, viewers were initially offered a deeply ingrained patrician form of public service broadcasting. According to Lord Reith, the BBC's first Director General, public service broadcasting was meant to "inform, educate and entertain". Only able to watch BBC, the new television owners generally got too much of the first two and not enough of the latter. Partly because of what was on offer, television's impact on cinema was not as pronounced as it might have been.

However, commercial television (euphemistically called independent television) launched in Britain in September, 1955, began to exploit the opportunities presented by a rapidly changing, increasingly consumer-driven society. For the first time, British television audiences got used to programmes with breaks for advertisements but more importantly, commercial television introduced viewers to programmes with a much broader appeal. Tellingly, the first issue of the *TV Times* published in 1955, had sections for panel shows, quiz shows and "light entertainment"- all of which were anathema to the BBC hierarchy. In a thinly disguised swipe at the BBC, the magazine's editor stated: "Viewers will no longer have to accept what is deemed as best for them. The new independent television programme planners aim at giving viewers what viewers want- at the time viewers want it."[33]

By then, it was obvious that increasing numbers wanted it. Indeed, just two years after the launch of ITV, the number of television licenses overtook the number of radio licenses in Britain for the first time. Within three or four years of its launch, ITV's share of the audience on any given evening could be as much as seventy-three per cent. Moreover, as Peter Lewis points out "there was no disputing that the working class audience, which provided ITV's massive surplus in the ratings, had clearly identified the commercial channel as 'Us' and the BBC as 'Them'."[34] As the majority of Boltonians were working class in the 1950s, it's fair to presume that most of those settling down to a night in front of their new television sets were enjoying the early staples of ITV's more populist diet like *I love Lucy* and *Dragnet*, giveaway prize shows like *Double Your Money* and *Take your Pick*, and one of the earliest talent shows, *Opportunity Knocks*. Ominously for Bolton's cinema owners, television was beginning to provide the same kind of undemanding escapism for a mass audience that light musical and romance films had done just twenty years previously.

This change in how increasing numbers of people chose to spend their leisure time was immediately apparent when Tom Harrisson came back to Bolton in 1960. He recorded the increase in the number of television licenses noting their year-on-year growth in the town:

TV Licenses in Bolton
1952: 12,000 (approx)
1954: 27,500 (approx)
1956: 41,500 (approx)
1958: 55,000 (approx)
1959: 62,000 (approx)[35]

Harrisson commented: "The thing that will most strike the man … as *new* in the air of Worktown or Worksop: television antennae." He also noted how quickly older television sets were thought of as antiquated before rapidly being replaced by newer models – one of the earliest examples of consumer goods which are expected by both the manufacturers and customers to be upgraded as more advanced models are subsequently launched.

Whatever model of television set Boltonians aspired to own, by the time Harrisson made his observation, they could be bought outright, rented, or acquired on credit through Hire Purchase arrangements from any number of specialist dealers. In 1959, amongst many others, James Lee's electrical store on Derby Street were advertising in the *Bolton Evening News* a 17-inch table top model for just a £1 deposit and a payment of 10/–6 a week (52 and a half pence); an affordable proposition at a time when average earnings for a manual worker were around £14 a week. More significantly, renting a television was becoming a money saving alternative to buying tickets at the cinema – a week's rental being roughly equivalent to the cost of just four cinema tickets for a family of four.

By the early 1960s, dozens of advertisements for different models of television sets in the *Bolton Evening News* could be seen alongside the advertisements for the town's cinemas. They bear witness to television's growing popularity and its eventual triumph over radio as the nation's favourite home pastime. Like most technological innovations, the relative cost of owning or renting a television steadily fell as newer models were introduced. In 1962, one store in Bolton was offering improved 19-inch television sets ("Where else can you get one this big!") for less than 10/– (50p) a week; already an enticing two inches of extra screen for sixpence less than a couple of years before. By then, Britain was well on its way to becoming the "armchair nation" of popular perception – no wonder Harrisson noted that the television transmitter on Winter Hill to the north of Bolton had become an important local landmark.

In the meantime, the BBC was responding to the challenge of ITV as television audiences continued to grow. In 1960, its new Director General, Hugh Carleton Greene, declared that the BBC must recover half the audience in parity with its rival station. Consequently much-loved programmes like *Dixon of Dock Green*, *Z Cars* and *Steptoe and Son* were broadcast by the BBC and quality continued to soar with ground-breaking dramas like *Up the Junction* and *Cathy Comes Home* proving that programmes could be entertaining and informative in equal measure. Meanwhile, the hours of broadcasting increased with the toddler's truce being replaced by an early evening slot featuring the popular magazine programme *Tonight*, children's programmes and news bulletins; the latter negating the role cinemas once had in providing news to a mass audience.

Ever since its invention, watching television has been routinely blamed for a number of society's ills. Whether it can truly be held responsible for increasing obesity, indiscipline amongst the young, lowering moral standards, buck teeth in children caused by resting their heads on their hands while watching it, or killing "the art of conversation", there is one thing that can be stated with absolute conviction: the arrival of the television age profoundly affected the nation's cinemas.

In 1950, there had been a healthy 1400 million admissions to British cinemas. By 1960, the number of cinema admissions had slumped to a lowly 500 million: well over half the number of just a decade earlier. Conversely, by 1959, an estimated sixty per cent of British adults were watching television for between three and five hours a night, depending on the season; a quite phenomenal leap in the same period. Worse still for the profits of the nation's cinema owners, by 1960, more than ninety per cent of British households had a television set.[36]

All across Britain, cinemas were struggling to stay in business as audiences melted away. Bolton's cinemas were in trouble like everywhere else and one by one they began to close down. Some were converted for different uses, others were unceremoniously demolished. Even before the slew of closures that marked the 1950s, Bolton had lost two cinemas; the Hippodrome stopped showing films in 1940 and the Embassy closed in 1947. In the years that followed, the trickle of cinema closures became a flood as their numbers in Bolton declined catastrophically. The Regal closed in 1955, followed by the Palace and the Empire in 1956. The following year was an *annus horibillis*: the Palladium, the Majestic and the Gem all closed, whilst the Belle burnt down which probably saved the owners the trouble of closing it. In 1959, the Crompton also stopped showing films subsequently becoming in turn the Casino Cabaret Club, later Copperfield's supper club, the Bees Knees discotheque and latterly a supermarket – a concise summary of the kind of conversions that were happening to cinemas all over the country.

Hollywood's film industry, as might be expected, fought back with a number of technical innovations to try and get people away from their televisions and back to the cinema. These included bigger, wider screens, better sound systems, new Technicolor processes, Cinemascope and 3D films: the latter something of a novelty experience. Unfortunately, they did not bring the kind of queues common in cinema's heyday partly because, as we have seen, the appeal of cinema in Worktown relied on much more than just the film on the screen. Only twenty years previously, the only time many Worktowners ever walked on a carpet was in a cinema. Now, increasingly better paid Boltonians were buying their own wall-to-wall carpets. In the 1930s, George Orwell had noted that unemployed men would readily pay the few pennies it cost to get into a cinema in winter just to get out of the cold; thirty years later Boltonians were replacing coal fires with central heating systems that warmed every room in the house. In addition, the relative affluence that marked the post-war years meant people often spent money on home comforts which made a night in watching "the telly" even more attractive. By then, aspirant Boltonians were simply less inclined to go out to sit on cinema seats which were in many cases less comfortable than their newly acquired "three-piece suites" at home.

With more home comforts, the role of cinemas as refuges from drab lives began to diminish. Indeed the escapism which had been such an attraction in cinema's golden age was challenged in the late 1950s and early 1960s by some British filmmakers who were making more realist, "kitchen sink" films like *Look Back in Anger*, *A Taste of Honey*, *Saturday Night and Sunday Morning* and *A Kind of Loving*; the latter partly filmed in Bolton. In spite of their cultural importance and indisputable quality, they were unlikely to have people queuing around the block to see the kinds of streets they could see just outside the cinema. Worse still, that sort of drama could just as easily be produced for television as Granada television's hugely successful *Coronation Street* was proving.

As the 1960s began, there was precious little to encourage Bolton's remaining cinema owners; the Carlton, the Rialto, the Tivoli and the Ritz all went out of business in the first year of the new decade alone. Only twenty years previously they had survived because even films of dubious quality would play in the town's cinemas time and time again. With few alternatives and for want of anything better to do, people would still go out to see them. But with television sets in their own homes showing the same sorts of films, they no longer had to.

Like Bolton's other first run cinemas, to some extent, the Odeon found itself better placed to weather the storm, partly because it still took many years for a film to make the transition from cinemas to television screens. The Odeon's fortunes were also helped by a change of ownership. After Oscar Deutsch's premature death from cancer in 1941, the powerful Rank organisation acquired the Odeon chain completing the purchase in 1947. Although Deutsch's cinemas were still called Odeons, their prestige was bolstered by Rank which at the time was also involved in manufacturing as well as film production leading to more investment in new developments like the aforementioned Cinemascope which first came to the Bolton Odeon in 1953.

Despite the worrying trends for cinemas everywhere, the Odeon celebrated its twenty-first birthday in August, 1958, in some style. The Odeon's facade was decorated with bunting and special guests were invited to a reception in the restaurant. The film chosen for the coming of age party was *A Night to Remember*, a dramatic reconstruction of the sinking of the RMS *Titanic*. In keeping with the evening's nautical theme, there was a display featuring a ship's binnacle in the restaurant whilst outside, the Mayor inspected a Guard of Honour provided by the Bolton Sea Cadets. The audience were treated to recorded messages from a number of well-known actors including John Gregson, Norman Wisdom and Brian Worth. Kenneth More, who played Second Officer Lightoller one of the leading characters aboard the stricken liner, sent a congratulatory telegram. Naturally for a birthday party, there was a cake – a gigantic replica of the Odeon in sponge, sugar and icing – which later provided a welcome treat for some of the town's less fortunate children when it was shared amongst local orphanages. In one final nautical twist, the Sea Cadets, in common with the Titanic's passengers, wore life jackets throughout the screening of the film![37] While hardly the most cheerful choice for a birthday party, *A Night to Remember* was at least prescient, for in the years that followed, the Odeon's owners found they were simply rearranging the deck chairs on their own doomed ship.

In 1960, the Odeon's stage was extended and the dressing rooms improved. At the same time, the organ was removed to Walmsley Church to the north of Bolton; presumably without the up-lit console – this often forgotten aspect of cinema vanishing along with attendants in pageboy uniforms and pill-box hats. With the Odeon modernised and upgraded, the stars of the day arrived to entertain the town's teenagers. Amongst others, Cliff Richard, Roy Orbison, Dusty Springfield and Gene Pitney all appeared "live, on stage" and provided an injection of much needed glamour and modernity to the Odeon's ageing auditorium; a strategy which for a time masked the declining cinema attendances.

The modernity peaked in April, 1967, when Jimi Hendrix – far and away the most important artist to ever appear live at the Odeon – gave a mesmerising performance although due to his relative obscurity at the time, he was only a supporting act for The Walker Brothers and Cat Stevens (before his conversion to Islam). Rather incongruously, all three of these influential artists appeared below the special "guest star" billing afforded to the hirsute balladeer Engelbert Humperdinck.[38] Just the sheer novelty of the sounds coaxed from Hendrix's Stratocaster guitar that night meant when he finished his performance the audience were initially unsure how to react and a bemused silence ensued. According to one local musician fortunate enough to witness this footnote in rock history, the embarrassing interlude lasted for several moments before the audience at last burst into wild applause.[39] Although the most expensive ticket that night was priced at 15 shillings (75p), the cheapest could be purchased for 5 shillings (25p). Given Hendrix's subsequent elevation to the pantheon of rock music greats, it would appear to have been a bargain at ten times the price.

In the same year Hendrix appeared, the Odeon's exterior was modernised. The final cost of the alterations was £60,000; the same sum it had cost to build the whole cinema thirty years before. The Odeon now sported an angular, brightly lit canopy, new entrance doors and an enlarged foyer. Unfortunately, the alterations to some extent spoiled its art deco proportions and stylised curves but for the time being at least, the cinema was a little more *a la mode*. Along with new blue seats and carpets chosen to complement the introduction of softer amber lighting, it seemed the Odeon was primed and ready to embrace the contemporary cinemagoer.

Somewhat depressingly, Bolton's other cinemas weren't. The Windsor and the Theatre Royal both closed in 1962. They were followed into oblivion by the Royal five years later. Besides the new look Odeon, only three other cinemas were left in Bolton as the decade came to an end: the Lido on Bradshawgate; the ABC (still called the Capitol by many older Boltonians despite the name change in 1962) and the Queen's. This surviving quartet, found they were not only competing with television but also a growing number of other leisure pursuits too, not least the quasi-gambling pastime of bingo which experienced a huge surge in popularity in the early 1960s. Ironically, although bingo was often lambasted as a boring pastime mainly for the elderly, it became a lifeline for some ailing cinemas which could be converted into bingo halls with a minimum of fuss and expenditure.

The owners of the town's remaining cinemas found they were trying and often failing to keep pace with a rapidly changing society. This was most apparent at the Queen's, the oldest and frankly the least stylish of Bolton's rump of cinemas. After a brief closure in the 1960s it reopened. Significantly, when it did, the Queen's concentrated on showing Asian films to cater for the town's growing immigrant population; in itself an interesting marker of the changing identity of Bolton. Just twenty years before, the only place most Worktowners ever saw a black person was on a cinema screen, now they were their neighbours, work colleagues and friends as Bolton gradually became a multi- ethnic town.

Bolton's handful of remaining cinemas struggled on into the 1970s. They had once belonged to a cluster of cinemas that had all been profitable as a result of the symbiotic relationship that developed between them. As we have seen, by changing their programmes regularly – some twice within a week – they had been able to offer a wide enough choice to satisfy even the most enthusiastic film fanatic. Unfortunately, with the disastrous reduction in screens across the town there was much less choice on the screens for the dwindling numbers still prepared to go out to the cinema to watch films.

In subsequent years, audiences only continued to decline. Following the introduction of BBC2 in 1964, people could enjoy a range of programmes on one of three television channels. As if things weren't bad enough for cinemas, in 1967, BBC2 became the first television station in Europe to regularly broadcast programmes in colour. As colour transmissions became the norm, cinema's last remaining advantage over the "one eyed monster" disappeared. Black and white sets were soon relegated to bedrooms or went to the tip as colour television sets colonised the "front rooms" of Bolton's houses. Sadly it seemed, cinemas now offered nothing television couldn't. In one final ironic twist of the knife, Leslie Halliwell – the most passionate advocate for the delights of a night at a Worktown cinema – was choosing the films to be broadcast by the television industry that was largely responsible for killing them off.

The Bolton Odeon suffered a further indignity in 1972 when its spectacular auditorium was divided into three smaller screens in a desperate attempt to keep it profitable. The creation of this new "entertainment complex" cost a mere £30,000 and was quite remarkably achieved without closing the cinema for a single day. It was the first Odeon and only the third cinema in the whole country to be converted in this way. In a strategy designed to maximise the use of the building, the Odeon could now offer a choice of three programmes in one location simultaneously. Screen 1, previously the circle, had 879 seats whilst Screen 2 and 3 were created by the division of the rear of the old stalls. Both smaller auditoriums had the same capacity (150 seats) and only differed in the colour of their furnishings; Screen 2 was turquoise whilst Screen 3 had a bronze colour scheme.[40]

In a quirky publicity stunt, the newly converted Odeon was declared open by three sets of triplets. In praising the new look Odeon, Alan Mason, its manager, told the *Bolton Evening News*, "One advantage for instance, is that mum and dad can see an adult film in one cinema while the kids can see a film to suit them in another". Given that the Lido across town, was trying to survive by offering a different kind of "adult" film with titles like *Sextroverts* and *Erotic Fantasies*, perhaps Mr Mason might have chosen his words more carefully.

Just a month before the newly converted cinema opened, the writer of a letter to the *Bolton Evening News* commented with equal amounts of surprise and satisfaction that he had witnessed people "actually queuing around the cinema", a long forgotten phenomenon the author of the letter thought he "would never see again". In this instance, he was referring to the latest James Bond blockbuster, *Diamonds are Forever*. He concluded that "if you give the public the sort of films they want, they will flock to see them."[41] Sadly he was wrong. Even if there were enough glamorous spies to fill cinema screens it is unlikely it would have made much difference. In fact, the letter served only to underline the problems. After all if a queue at the Odeon – an everyday sight in cinema's heyday – was now so unusual to warrant putting pen to paper, it was clear proof that Worktown's last remaining cinemas were in serious trouble.

With decline all too apparent, the Odeon's managers organised a number of activities and publicity stunts to encourage people to patronise the cinema. These included Saturday children's clubs; permitting two local women to stay alone overnight in the cinema whilst watching horror films; imploring parents to visit the cinema on bonfire night by warning

"Don't risk the fireworks bring 'em to the pictures", showing Asian films on Sunday mornings, regular midnight programmes of horror films with titles like *Torture Garden* and *Dracula has Risen from the Grave* (if only the town's cinemas could) and encouraging the Odeon's usherettes to support the "Keep Britain Tidy" campaign. In 1979, there was even a national film premiere although the premiered film, *A Hitch in Time*, was a Children's Film Foundation production which, as its name suggests, was aimed at juvenile film goers. Whatever the film's merits, it wasn't exactly the red carpet and Leicester Square. Although each of the initiatives was dutifully reported by the local press, it all appeared somewhat desperate.

Every so often, there were notes of optimism at the beleaguered Odeon. James Bond and Walt Disney films in general retained their popularity throughout the 1970s and occasionally some outstanding films bucked the trend. *One Flew Over the Cuckoo's Nest* deservedly ran for eighteen weeks in the winter of 1976 and *Star Wars* enjoyed a remarkable run of twenty-two weeks. However, these all-too-rare flashes of success only highlighted the overall decline. By the time the 1970s came to an end, the regular full houses of the Odeon's heyday were a distant memory.

The Odeon's struggles were shared equally by the town's other cinemas. The ABC closed in 1977 before being converted into a bingo hall and subsequently a squash club. Even showing Asian films couldn't save the Queen's; it finally closed in 1980. Both cinemas have since been demolished. On Bradshawgate, the Lido, like the Odeon, was in its death throes. Although it was never quite as grand as its more illustrious contemporary, the Lido was still a fine example of art deco architecture. Externally, it had the streamlined motifs associated with cinemas of the age, whilst inside, the proscenium arch with its frieze depicting the gondolas and canals of Venice, soared above a stage forty feet wide and twenty-three feet deep. With an impressive nine changing rooms the Lido was admirably suited to live performances and it had a reputation for variety shows and annual pantomimes. The famous music hall duo, Flanagan and Allen once appeared there as did George Formby when he made an unscheduled appearance on stage just before one of his films, much to the delight of the astonished audience. Arguably though, the highpoint of live appearances at the Lido occurred in 1947 when Laurel and Hardy – Hollywood's most famous double act – appeared in person as part of a British music hall tour.

Alas when the ill winds of change blew, the Lido's past glories also meant nothing. Like the Odeon, it had been subdivided into three cinemas in the early 1970s, Studios 1 and 2 being created from the old circle whilst the original cafeteria was converted becoming Studio 3. In 1973, the original stalls became Scamps discotheque with Bolton's aspiring John Travoltas cavorting on the spot where the iconic Laurel and Hardy had entertained a full house only thirty years previously. By 1980, there were just two cinemas left in Bolton – both of them shadows of their former selves.

In late 1981, plans were submitted to convert the Odeon into a bingo hall much to the dismay of Bolton Film Society whose spokesman argued that Ashburner Street would become a "bingo boulevard"; a fear not entirely unfounded as another other bingo club was already open just yards away. His impassioned pleas were to no avail. In January 1983, the Bolton Odeon, the cinema that more than any embodied the golden age of Worktown's picture palaces bowed to the inevitable. After showing *Mary Poppins* on Screen 1, Woody Allen's *A Midsummer Night's Sex Comedy* on Screen 2 and *Flash Gordon* and *Battle Beyond the Stars* on Screen 3, the lights were finally turned off. The Bolton Odeon had screened its very last film.

In February 1985, after a £350,000 facelift the Odeon followed the somewhat depressing pattern of dozens of other cinemas when it reopened as the Top Rank Bingo Club. Quite what the genteel ladies in Humphrey Spender's photograph would have made of a pastime which at that time was mostly associated with working men's clubs and more down-at-heel holiday resorts can never be known, but it's difficult to believe they would have approved. That it was opened by the pug-like, unglamorous actor Paul Shane from the hit TV show *Hi-De-Hi* simply compounded the misery. Where once had thundered some of the greatest epics in cinema history, an unlovely, renovated interior now reverberated to the cries of "full house" and "eyes down for a line". Later renamed the Mecca Bingo Hall, the refurbished Odeon continued to provide "entertainment" (mainly it has to be said for Bolton's senior citizens), for nearly nineteen years. Despite this final humiliation the Odeon couldn't be saved, for even bingo was being re-branded and marketed to a younger generation of players who demanded modern, purpose built bingo halls with their own car parks, bars and upmarket catering facilities. Finally, in November

2004, the Odeon was put out of its misery when the last game of bingo was called and the doors were closed for the very last time.

Things were no better at the Lido. In the early 1990s, the Dance Factory nightclub – the successor to Scamps – eventually closed as glitterballs and discotheques were usurped by rave culture, superclubs and the "Madchester" scene. By the mid-1990s, a Laser Quest fantasy battle arena was occupying the stalls where the nightclub had previously been. For the next few years, "Staying Alive" took on a whole new meaning as children firing infrared guns charged around shooting one another and occasionally hosts of zombies on what had been the dancefloor, now a luminous, dystopian battlefield. Blissfully unaware of the combat taking place below their feet, the last cinema screens in Bolton – by then owned by the Cannon chain – showed films to a handful of customers. In 1998, disembowelled and hardly recognisable as a cinema any more, the Lido, the last Worktown cinema to actually screen a film, also gave up the ghost. Appropriately, it closed after a special showing of the classic film *Casablanca*. When the reels of film from the wartime masterpiece were packed away and the projector switched off, the last fragile link with the picture palaces of Worktown was severed once and for all. In March 2006, the Lido was demolished and replaced by a block of flats.

For a while longer at least, the Odeon enjoyed a stay of execution. In the late 1990s, discussions took place about possible listed building status and most would say in this case, deservedly so. The Odeon's importance to the architectural heritage of Bolton was never in question however its plight reflected the challenges facing so many of Britain's old cinemas. All over the country they needed innovative strategies to revive their fortunes as it was painfully obvious their glory years as cinemas were over. The problem of preserving these architectural gems which had been dramatic focal points on the nation's high streets for generations, rightly garnered attention from English Heritage. Tragically however, when it came to the Bolton Odeon, all the talk and good intentions came to nothing. Although there was a wave of sentiment expressed in the letters pages of the *Bolton News* and various suggestions as how it might be redeveloped as a cinema or arts centre, the Odeon was eventually sold to the Woodthorpe Homes property group.

As a result, Bolton's best example of 1930s architecture was earmarked for demolition and redevelopment. Bolton Council was apparently content to ride shotgun with what many regarded as an appalling act of civic vandalism and short-sightedness. In supporting the redevelopment of the site, a council spokesman told the *Bolton Evening News* reporter: "This scheme is part of the wider cultural and innovation quarter for the town centre [sic]. Hopefully it would fit in quite nicely with the concept of a culture and leisure area." In one final risible comment he added "I've seen the drawings and they look very impressive." It was all over bar the shouting. At the stroke of a bureaucrat's pen, Bolton Council achieved what the German Air Force couldn't and on February 18, 2007, watched by a few shoppers in the open market, the wrecking balls began to reduce the Odeon to rubble. Unlike many Boltonians who outlived it, the Odeon had not quite made three score years and ten.

Sentiment aside, the Odeon could not have been saved as a cinema any more than any of its contemporaries. Marooned in a declining town centre, it was a product of the society Mass Observation came to investigate. The letters in the *Bolton News* expressing dismay at the loss of the town centre's last cinema were arguably only expressions of nostalgia, for in reality there are more cinemas in Bolton now than ever before. The multiplex cinemas at the Valley and Middlebrook retail parks, both of which opened in 1998, between them boast a staggering twenty-seven screens and were part of a rebranding of cinema that led to something of a renaissance of cinema-going.* They both offer virtually 24-hour programmes, the seating is spacious and comfortable, they are equipped with the most up-to-date projectors and sound equipment, their locations alongside restaurants and bars offer a more sophisticated evening out, and most importantly of all, they are easily accessible by car. However, unlike Worktown's cinemas, their bland uniformity and uninspiring box like appearance renders them characterless and soulless.

To preserve the Bolton Odeon for future generations required vision and imagination: in this instance, there was neither. Appallingly, over a decade after it was demolished, the site of the Odeon remains undeveloped. A sign on one of the hoardings surrounding the empty space proclaims: "Watch this space for town centre living, offices and leisure including a hotel, bars, restaurants, shops and cafes." Quite what the pretentious babble is all about remains to be seen. Seventy years ago – in a different

---

* In 2016, the town got a further nine screens after the Light cinema opened in the Market Hall.

era, in a totally different town – Humphrey Spender took his photograph of Bolton's most esteemed cinema from the same spot. A few of the black tiles that can be seen in his picture are still visible just under the hoarding. Along with the piles of rubble and the weed strewn wasteland, these tiny cracked tiles still shining above the pavement are the last poignant reminders of the twenty-one vanished cinemas of Worktown whose glamour, magic and romance once helped people forget that waiting for them outside was the grimiest of towns.

WASH DAYS, BATH NIGHTS

Wash day.
Humphrey Spender

Two hundred gigantic mill chimneys dominated Worktown's skyline. Alone they would have been enough to cover the town in soot, but there were another 50,000 domestic chimneys on the roofs of the houses as well. All together, the chimneys belched tons of noxious black dust into the raw, damp air every day so there was always a dirty cloud over Bolton making the sky grey even when the sun shone. But of course, "what goes up must come down" and the cloud of soot fell back down from the sky to settle like an unwashed blanket over the buildings, the roads and even the faces of the Worktowners. The inescapable griminess meant everyone who lived in Bolton faced a titanic weekly battle to keep themselves and their houses clean. If it is true that "Godliness is next to cleanliness", it was certainly hell to achieve in Worktown.

Tom Harrisson and his team of Observers living in Davenport Street soon found out how dirty Bolton was. Harrison noted that even the trees have "black stems"- something most Worktowners would have hardly noticed let alone commented on; after all, they were used to it. The playwright, J.B. Priestley, on witnessing the scarred industrial landscape between Bolton and Manchester for the first time thought that it almost challenged people to live in it while the English novelist, William Gerhardi, thought Bolton "…..looked like the bottom of a pond with the water drained off. In here, were the people who if they could endure this, could endure anything."[1]

The students, intellectuals and left wing idealists investigating Bolton for Mass Observation had actually volunteered to endure it but unlike the Worktowners who expected to live all their lives amongst the dirt and grime, at least the Observers were free to leave when they could stand it no more. Describing the revulsion they felt, Tom Harrisson said: "Of 42 southerners who came up to work with us in winter, 39 found Worktown 'ugly','awful', often intolerable. In winter you are living in a town without greenery or unindustrial life."[2] By and large, those who stayed in Davenport Street for any length of time only put up with "slumming it" because they knew they would eventually return to comfortable lives far removed from the world they had briefly inhabited.

Humphrey Spender disliked spending any time at all in Bolton only ever coming to the town for short spells. Apart from the loathsome living conditions in Davenport Street, Spender was always uncomfortable about the invasive, voyeuristic nature of the Worktown project. As far as he was concerned, he was recording a type of hardship and poverty far removed from his own privileged background. Nevertheless, Spender continued taking photographs maintaining the secrecy essential to the project by concealing his lightweight Leica camera under his coat. In spite of his best efforts, there were however some hostile confrontations when initially unsuspecting people noticed what was going on and the threat Spender's camera posed to their privacy.

Because of the potential for unpleasantness, the Worktowners in Spender's images are almost always recorded out and about in public places. Indeed, producing a visual record of the daily routines taking place behind closed doors was difficult if not impossible which inevitably results in an imbalance between domestic and public life in the

Worktown photographs. This disparity was not helped by the fact that the Lancashire working class could be fiercely private in the company of outsiders and would probably have had suspicions about any stranger – let alone an erudite, middle class one like Humphrey Spender – wanting to take photographs inside their homes. There is however, one memorable exception. Although it is not exactly clear why, Spender did take a photograph of a baby being bathed by its mother in front of a coal fire; a particularly fascinating image as for obvious reasons it could only have been taken by invitation. Moreover, it is the only interior of a Worktown home that can be seen in over 800 photographs Spender took in Bolton.

Despite the challenges of recording such domestic activities, Spender still managed to produce a visual record of several chores that were part and parcel of everyday life in Worktown. His images of women pegging out laundry, of clothing billowing in the wind on back streets and of housewives scrubbing pavements and doorsteps are reminders of once familiar routines in Lancashire's mill towns. Spender's photographs of them are of immense importance because although they feature what on the surface appear to be mundane, everyday activities, they are testament to a shared dignity and pride which once characterised Bolton's working class communities.

In a town where poverty was never far away, it was these conspicuous displays of cleaning and polishing inside and outside houses that were the foremost way families demonstrated their self-respect and independence to everyone else. Indeed amongst poor people, one way they could hold their heads up within the community was by showing their neighbours that even if the household was experiencing hardship, everything was still kept spotlessly clean. Consequently, drying laundry in the back streets each week, possessing "Sunday best" clothes which were clean and ready to wear, making sure that doorsteps and the flagstones immediately outside each house were scrubbed and keeping the ranges used for heating and cooking clean and maintained all had a deeper symbolic importance.

As an anthropologist, Harrisson was bound to be intrigued by their significance, an interest that cannot be divorced from his wider exploration of the expectations of women in working class communities. In Worktown, the considerable burden of running a house was not shared equally by all its members. It was women who kept homes clean and it was usually women who criticised those who didn't. Men might be undomesticated, lazy, or even absent in the pub, but ultimately it was *she* who got the plaudits if a household was thought to be clean or *she* who was blamed if standards fell below those expected of the people living on any particular street.

This attitude prevailed at one time because there was an entrenched belief amongst most men – and it is also worth emphasising, most women as well – that homes were the housewives' domain and by extension keeping them clean was seen as women's work, something they were constantly reminded of. "As soon as a woman knows of the wonderful results she can get by using ACDO on washdays she becomes a confirmed user" ran a typical advertisement of the time, whilst the makers of Pinkobolic Soap happily informed their potential customers that it removed "all fear of dirt and germs for the housewife." Another soap manufacturer told potential customers: "Do as thousands of other women are doing and change to this amazing 'no scrub' soap today."[3] Such unsubtle messages appear again and again in advertisements of the mid twentieth century which continually reinforced the domestic expectations of women nearly as much as promoting the qualities of the products being advertised.

It is therefore hardly surprising that Mass Observation found that apart from regular visits to the nearby shops, women were rarely seen on the streets during the day. Rather than going out, they were expected to be attending to household chores, most of which involved cleaning. An Observer questioned one woman about the order in which she cleaned the rooms in her house each day: "I asked about where they started – if they started from the front room. 'No you must start from the top and work down'. Why:-It works better-the dirt doesn't float around and makes it that you haven't to do things twice over."[4]

As most of Worktown's terraced houses weren't very big, it would be tempting to think that even doing it "twice over" would not be so tiresome but keeping even tiny homes clean took an inordinate amount of time and effort partly because cast iron ranges with built-in water heaters dominated the main living room of each house. Coal fires were lit in them every day because as well as warming the occupants in colder weather, their ovens were the only means of preparing hot food. One Boltonian later recalled their contribution to the general muckiness: "The gases soot and carbon smuts that squirted out of these tiny volcanoes filled the room, the air, our clothes and lungs and caused the constant battle for cleanliness."[5]

Tom Harrisson was fascinated by the expectations of Worktown's women in relation to domestic chores noting that not only did they bear the burden of housekeeping, they also spent a great deal of their time in "keeping up appearances" to the outside world. To help keep them up, women had two main priorities: the brass latches on the front doors which were always highly polished and the doorsteps next to the pavements which were scrubbed clean before being marked with a donkey stone. On witnessing their cleaning routines, Harrisson commented: "Despite the grime of the atmosphere, curtains are always spotlessly clean and the doorsteps, rubbed to a pure white or brilliant yellow with a 'donkey stone', are a joy to the eye. Woe betide the negligent housewife whose doorstep disgraces the street by falling below the general standard of cleanliness, and a really energetic woman will go beyond her step and holystone a strip of the paving flags in front."

It was this communal pressure that helped bring about row after row of scrubbed doorsteps, gleaming doorknockers and unblemished net curtains, all of which gave Worktown's streets an undeviating, regimented appearance. The identical sash windows adorning the houses only added to the overall uniformity and incidentally to the list of chores for the housewives who were expected to keep them spotlessly clean as well. In this case, there was at least some relief for the housewife as washing the upper windows was normally done by a paid window cleaner because of the need to use ladders – the only domestic cleaning task in Worktown women were not expected to do.

As most terraced houses didn't have a garden let alone a driveway, their windows, doorsteps and door knockers abutted the pavements where people walked. Being so readily on show to any passing "busybodies" or "nosy parkers" was of course another imperative to keep everything spick and span. Because working class people lived in close proximity to their neighbours on either side and directly facing on narrow terraced streets, inevitably housewives competed amongst themselves to maintain the cleanest household – an unspoken rivalry often simmering just below the surface of neighbourliness with one Observer writing of the women living on Davenport Street: "competition goes on with cleaning the front, who's can be the cleanest."[6]

The competition involved in cleaning was most apparent in the way women treated their front doorsteps. Harrisson noted the ritualistic aspects of doorsteps and the way the donkey stones of urban folklore were used to clean them. Although the cleaning stones used for scrubbing steps were always called "donkey" stones, in fact, only one manufacturer, Read's, could truly claim the name. After becoming established in Manchester in the nineteenth century, Read's company chose a donkey as their trade mark which was duly stamped in relief on each of their products. Thereafter, the name stuck for all cleaning stones despite the northwest at one time being home to eleven factories making stones, none of which had donkeys on them. Most donkey stones were white in colour although some came in a dark cream hue and a golden yellow.[7] Although the stones were relatively inexpensive costing only half a penny each, they were often given away by "rag and bone" men in exchange for old rags and other unwanted things so in reality, they mostly cost nothing at all.

Whenever there was a dry day in Worktown, housewives scrubbing away at their doorsteps was a familiar sight – an activity recorded in several of Spender's most evocative photographs. This task began with women washing the surface dirt off the steps before dipping their donkey stones into buckets of water and scrubbing away at the doorstep over and over again. When the step was spotless, it was only declared finished after the housewife had drawn a line around it with her donkey stone. Although the purely decorative effect never lasted very long in Bolton's grimy atmosphere, the thin white, cream or yellow stripe etched where the step joined the pavement had a deeper significance on working class streets. Regular cleaning is obviously necessary for healthy living but donkey stoning a stripe around the step serves no discernible purpose apart from letting the neighbours know that the cleaning has been done. A cursory glance at Spender's photographs of Bolton's streets shows this symbol of respectability and self-esteem is rarely missing from any doorstep.

Mass Observation searching for patterns in the mosaic of human experience explored the seasonal aspects of domestic routines. One twenty-two year old woman told an Observer that she was doing her "spring" cleaning – an odd concept in itself as women were almost always cleaning anyway. When asked what this meant and why it was done at that specific time of year she replied: "for the summer – you get out the summer cushions and the light curtains instead of the heavier ones."[8]

It was of course one thing to document Worktown's repetitive cleaning routines, another to have to do them. It is scarcely believable that at the time of writing, there are still significant numbers of people who are able to recall first hand the drudgery involved in one of Worktown's most arduous tasks: the washing and drying of a household's clothing, bed linen and curtains. It was a weekly routine reserved for Mondays, the day set aside for it in working class communities and it was so ingrained that the term "Washday" was often used instead of Monday to mark the first day of the working week; a day that for most women brought only hours of toil using an arsenal of long-forgotten equipment – coppers, dolly tubs, possers, washboards, mangles, carbolic soap, soda and "Dolly Blue".

Preparations for Washday began in earnest on Sunday nights when grubby shirt collars and cuffs were soaped ready for the next day's early start. At the same time, any especially dirty laundry was put in big wash tubs to soak overnight. Washday proper started at dawn with the housewives filling buckets of cold water from a single brass tap located above shallow earthenware sinks known as slopstones. The water was then poured into the coppers; primitive gas heated boilers with wooden lids which came complete with ladling cans and pairs of wooden tongs.[9] When the water reached boiling point, "the whites" – mainly shirts, tablecloths, bed sheets and handkerchiefs – went in separately to other laundry for the "long boiling" which was meant to get whites spotlessly clean.

In the meantime, as coppers boiled away, the "coloureds" were sorted into different piles – from the cleanest to the dirtiest in order to prepare them for washing. After transferring buckets of hot water from the coppers to the dolly tubs used for washing clothes, the least grubby laundry went in first so the water might stay as clean as possible for as long as possible; an economic imperative because hot water was an expensive commodity in working class homes. Next the women used possers, dollies or even simple wooden sticks to stir and agitate the heavy, laundry loads over and over again-an exhausting activity as each batch of laundry generally required several rinses to get it clean. All the time, the women inspected the saturated garments by lifting them up from the tubs with their sticks and possers, or sometimes even huge wooden tongs before plunging them back in the water for another wash if required.

As the housewives laboured over the tubs, the water became dirtier and cooler. Only when each load of washing was finished to the housewives' satisfaction, was it taken out before another load of the incrementally dirtier laundry was added. All the while, the women were furiously rubbing any deeply stained garments against the ridges of washboards-sheets of corrugated iron or glass encased in wooden frames – to pummel the dirt out of them.

In the meantime, the whites were boiling in the coppers. They were only declared finished after a final soaking in water that had tablets of synthetic ultramarine known as Dolly Blue dissolved into it. These little tablets along with baking powder were added in muslin bags and ensured the garments retained a "bluey whiteness"; an important part of any self-respecting housewife's laundering routine especially as white cotton garments tended to go yellow with age. The tablets of blue manufactured by companies like Reckitt's, and a Bolton based company, William Edge, all promised "snow white linen" and they were considered an essential addition to the paraphernalia of Washdays.

When all the washing was at last clean, it was time to get it all dry. The first stage involved wringing the cold, wet garments out by hand before housewives fed them through a mangle, a feature of every scullery in Worktown. Although these primitive machines came in different sizes and designs including some that could be converted into tables when not in use, all shared the same characteristic: yet more physical effort was needed just to turn the rollers which squeezed as much water as possible out of the washing. It was common for children to help mothers on Washdays and it was also common for them to trap their fingers in the mangles' rollers through not being deft enough or on occasion, playing with the machines. As a result of their labours on Washdays, the hands of women became hard and calloused over time. Hardly surprising then that their condition was once a measure of social class in Britain – the rougher the hands, the more working class the woman.

When all the damp clothes and sheets were at last ready for "pegging out", women lugged the laundry outside and down the back yards before hanging it on the lines strung between the walls of the narrow back streets. Even then, there was much to do because housewives had to sort and hang each garment in a different way to maximise the breeze blowing through it. Shirts were pegged tightly by the collar, pillow cases anchored at the open end so they billowed in the wind and sheets bent double over the line, all held in place with dozens of little wooden dolly pegs. In order to make ironing the laundry easier afterwards, long wooden props up to nine feet in length raised the washing higher into the breeze to help blow the creases out.[10]

Such was the persistent grime in the atmosphere in Worktown, the washing lines themselves quickly became dirty – yet another frustration for the housewives. Thankfully, the *Bolton Evening News* was on hand to offer advice in its weekly column featuring domestic tips – "for women" of course – which advised them that their washing lines could be "easily cleaned" by rolling them round and round the washboard whilst scrubbing them.[11] After hanging the laundry out to dry (presumably on washed lines), coal deliveries and dirty children playing games on the back streets all threatened to undo a day's unremitting toil. If that wasn't irritating enough, some Boltonians recalled that the washing hung out on the back street was just as likely to get grubby from being outside due to the constant chimney smuts and soot falling from the sky. Rain was yet another nuisance on Washdays and whenever the sky blackened and the first raindrops fell – a not uncommon occurrence – the yells of "it's spitting! It's spitting!" shouted over the walls of the backyards led to a stampede and the speed with which a week's laundry could be brought back inside by the panicking housewives became part of mill town folklore.

Because getting a family's weekly laundry clean was so arduous, it is hardly surprising that it took up most of the day and there wasn't much time to do anything else on Washdays. Monday's evening meal- called "tea" in the industrial north- was often cold meat left over from Sunday; a reflection of the demands of washday as much as the economics of the household budget.

Advertisements on hoardings and in the *Bolton Evening News* in the 1930s promoting various cleaning products are reminders of what Washdays once involved because the various manufacturers' claims for the efficacy of their products show just how much hard work was once involved. The makers of Rinso soap advertised that their product ended the need for "long boiling and hard rubbing" before claiming somewhat fraudulently that as a result "Hard work on washday is a thing of the past." They were similarly overly optimistic about the effectiveness of another of their products claiming "Today women are finding that they need no longer be tired out and nervy on Monday evenings. That's because they no longer have to rely on hard rubbing to get their clothes clean." Unfortunately, most of the time they did and to make matters worse, manufacturers often used photographs of unruffled, pretty women smiling over their dolly tubs to promote their cleaning products which can only have infuriated the hard-at-it housewives sweating over piles of laundry in damp sculleries.

One laundry business's advertising rhetoric went as far as promising to abolish Washdays altogether. "Don't get us wrong, we haven't discovered the Elixir of Life but are referring to that old Bolton pastime of pegging out the clothes when it's fine, dashing in with them when it rains, crawling out with them again when it stops raining and tottering them in again" their advertisement stated before warning "There are more cases of backache caused among Bolton's housewives by bending over washtubs than by getting into baby cars. But to abolish bathtub backache, it is only necessary to send your wash to us."[12] Unfortunately most women couldn't afford to, so they were stuck with the "long boiling" and the "hard rubbing", and if "crawling", "tottering", "hard work", "nervy", "tired out", "backache" and "exhausting" was the routine vocabulary of Washdays, it says everything about what Worktown's housewives were expected to do.

If getting their laundry clean was difficult enough for Worktowners, so too was keeping themselves clean. Bathrooms were non-existent in the "two-up, two-down" terraced houses – the bulk of the accommodation for Bolton's army of mill and factory workers. Consequently, adults, adolescents and children took their weekly baths downstairs in the living room in front of the fire or range and usually, all the family had a bath on the same night. As a result, like Washdays, "Bath Nights" were a weekly ritual, more often than not on Saturday nights.

This pattern may at first appear odd, but setting aside a specific night for bathing was essential in houses without the convenience of running hot water. The absence of what today is considered the most basic of amenities meant taking a bath in Worktown demanded a colossal effort involving the whole family. The "tin" baths of urban folklore used for bathing were actually made of zinc and they were generally found hanging from large hooks on the walls of backyards, sculleries, and occasionally the cellars of houses large enough to have one. To make carrying the baths easier –especially when the dirty water was being thrown away – they were manufactured with two large handles one on either side. After plonking the bath on the floor as close to the fire as possible, water was boiled in the scullery and carried in buckets, kettles and pans to the bath by family members working in relay.

Due to the tiresome fetching and carrying and also the expense of producing enough hot water, a hierarchy born of necessity resulted with children usually bathing first followed by their parents who got in the same water when the children had finished. Furthermore, as the members of the household took their turn – and it should be remembered that large families with four or more children were quite common in Worktown – water continued to be boiled ready to top up the bathwater as it cooled. So luxurious was hot water recalled one Worktowner, Joyce Allen, after all the members of her family had had their baths, even the family dog was thrown into the bath before the dirty water was finally used to wash the flags in the back yard.[13] Whilst a tin bath filled to the brim with hot water might have felt warm and luxurious to smaller children, they were considerably smaller than most modern baths and in terms of adults and adolescents, as much of their bodies could be out of the water as actually in it.

Judged against contemporary norms, a once-a-week bath might suggest Worktowners were found wanting in terms of personal hygiene, however it is worth pausing briefly to consider the context of these routines. The north of England is not exactly noted for its warm climate which meant for most of the year, family members would take their baths before drying themselves with damp towels in carpet-less, freezing cold houses with only the most rudimentary comforts. Boltonian, Brenda Hall, later recalled the kind of discomforts working class people experienced: "Imprinted on my mind from those times is the cold blue linoleum on the bedroom floor across which I walked to trace with a finger the fern patterns in ice on the windows. Nobody had central heating … though there was a cast iron fireplace in the bedroom the only time a fire was lit was when somebody was ill and they had to stay in bed."[14]

Mrs Hall's memories are far from unusual. Before the Second World War, the vast majority of Worktowners lived in homes that were frighteningly primitive in comparison with most contemporary houses. In 1921, only twelve per cent of British homes had electric lights. Even in 1933, only one house in every three had a supply of electricity and of course it was more affluent households – not the homes of the working class –

that first enjoyed the benefits of a safe, convenient power supply. After the national grid was established in 1937, the use of electricity did become more widespread but nevertheless, even as late as 1944, only two out of every three British houses had electricity.[15] The absence of electricity might be considered hardship enough, but as we have seen, houses could also be extremely cold before the advent of virtually draught proof UPVC doors, double glazed windows and efficient central heating systems – all now largely taken for granted.

Furthermore, at the time of the Worktown investigation, most of the floors in terraced houses were covered in cold linoleum because carpets were relatively expensive, inside walls were often damp and crawling with cockroaches which reputedly were only bold enough to appear when the lights were turned off and beds with overcoats piled up on top of the blankets to keep their sleeping occupants warm on cold nights were a common sight. To compound the miseries, large families were usually crammed into houses that were tiny compared with many modern homes. Little wonder that a bath once a week was quite enough. Indeed, the fact that relative cleanliness *was* achieved by the weekly domestic routines in Worktown is quite remarkable by any measure. It is telling that many of the middle class academics who joined Tom Harrisson in Davenport Street were genuinely shocked and appalled by the living conditions in Bolton. Such was the dislocation from their normal experience, they even considered 85 Davenport Street to be miserable, down-at-heel, and damp although it was actually more spacious and of a better build quality than many other houses in the town.

It is worth noting however, that just because the Worktowners only had a bath once a week, it didn't mean they didn't wash daily in the scullery using the cold water tap although whether products like Wright's Coal Tar Soap ever really succeeded in keeping "a man looking fit and fresh" for very long as their advertisements claimed remains open to question. For women, products like Icilma's dry shampoo – "Just sprinkle on and brush out" – were widely promoted to help to keep hair cleaner between the weekly baths, and in a rather unpleasant contrast the Brylcreem company was happy to advertise that their hair styling cream for men contained "no soap." No wonder antimacassars, small easily washed cloths, were commonly found draped over the backs of settees to prevent greasy stains getting on the cushions from the heads of those sitting on them.

There was however, one small shred of comfort for the Worktowners enduring the begrimed living conditions. At least Bolton's industrial base was principally cotton spinning rather than coal mining for it was universally acknowledged that conditions in mining towns were far worse than anywhere else. Despite the cotton industry's dominance, there were several coal mines in Bolton that employed thousands of miners. Almost unbelievably in a town as grubby as Bolton, miners stood out from other workers on their way home from work because of their dirty faces. This indignity resulted from the fact that employers rarely built bathing facilities at their collieries for miners to wash themselves after a shift. At the height of Britain's industrial might – an economy that was dependent on coal miners as much as any other industrial workers – spending every day caked in filth was simply dismissed as an occupational hazard, which in retrospect is all the more appalling considering miners were doing one of the country's most burdensome and dangerous jobs. Although the building of pithead washing facilities could have gone some way to giving miners a semblance of respect at the end of each working day, their employers dismissed the possibility of building them at most collieries as they argued it was simply uneconomic when no seam of coal lasts forever.

Washdays and Bath Nights and all they entailed only began to disappear after the Second World War although as Worktown remained unchanged in many respects for at least another twenty-five years, some routines persisted for longer than might be expected. It is worth re-emphasising that the Worktown that was observed by those in Davenport Street was essentially a product of Victorian times. Taking a Worktowner celebrating their sixtieth birthday in 1938 as a representative example, he or she would have been born in 1878. In terms of the house they most likely lived in, the plumbing or lack of it, the outside lavatories and tin baths, the coal fires and absence of electricity and running hot water, little had changed since they were children growing up in the autumn years of Queen Victoria's reign. On the other hand, by the time someone born in Worktown in 1938, reached the same milestone birthday in 1998, most of the domestic routines and living conditions they experienced in their early lives had completely vanished.

Washdays began to change after two factors came together at roughly the same time. First, the development of more practical domestic washing machines, and second, a growing number of people with enough disposable income to buy them. Electric washing machines had in fact been available since Edwardian times but they were all of beastly dimensions. In addition, they were often unreliable and along with the incompatibility of water and electricity, not entirely safe. But far more importantly, for the first half of the twentieth century, washing machines were prohibitively expensive so their impact on working class people was bound to be negligible. Indeed, when the Happy Homes Exhibition took place in Bolton's Drill Hall in Silverwell Street between September and October 1938 – an event photographed by Humphrey Spender and the subject of a number of Observer's reports – amongst advertisements for radiators, vacuum cleaners, clocks, irons, cookers and even refrigerators, significantly, there is not a single one for washing machines.[16]

After the Second World War however, washing machine manufacturers improved the design of machines making them safer and smaller. More importantly, washing machines started to become increasingly affordable due to the numbers of them rolling off the production lines. In the main it was American companies that were leading the way taking advantage of the fact that the European economies which had been most shattered by the war were beginning to recover meaning people had more money to spend on labour saving applicances.

Alongside innovations in washing machine design, a range of new and very effective synthetic detergents using petroleum by products were also being developed. *Fab* launched in 1949, was the first, followed by *Tide* in the following year. During the 1950s, *Surf*, *Daz*, *Omo* and perhaps the most familiar and enduring, *Fairy Snow*, were all launched.[17] All these washing powders soon became household names as well as staple items on the shelves of corner shops, Co-op stores, and the early supermarkets. Their familiarity to the British public by the end of the 1950s was evidence of the growth in the ownership of washing machines as British society became more affluent. By then, post-war government propaganda films were claiming that the "The four foundations of modern living" were the fridge, washing machine, cooker and hot water boiler and if advertisements in the *Bolton Evening News* during these years are anything to go by, many working class Boltonians were no strangers to the benefits they brought.[18]

In the mid-1950s, the beginning of the consumer boom, Bolton's hardware shops were beginning to stock a range of washing machines for the increasing number of people able to buy or rent them. As well as selling an ever-widening range of models, Bolton electrical goods showrooms were offering free demonstrations of how to operate washing machines; not entirely a sales gimmick as most of the young housewives the advertisements were hoping to attract had been children in Worktown and had never seen a washing machine, never mind used one. Presumably after being taught how to use it, an Hoover washing machine could be acquired for an initial deposit of ten shillings (50p), followed by a weekly rental of seven and eight (approximately 38p).

For those who preferred to buy a machine outright rather than rent one, Bolton's stores were advertising washing machines for sale at £87. As a further enticement, some machines were being offered on Hire Purchase terms requiring 104 weekly payments: an early example of the kind of credit being made available to working class people that was fuelling demand for things like washing machines.

The first domestic washing machines to sell in significant numbers were twin tub appliances which as the name implies, featured one tub for washing, the other for wringing out the moisture. These pioneering machines were still relatively labour intensive as they came equipped with two hoses – one which needed to be attached to a tap so the drum used for washing could be filled with water while the other was used to empty the tub after drying. Before fully plumbed in washing machines became ubiquitous, twin tub machines still required considerable attention during the wash cycle leaving one local supplier of washing machines advertising in the *Bolton Evening News* to concede that "Even the best washing machine can only do part of the job!". Nevertheless, by the end of the 1950s the time and labour needed to do the weekly washing was changing fundamentally.

Of course not everyone was able to join in the Washday revolution immediately. Like most new technological developments when first launched to consumers, washing machines were relatively expensive. In 1959, the average wage for a British manual worker was £13 a week so a washing machine would cost approximately five times the average weekly wage. Putting this figure in context, fifty years later, many washing machine models could be bought for less than £200 – considerably less than the weekly minimum wage stipulated by the government. Because of their relative expense, washing machines in the immediate post-war years represented a major investment for most households although it would be safe to presume any older housewives with memories of Worktown's washdays can only have considered such an investment, money very well spent. Naturally, not every family was in a position to afford one so they became something to aspire to and save for, especially for young couples who were getting married and setting up their first homes. When they could finally afford their first washing machine, some younger women understandably experienced pangs of guilt when they recalled that their own mothers had never been fortunate enough to own one.

In the same decade, climatic factors led to changes which would have a more indirect but equally important effect on Washdays. In December 1952, a peculiar combination of damp air and lack of wind led to the Great London Smog; an impenetrable thick mist which descended on the capital city created by a combination, of smoke, soot and fog. It lasted for five days and resulted in the deaths of some 4000 people. In 1956, the government responded with the first Clean Air Act which aimed to control domestic sources of smoke pollution by introducing smokeless zones. "Should new tenants be made to burn only smokeless fuel?" asked a newspaper reporter in the *Bolton Evening News* in August 1958, which suggests there were some reservations about the new fuels. Clearly one councillor didn't share them claiming that "Bolton led the country in the fight against smoke pollution." But then again Bolton ought to have led the fight given that it probably had more to gain than any other town in the country. As a result of the much overdue legislation, the new fuels burned in smokeless zones began to make Bolton's air cleaner overall.

In 1968, there was further government intervention. The Clean Air Act: Tall Chimneys was intended to help disperse air pollution more effectively from factory chimneys. Perhaps no town anywhere in Britain benefitted from the new regulations as much as Bolton whose forest of factory chimneys was still an awe inspiring sight in the 1960s. Rather more sadly for those of a romantic inclination, in August 1968 the last British steam locomotive to carry passengers made a return journey from Liverpool to Carlisle finally bringing the country's age of steam locomotion to an end. For all the nostalgia surrounding them, steam trains were filthy things and they had contributed more than their fair share to the griminess of Worktown. As Worktown's industrial base began to decline, smoke-filled railway sidings, warehouses and distribution depots in Halliwell and on Crook Street amongst others were deemed surplus to requirements and they closed. Although it was an indication that the cotton industry was in terminal decline, it at least brought one benefit to the town: much cleaner air. Meanwhile gas and electric fires had started to replace coal fires in many homes and along with smokeless fuels, it meant the sunny days when there was a haze in the air and the shadows were indistinct began to at last recede into folk memory.

So too, the dolly tubs. When in April 1958, a competition in the *Bolton Evening News* offered "lucky housewives" (no change in who was expected to do the washing) an opportunity to win one of a hundred sparkling new Hoovermatic washing machines, it was as much evidence of the way washing machines were becoming commonplace as the generosity of the competition's organisers. For the unlucky majority who did not win one, there was by then no shortage of places in Bolton to buy them. There were some fourteen Hoover washing machine dealers in the town centre alone by the late 1950s which included department stores like Whittakers, bigger retail outlets like the Co-operatives and smaller independent dealers like Bullough's and the Thomasson Brothers, both trading from stalls located in Bolton Market Hall; a quite remarkable contrast with the Worktown of just twenty years previous where shops selling washing machines were virtually unknown. In 1957, only one in five British households had a washing machine. Within three years, there were an impressive fifty per cent of households with washing machines; figures that suggest at least half of Bolton's housewives could celebrate the dawn of a new decade by at last getting rid of their dolly tubs.[19]

With full employment and rising wages marking the early 1960s, advertisements for washing machines became common staples of the "small ads" pages in the *Bolton Evening News*. In 1963, Servis a British manufacturer launched their first fully automated washing machine-a significant breakthrough in washing machine design.[20] In the same year, the Hoover Company were boasting that only they had made five million washing machines; an extraordinary figure which by definition must have saved precisely the same number of women across the world incalculable hours of back breaking work.[21]

As the 1960s came to an end, whether it was a Hoover or a Servis, a top-loading or a front-loading, a twin tub or an automatic, washing machines had become a routine addition to kitchens. Moreover, with growing affluence some washing machines were even being put in "utility" rooms; a word gaining wider currency amongst Bolton's home owners and it barely needs saying, one that had been completely unknown in Worktown.

For the employees of William Edge and Sons based in Halliwell on the outskirts of Bolton, the growth in washing machine ownership was a cloud that came without a silver lining. In 1968, the company finally stopped production of Dolly Blue, their "magic" bags of ultramarine that had once made the Worktown housewives' "whites whiter." Although undoubtedly unsettling for the 200 workers who were made redundant, it was further evidence that the old rituals of Washday were disappearing.

By the early 1970s, in Bolton as everywhere else, washing machines were no longer thought of as the preserve of the better off. In a quite extraordinary social change, many of the young mothers happily using their washing machines, at a time of their choosing, on several days of the week, had themselves grown up in households where they had watched their own mothers toiling over dolly tubs every Monday. The chasm between the experiences from one generation to the next grew even wider as space-saving, front-loading machines with fully automated programmes to make washing laundry even more efficient came onto the market in increasing numbers. Moreover, by then, they were becoming relatively inexpensive compared to other household items. To exemplify this social progress, in 1974, the Asda superstore in Astley Bridge was advertising automatic washing machines for sale at £59.95 while in comparison, new colour televisions in the town's electrical stores were costing as much as £175.[22]

Inevitably there were drawbacks inherent in the social changes surrounding cleaning routines. In 1979, Eli Whalley, the very last surviving manufacturer of donkey stones finally ceased production. When the factory in Ashton-in-Makerfield closed, a century old tradition of using donkey stones to scrub doorsteps passed quietly into history taking with it a century old tradition of women competing to have the cleanest one. Scant comfort for the redundant employees admittedly but at least the factory where they worked had outlasted the "rag and bone" men who had used their donkey stones as currency. Apart from the iconic *Steptoe and Son* comedy programme which kept memories of them alive, these wheelers and dealers had disappeared from Bolton's streets during the 1960s as rising prosperity brought in its wake a more "disposable society" more inclined to throw things away.

Other aspects of Washday were also disappearing. The tedium of getting laundry dry was ended by the affordability of tumble dryers, an historical narrative which shares much in common with the story of washing machines. Tumble dryers had been around for most of the twentieth century but like washing machines, the prohibitive cost of the first dryers meant working class people could not afford them. After the Second World War, improvements in designs led to tumble dryers becoming both practical and more affordable. As a result, the outdated mangles were consigned to the tip or museums as housewives enjoyed the convenience of drying clothes without blistering their hands, checking the children's fingers were alright or constantly glancing heavenwards for fear of rain. Technological breakthroughs also made their mark on dryers and before long, they reduced in size and perhaps more importantly, they became much quieter – noisiness in operation being one of the main drawbacks of the early machines. These improvements helped make dryers more practical to use and when programmable features became widespread, the old washing lines with their laundry flapping in the wind, once the outward facing badge of a family's respectability in Worktown, started to disappear.

By the 1980s, Bolton's housewives or just as likely in more egalitarian times, their husbands, were the beneficiaries of a transformation their parents could scarcely have imagined. Aided by programmable washing machines and dryers, doing a household's weekly washing had become virtually effortless. Simply open the door of the washing machine, throw in the laundry, put in detergent and softener, flick the switch, and then go and do something else. Shortly after, remove the damp washing, put it in the adjacent dryer, flick the switch, and then go and do something else. A whole week's worth of laundry could now be done in a fraction of the time and with significantly less effort than had been required for only one set of bed sheets in Worktown forty years previously. Moreover a household's laundry could be done on any day and at any time, including during the night to take advantage of cheaper electricity tariffs after "quartz technology" and computerised control enabled precise, remote programming of washing machines and dryers; technological innovations which first appeared in the mid-1980s.[23] In a remarkable transformation, Bolton's housewives had gone from dolly tubs to digital control within two generations.

It hardly needs saying that the impact of this change was most keenly felt by women. In the 1960s, despite more enlightened times, Worktown's gender roles held sway and generally it was women who remained responsible for most or all of the domestic chores in working class households. The growth in the ownership of washing machines and dryers alongside other time saving appliances was a phenomenon that enabled many women to go out to work full time, part of the reason why Britain's economy boomed at that time. Moreover, opportunities were widening for women (and men) in a more diverse employment market which demanded new qualifications and skills. With less time required for completing domestic chores and of course, changing attitudes, a generation of women were better positioned than ever before to pursue educational opportunities or full-time careers in well paid occupations; something which had been impossible for most women shackled by time-consuming domestic chores in Worktown and moreover, the universal expectation that they would be the ones who would do them. In this respect, it's fair to say that Bendix, Hoover, Servis and Hotpoint did just as much for the cause of women's emancipation as any impassioned feminist arguments of the time or any number of their bras supposedly burnt in protest.

As Worktown's Washdays were disappearing, so too the rituals of its Bath Nights. By far and away, the most significant factor in their disappearance was the national slum clearance programmes of the mid twentieth century. This enlightened legislation began with the Housing Act 1930 which aimed to rid British towns of their worst housing stock – the hideous legacy of Victorian industrialisation of which Bolton had more than its fair share. This fundamental change in the kind of houses ordinary people might live in signalled the beginning of the end for tin baths in front of fires because when new houses were built to replace the demolished slums, they all had toilets and bathrooms installed from the outset.

However, slum clearance in Bolton was not without its challenges. In November 1962, the council's programme fell behind schedule partly due to the reluctance of many people to leave areas they had lived in all their lives. This problem was worse in Bolton than other comparable towns because of the unusually high number of owner-occupiers, many of whom were understandably reluctant to surrender their property. The slow pace of clearance in the town brought unwelcome attention from the government who urged Bolton Council to do something "more than it has been about its slums."[24]

Although the editor of the *Bolton Evening News* agreed that the town needed to rid itself of "the shame", he then added somewhat defensively that "many of the houses designated as 'slums' are cosy and comfortable inside." He continued to excuse the slow progress by saying that "the fact that a house is imperfect (having an outside toilet for instance) does not necessarily mean that it is a 'slum'." He may have had a point, but the absence of an inside lavatory also meant the absence of a bathroom which would probably be "slum" enough for most people. Thankfully for those Boltonians still living without inside lavatories and bathrooms, the initial plan for 2488 of the worst houses to be demolished was reformulated to encompass the demolition of 3670 dwellings before 1967.[25]

As the houses came crashing down, new houses were springing up on estates built on green fields all around the edges of Bolton. At the same time there was substantial redevelopment of the areas where terraced houses, back yards, and cobbled streets had been ubiquitous bringing different types of houses and in some cases, high rise tower blocks. This change in where many Boltonians lived and the type of houses they expected to live in simply mirrored national trends. Nine million new houses were built in Britain in the thirty years after the Second World War and of course they all boasted indoor bathrooms. Bevan's Housing Act of 1948 made a significant contribution to this social progress by stipulating a generous contingency for the building of council houses with spacious rooms and more crucially, indoor bathrooms. As a consequence, by 1964, eighty per cent of households renting from a local authority enjoyed the sole use of a sink, a fixed bath, a washbasin, a hot water supply and a toilet.[26] Initially, some people were overwhelmed by the change in their circumstances. One Boltonian after moving to a new house later recalled "there was a tiny kitchen with a sink and gas cooker and a passage that passed behind the lavatory to a room made wonderful by an enamelled cast iron bath and a wash basin, both even had taps. It took weeks to accept that hot water ran from one of them."[27]

It should be remembered that there had in fact been substantial numbers of council houses built in Bolton before Bevan's legislation. In the 1930s, large Corporation estates as they were first known had been built in Breightmet, Hall-i-th-Wood, Johnson Fold, and Tonge Moor. Attitudes towards the new estates were explored by Mass Observation and make for interesting reading. One woman told an Observer: "I would like to move. It is so nice up there, there is a garden for the children. And a bath and I would like to have a nice house"; a comment that challenges the often held view that old working class communities were broken up with people being forced onto new estates against their will.

In another report, one Observer wrote: "Again reverting to generalisations, the popular conception of certain sections of the public that working class tenants of estates do not avail themselves of their new amenities is erroneous. It has been said that coal has been stored in the bath, etc. But this is totally untrue of the large majority of estate tenants." Whether the oblique reference to a "majority" meant there were a minority who did put coal in the bath is open to question, however it goes a long way to contradicting a sneering myth of the time; that working class people would only keep coal in the bath if they were fortunate enough to get one. Perhaps most significantly of all, the importance of keeping up appearances and communal pride that characterised Worktown's streets was also maintained on Corporation estates with one Mass Observation report concluding when working class people moved to the new housing "with very isolated exceptions a pride in living and appearances is adopted."

Over time, bathrooms became normal in Bolton's surviving, better built terraced houses. Most of them were "renovated" or extended with bathrooms being relatively easily incorporated into old properties after a stud wall dividing the second bedroom created a new room with enough space for a bath, toilet and sink. Strictly speaking, thousands of Bolton's surviving terraced houses which are still sometimes called "two-up , two-down" became "three-up, two-down" at some point in the mid twentieth century – a small bathroom alongside two bedrooms upstairs being more normal with the original landings reconfigured to provide space for three doors. Because bathrooms are now universal in what remains of Bolton's nineteenth century and Edwardian terraced housing, quite possibly many of the current occupants are unaware of the revolution of only half a century ago.

As a result of that revolution, tin baths, the most potent symbol of Worktown's Bath Nights, became part of working class folklore but despite the relentless social progress that was made, not as quickly as might be thought. Although "The times" may have been "a-changin'" in 1960s Britain, they were not "a-changin'" as fast as many people still shivering through Bath Nights would have liked. Whilst the decade is usually associated with the "white heat" of technology and radical social change, in 1964, only sixty-one per cent of British owner occupiers and only just over half of private tenants enjoyed the pleasures of indoor bathrooms.[28] The slow pace of progress was especially apparent in the old manufacturing districts; the places where a significant proportion of the population still lived and worked despite the popular myth that suggests everyone was driving around London in minis adorned with union jacks. The reality of the "swinging" decade was rather more humdrum for most Boltonians. Indeed, throughout the 1960s, Bridgeman Street Public Baths at the southern end of Bolton remained firmly anchored in Worktown still offering "slipper" baths with an unending supply of hot water for a small charge presumably for people without indoor bathrooms.

Similarly, the feature film, *The Family Way*, made in and around Bolton in 1966, confirms that some aspects of Worktown's domestic routines endured long after Mass Observation recorded them. When it was made, there were still plenty of locations to film the central characters working in local mills and factories that had hardly changed since Spender photographed them. However, *The Family Way's* plot about an unconsummated marriage and a glimpse – probably all too brief for some members of the audience-of Hayley Mills' bare bottom – suggests more daring social conventions were starting to permeate Bolton's terraced streets. However, the modernity jars somewhat as the recently married young girl played by Mills is discovered in a tin bath in the kitchen by her brother-in-law. Kitchen sink drama indeed. Admittedly, the film is fiction but like all convincing dramas, it is rooted in some reality. For a post-industrial society which has known nothing but indoor bathrooms, it is astonishing to find that tin baths were still commonly used – especially in poorer households – well into the 1970s as any cursory search of nostalgia/folk memories forums on the internet will confirm.

Even when people were away on holiday – a time when it might be expected they would have more time to relax and could enjoy a little pampering – using a bathroom was not necessarily included in the holiday experience. Quite remarkably, as late as 1967, the bathrooms in some of Morecambe's guest houses remained locked throughout the whole of the summer season – a draconian measure that was deemed necessary according to a spokesman for the Morecambe hoteliers because otherwise their guests would try to take a bath each day![29] Even holidaymakers lucky enough get into a bathroom in the 1960s often still paid for the privilege, an extra charge for taking a hot bath being far from unusual.

The hoteliers' attitudes were however becoming outdated. Perhaps the only reason they lingered on was the fact that old attitudes towards bathing remained stubbornly entrenched amongst a generation who had endured the miseries of wartime rationing and the austerity years. Although bathtubs with an endless supply of hot water were becoming part of everyday life, indulging oneself in a bath filled with steaming, hot water was somehow perceived to be an unnecessary luxury to a generation still haunted by the expense of boiling water in Worktown – attitudes which were encapsulated in the comment of one Worktowner who said to an Observer after moving to a corporation house: "Yes a bath is alright but you must heat it if you want it. Who can afford it."[30] Even in the late 1960s, to save time but equally likely money, when I was a child "stand up" baths were quite a regular occurrence in my house; a joyless experience which involved washing all over whilst standing up and shivering in a bath filled with only six inches of water.

Because this frame of mind persisted, the totemic aspect of a regular night set aside for having a bath lingered on even after indoor bathrooms had ended the rigmarole of tin baths in front of fires. Oddly enough, for much of the 1970s and 1980s, people still only had one bath a week. By that time, Sunday night had become the preferred option replacing the old Saturday night routine that had preceded the wearing of "Sunday best" in Worktown – a notion which had died out anyway thanks to people owning more clothes, a more relaxed and casual approach to dress, and of course a general decline in church attendances. For a generation enjoying (or enduring) their adolescence in the 1970s, the signature tune of Alan "Fluff" Freeman's Sunday night radio show "At the Sign of the Swinging Cymbal", was a different kind of symbol: it reminded many a teenager that the weekend was over and it was time to have a bath in readiness for school the next day.

In turn, the Sunday Bath Night also disappeared after showering gradually became the nation's preferred bathing routine. This took a while to happen partly because British people were at first slow to embrace other alternatives to baths. American record producer, Tony Visconti on arriving in London from his native New York in the late 1960s later recalled the unpleasantness of washing himself in dirty water: "I also had to get to grips with washing my hair in the bath – why don't they have showers in this country, was all I kept thinking?"[31]

He obviously wasn't the only one thinking it because within twenty years, the routine of showering crossed the Atlantic. This happened partly because people became accustomed to showering every day when they went on holidays in other parts of the world, but mostly as a result of a gathering momentum extolling their virtues from a hygienic, economic and environmental perspective – arguments that were given an unexpected boost by the legendary summer of 1976. As the sunshine blazed on and on, record temperatures were recorded, reservoirs ran dry and stand pipes were used to ration water. Dennis Howell – not surprisingly, the only Minister for Drought Britain has ever needed – exhorted the British people to fill their baths with only five inches of water before sharing it with a partner: a better endorsement for the pleasures of showering would be hard to imagine.

As the 1970s drew to a close, shower heads fed by electric heaters with fitted shower curtains or glass screens appeared in ever increasing numbers over baths, a home improvement that was enthusiastically embraced partly because installing a shower of this type required little or no extra modification to existing bathrooms. But perhaps the most important factor that made showering so common was how it benefitted people living busier lives. Showers are not only more economic, they are also quicker than running a bath; especially important in households where both adults work full time – a pattern that became far more common as the century progressed. Consequently, showers have taken over from baths in most households bringing with them new routines with white collar workers often showering *before* going to work while those in manual occupations usually shower *after* work. Quite extraordinarily, by the time the twentieth century ended, Boltonians could be showered, dried, and dressed in less time than it had taken their grandparents to fetch the tin bath in from the back yard. But far more significantly still, indoor bathrooms meant personal hygiene with all its benefits had become a daily rather than weekly routine.

Given all the hardships of keeping clean in Worktown, it would be pleasing to think that the infant shivering in the tin bath or the women hanging out washing in dismal back streets in Spender's photographs lived long enough to enjoy the comforts of modern bathrooms and the convenience of washing machines and dryers. They deserved to, for there is a heartrending pathos about the housewives of Worktown scrubbing away at their steps as the soot fell relentlessly from above. They did it time and time again because keeping clean in the dirtiest of towns was an expression of their shared dignity and pride – a pride forever enshrined in what was the most humdrum of symbols: donkey stoned stripes on spotlessly clean doorsteps.

The same kind of fierce, communal pride was present amongst their husbands and sons too. But they showed it in an altogether different way by gathering all in one place and always at the same time: three o' clock on Saturday afternoons.

BURNDEN PARK

Spectators on the terraces of Burnden Park.
Humphrey Spender

Just as white stripes on doorsteps united Worktown's women, the white shirts of Bolton Wanderers Football Club united their men. Supporting their football team was just as much a Worktown habit as cinema going, church festivals, drinking in the pub and Washday. Describing the importance of Bolton Wanderers to Worktown, Tom Harrisson noted that: "nothing else matters much except the progress made by the town's football club whose stadium draws each Saturday more people than go into the pubs or churches."[1] This enthusiasm for football went far beyond sporting interests because when Harrisson wrote those words, Burnden Park, the home stadium of Bolton Wanderers Football Club, was the physical embodiment of Worktown's collective identity.

Fittingly for a town whose identity was synonymous with dark satanic mills, Bolton Wanderers played in a stadium which rose like a breakwater from an ocean of industrial detritus that had washed up around the town's southern perimeter. To the north of the ground, the soot-rinsed town centre; to the west, factories, mills, terraced houses and chimneys; eastwards, a dingy valley full of warehouses, sheds and mills cut in two by an equally dingy canal; on the southern side, a tide of industrial slurry that flowed virtually uninterrupted all the way to Manchester. In all respects, the location of Burnden Park was robust confirmation – as if any was ever needed in Worktown – that it was indeed "grim oop North".

It was grim in the ground too. Steam locomotion, the colossus that sculpted industrial Bolton, seeped into the very stadium itself courtesy of the locomotives that belched smoke over the crowds from above the steep terrace enclosing the northern end of Burnden Park. This part of the stadium was unique amongst British football grounds, for the steps where the spectators congregated were cut into the side of a huge railway embankment. The gigantic curving terrace even had its own signal box – a quirky but utilitarian feature as the supporters who gathered on it were massed below the main railway line connecting Bolton to the towns of east Lancashire. At one time, the unimaginatively named "Embankment" end of the ground alone could accommodate an astonishing 16,000 spectators. Due to the absence of any kind of roof, the Embankment offered an uninterrupted view of the action for a huge proportion of the people in the stadium and even some who weren't because as Harrisson noted, the train drivers often slowed down to give themselves and their passengers a glimpse of the football match before continuing to Trinity Street, the town's main train station.[2]

Opposite to the Embankment, the eponymous Great Lever End provided a further terrace for standing spectators. Although "The Lever End" was much smaller, there was at least a roof to provide some shelter from the damp Lancashire winters. Completing the stadium were two further terraces which ran along the full length of the pitch on either side. The smaller of the two backed onto the Manchester Road, while on the opposite side the Burnden Terrace towered above the Croal Valley and the Bolton to Manchester canal. The sides differed from the "ends" as they both had grandstands with seating just above the standing terraces that gave the spectators in them a more balanced, panoramic view of the pitch and a slightly more genteel match day experience. Shockingly, in common with most British football grounds at the time, the grandstands at Burnden Park were almost entirely made of wood – not the safest of construction materials at a time when smoking cigarettes was far more prevalent.

With terraces large enough to accommodate thousands of supporters at a time, football clubs were important in industrial towns because they offered an afternoon's entertainment at an affordable price. When the Worktown investigation took place, the price of admission to a football match was comparable to the price of a cinema ticket. Even a ticket for the 1933 FA Cup Final, the traditional climax to the football season and the Holy Grail for most football supporters, only cost 2/–6 (30p) at a time when a skilled craftsmen might earn around £4 a week.[3] Because football was so affordable for all but those on the lowest income or the unemployed, most professional clubs throughout the country were indelibly woven into the social fabric of the towns and cities they represented.

This bond with working class people was forged after football was well and truly wrested from its upper class origins by the teams which developed in Britain's manufacturing districts in the late nineteenth century; a bond still discernible in the nicknames of football teams which often refer to the artisan tradesmen who first formed the clubs. "The Gunners" because of Arsenals connection to the Woolwich Arsenal; "The Railwaymen" of Crewe Alexandra, a railway town; and "The Hatters" of Stockport County because of the town's hat-making tradition. And so on. In Bolton Wanderers' case however, the origin of their nickname, "The Trotters", is rather obscure. Some claim it is just another word for "wanderers"– teams that will go anywhere for success, others that it refers to pig's feet, a local delicacy known as trotters supposedly eaten by the players after training, some believe there was a pig pen next to one of the club's first grounds forcing the players to retrieve stray balls from amongst the pigs and lastly, trotter is a local colloquialism used to describe somebody who is a practical joker. Whichever of the stories rings most true, all of them have a working class pedigree.

Other aspects of footballing tradition also reveal similar provenance. Football was played at three o'clock on Saturday afternoons for no other reason than it allowed manual workers who were engaged in Saturday morning shifts in mills and factories to watch matches. The day and timing of matches also differentiated football from more middle class sports like cricket and tennis where fixtures were often played midweek – a factor which all but ruled out factory workers from watching because until the late 1930s, they were not entitled to paid holidays and their annual holiday week was inflexible as it was a fixed week in the calendar year.

Football's bond with working class communities was further strengthened by the close proximity of the grounds to the most densely populated areas from which teams drew their support. Most professional matches were contested within a bus or tram ride – sometimes walking distance – of where most of the "home" supporters lived, in marked contrast to the county cricket grounds, race courses or the premier tennis venues which might be some distance away. It was the supporters' proximity to their clubs' grounds which helped to promote the fierce tribal loyalty most in evidence at "derby" matches between teams from the same town or the nearest neighbouring one.

One Observer noted the ritual of football watching amongst men who had just finished work for the week writing: "On arriving home at midday on Saturday, the spinner or overlooker swallows a hasty meal and dashes off to the match."[4] On arriving there usually via the pub, he would join thousands of other mill and factory workers who had done much the same. After going through the turnstiles, whether from habit, economics, superstition or simply because they met their friends at the same time, most supporters made their way to the same preferred spot for each game which often necessitated – certainly at the time of Bolton Wanderers' heyday – getting into the ground with at least half an hour to spare before the kick-off. In the 1930s, with crowds regularly in excess of 50,000, the charged atmosphere created by huge numbers of supporters standing together offered both an exciting spectacle and an emotional safety valve for manual workers whose daily lives were at best routine, and at worst, grindingly monotonous.

The relationship between supporters and local teams is captured in L.S. Lowry's memorable painting *Going to the Match*. Depicting crowds of Lowry's signature match-stalk figures hurrying to a football ground already bursting at the seams, to the delight of many Bolton Wanderers' supporters it reputedly depicts a match day at Burnden Park. It is not however, an accurate portrayal of the ground as the Embankment appears to be at the Lever End and there are no railway lines; disparities that simply result from the fact that like much of Lowry's work, the painting is a composite of different elements. When it was bought on behalf of the Professional Football Association for some £2,000,000 in 1999 – at the time a record sum for a Lowry painting – the PFA's chief executive, Gordon Taylor, by happy coincidence an ex-Bolton Wanderers player, declared that the painting's appeal lay in the fact that it represented the "heart and soul of the game."[5]

Figuratively speaking, Bolton Wanderers' "heart" began to beat in the nineteenth century, its "soul" found in the generations who shared the constantly changing fortunes of the club that represented *their* home town. In common with other long established clubs, Bolton Wanderers' genesis can be traced to the Victorian obsession with masculinity; a notion expressed in the competitive team sports played in English public schools. In 1874, J.F. Wright, the vicar of Christ Church in Bolton, possibly influenced by the growth of "Muscular Christianity" – a philosophy preaching the spiritual value of sport – decided to form a football team. To that end he persuaded Thomas Ogden, a regular churchgoer, to collect sixpence each from any potential players in his congregation. Whether Reverend Wright was really enthusiastic about football or equally possible, was simply trying to divert virile young parishioners from other temptations remains a mystery, however what can be stated with certainty is that enough money was collected, a football was bought, and Christ Church Football Club became one of the country's first football teams.[6]

In 1877, Christ Church F.C. changed its name to the Bolton Wanderers. Four years later, the club moved to the Britannia Hotel on Pikes Lane which became their new home ground. In 1888, as the sport was gathering momentum throughout the country, Bolton Wanderers became one of only twelve founding members of the Football League which gave birth to the modern game in England and over time the whole world. The Pikes Lane ground however, proved unsuitable partly due to drainage problems and also because of the growing numbers regularly watching the Wanderers whose successful exploits on the pitch resulted in too many matches when the ground could no longer accommodate all those who wanted to get in. This forced the club's owners to look for a new home again; an imperative that was all the more pressing because an inconvenient hill adjacent to the Pikes Lane pitch meant that some people could comfortably watch the match without paying any admission fee!

In 1895, the wanderers proved worthy of their name again when the club moved to a new home ground constructed to the south of the town in the district of Burnden. Duly Bolton Wanderers welcomed Preston North End for a friendly match on 11 September 1895. The inaugural match at their new ground was followed just three days later by the Wanderers' first competitive league fixture; a match against Everton. At last the wandering was over for Bolton's football team: Burnden Park would be their "home" for over a century.

Meanwhile, all across the country football was becoming firmly established as the national game. In fact, Burnden Park was just one of many similar stadiums built in what some argue were football's "goldrush years"; a thirty year period of stadium building that began in 1895 when Everton's Goodison Park stadium was built and ended in 1923 with the completion of Manchester City's Maine Road ground. In the early part of the twentieth century, the professional clubs moving into these grounds were competing in two countrywide leagues and by then, like dance halls and cinemas which were also experiencing a similar growth spurt, football was firmly ingrained in working class popular culture.

After the restrictions placed on sporting fixtures during the First World War came to an end, football's popularity only continued to grow. So did the Wanderers' popularity as they enjoyed one of the most successful periods in their history. They won the F.A. Cup three times in the 1920s including a famous victory over West Ham in the first ever final played at the new (now "old") Wembley Stadium. The team's fortunes on the pitch however were more variable in the decade that followed. The Wanderers were unable to repeat their cup triumphs and they were actually relegated for the first time in 1933 playing in the second division for two seasons. Footballing disappointments aside, in the 1930s, crowds regularly exceeding 50,000 were common at Burnden Park; a period which included the highest attendance ever recorded when 69,912 supporters watched a game against Manchester City in 1933. Tellingly, of the sixteen highest recorded attendances in Burnden Park's history, four of them occurred during the 1930s.

With match days of such importance, inevitably Tom Harrisson made a point of observing one. Quite what the erudite, public school educated

Harrisson thought of such an alien experience must remain a mystery as in keeping with the aims of his project, he was there to be an objective rather than subjective observer. Nevertheless, his ten pages long, handwritten report dating from 20 March 1937, is compelling because it is a unique insight into the behaviour of typical football supporters watching a game; a distinct contrast with most other reports about Burnden Park which naturally focus on the action on the pitch with only the odd reference to those watching. Harrisson's report on the match between Bolton and West Bromwich Albion describes the mood of the supporters, the individual comments they made, the way supporters dressed and the social composition of the crowd. The home team had not won since December causing some apprehension amongst the home support, but Bolton eventually won the match 4-1 and according to Harrisson's report, the crowd left "jubilant."[7]

An anthropologist by profession, Tom Harrisson was bound to be fascinated by the primeval tribal behaviour he witnessed at Burnden Park. He noted for as long as the game lasted, "feelings are rapidly changing, up comes fury, exaltation, sarcasm" accompanied by equal amounts of disagreement, argy-bargy, and bickering. Harrisson also took time to record individual shouts from the crowd directed at the players of both teams labouring on the pitch below: "Hit 'im", "come on Andy", "no use at all", "Nasty, Nasty", "Foul. Right in the back, hit 'im in the kidneys", "What a bloody shot", "They're not shooting that's what it is" and "Come on ye pancake"; the latter, a rather tame insult by the vicious standards of many a football supporter. There was of course, partisanship aplenty. Harrisson recorded that "when a Bromwich player handles the ball all hands in crowd shoot up demonstrating to one another what he did. When a Bolton player handles 'no one says a word!'"[8] Harrisson also saw how the supporters could easily turn on their own noting "the vindictive nature of the crowd … all tell the players what they should have done" before concluding that the match was the only place men could shout in Worktown as they couldn't at home or at work.

The footballers Harrisson saw playing that day were earning at most £8 a week, the maximum wage imposed on players in the late 1930s. This was roughly double the industrial wage at the time. Given the scale of Bolton's industrial base, we can safely assume therefore the players Harrisson saw were at best only earning twice as much as the vast majority of those watching them. For this reason, famous footballers in the mid years of the twentieth century tended to be hailed as proletarian local heroes. Sporting immaculately Brylcreemed hair, square of jaw and with muscular arms folded across barrel chests, most looked like they had just finished a shift at the local mill or down the pit, which in many cases was not too far wide of the mark. Whatever the rights and wrongs of the enforced wage restraint, the fact that footballers' earnings did not distinguish them too much from other workers was important in cementing the ties between supporters, players, and of course, the town they represented.

Six months after Harrisson made his report, Humphrey Spender took his camera to Burnden Park. In contrast to Harrisson's written observations, Spender's visit resulted in an important visual record of football supporters standing on the terraces; a significant departure from most other photographs of Burnden Park (and other football grounds for that matter) which show the players on the pitch rather than the people watching them. Spender's photographs were actually taken at a reserve rather than a first team fixture; on this occasion, between Bolton Wanderers and Wolverhampton Wanderers – the first team being involved in a reciprocal match at Molyneux, Wolverhampton's home ground. Nevertheless, there was still an impressive 3000 spectators there on the day. Even though the attendance was obviously much lower than for a first team match, Spender's photographs capture the essence of an afternoon at the match on the cusp of what was arguably Burnden Park's golden age.

One of the most striking features of Spender's photographs is the almost complete absence of commercial exploitation. The only advertisements that are immediately apparent are for two local firms, Booth's steelworks and Magee Marshall Brewery – the latter something of a marriage made in heaven between two of the central interests of the 1930s working man: beer and football. Sponsorship on the players' shirts at that time let alone in the name of the ground was also completely unknown as were supporters wearing replica team shirts, a relatively modern phenomenon. Considering professional football was largely played in the winter months, another surprise is that scarves in club colours are not apparent. In fact, one of the more startling aspects of Spender's photographs is the conservative dress of the spectators at the match, something which had not gone unnoticed by Harrisson who recorded the preponderance of bowler hats and trilbies on the heads of those sitting in the grandstands.

By far and away, the most significant point of note is the total absence of women in the photographs. The football terraces of the 1930s were evidently a man's world. Any family ties were almost exclusively masculine – brother with brother, uncles and nephews, grandfathers and grandsons, and of course the most common relationship found at the match: fathers and sons. Taking their (male!) children to their first match and inculcating them into the terrace community was once an important rite of passage in working class families, a treasured shared experience that often continued over a whole lifetime with "dads and lads" continuing to go to the match together whenever possible.

The family bonds amongst supporters go some way to explaining why there were relatively few off-putting disturbances at football grounds before the 1970s. With delicious irony, John Lydon (Johnny Rotten), the lead singer of the Sex Pistols – a band not exactly remembered for their deference to authority – and a lifelong Arsenal supporter, recalled the essentially self-policing nature of the terraces he experienced as a child:

> It was incredibly family orientated and community based because you'd know everyone in there and they'd know you. Friends, neighbours, relatives, priests – a total community. Back then the locals wouldn't put up with any nonsense. If you were up to no good you would get a smack around your head from someone older telling you that you're out of order.[9]

With this kind of atmosphere prevalent at football grounds, it is perhaps not surprising to find that Harrisson on his visit to Burnden Park, found that there was "not very much bad language, except bloody." Given the routine swearing from supporters today, an extraordinary revelation unless of course Harrisson had unwittingly stood next to any clergymen who happened to be watching the match.

Two years after Spender photographed Burnden Park, the outbreak of the Second World War led to the immediate suspension of football matches throughout the country. Like the suspension of cinema, this was only a temporary measure before regional leagues were introduced to improve the morale of a nation waging war abroad and on the home front. Burnden Park did its bit for the war effort with the grandstands becoming storage space for the Ministry of Supply. Also doing their bit was the team. In a genuinely inspiring moment in the club's history, Harry Goslin, Bolton's captain, persuaded the playing staff to volunteer for service together and the "Wartime Wanderers" as they became known spent much of the war in the Royal Artillery Regiment. Tragically, Goslin the man at the heart of this brave enterprise, was mortally wounded in Italy in 1943. Fortunately, all the other players survived the war.

The war proved only a temporary lull in football's popularity for as soon as it ended, the crowds returned and the 1948–49 season saw support for British football teams reach its zenith with 41.3 million match attendances being recorded at grounds all around the country. The return of huge crowds however led to one of the darkest days in Bolton's history when Burnden Park acquired the unenviable distinction of being the scene of British football's first major crowd disaster.

On March 9 1946, Bolton entertained Stoke City for the second leg of an FA Cup quarter final. Although the official recorded attendance was 65,419, an estimated 85,000 spectators actually tried to get in to see what promised to be a fascinating encounter. Some supporters jumped over the turnstiles without paying, whilst others poured over the wall bordering the railway lines ripping up a retaining wall made of railway sleepers as they did so.

Both actions were sufficiently reckless to create a crush amongst the supporters nearest to the pitch. It is believed that the father of a distressed boy elected to leave the ground rather than endure the discomfort any longer and picked the lock on an exit gate to get to safety outside. This in turn led to a further deluge onto the Embankment through the now unlocked gate and as the teams came out, two barriers gave way and hundreds were trampled. As the chaos escalated, the match was briefly stopped before it was restarted quite unbelievably in front of several prostrate bodies laid at the side of the pitch – a measure deemed necessary to prevent further crowd problems. Because the match continued amidst the horror, many of those present, including my father and grandparents, insisted they were not aware that there was anything wrong until they had left the ground.

If many of those in the ground did not know what had happened, neither did the match reporter from the *Bolton Evening News*. "Amazing Cup Tie Scenes at Burnden Park" was the early edition's headline preceding only a detailed account of the ebb and flow of the game with no mention of fatalities. Within a couple of hours however, the "Final" edition of the evening paper made for grimmer reading. It confirmed that "at least 17 people were killed and many more injured".[10] Two days later, the newspaper revealed the full extent of the tragedy but remarkably for an event of such magnitude in the town's history, the Burnden Disaster still shared the front page with several other stories: "Germans knew nothing of Horror Camps", "Baby Thrown into Lake: Mother quoted" and more incongruously still, three photographs of just married local couples. Above their smiling faces, the main report confirmed that thirty-three people had been killed. Curiously, only seven of the deceased were actually from Bolton, the rest were from Atherton, Wigan, Barnoldswick, Leigh, Rochdale, Hindley, Littleborough, Ashton-in-Makerfield, Tyldesley and Manchester. The youngest victim, Henry Birtwistle who came from Blackburn was only fourteen years old.[11]

Besides the horrific death toll, a further 500 people had been injured, some seriously. One remarkable aspect of the Burnden Disaster is just how quickly it disappeared from the front pages of the town's newspaper and to some extent, the national consciousness. By the Tuesday after the match, there was very little coverage in the *Bolton Evening News* apart from a report about a relief fund which had been quickly established to help those most affected.[12] Instead, the disaster was already vying for column inches with headlines about a strike, an article about Eisenhower's decision to use the atom bomb, a murder story, petrol rationing, the Nuremberg trials and a photograph of a woman modelling the "latest styles in cotton fabrics". No wonder the Burnden Disaster subsequently acquired the sobriquet, the "Forgotten Disaster".

This may partly be explained by the fact that because the tragedy occurred less than a year after the Second World War ended, people were simply more inured to death and injury. Certainly the war was used to contextualise the disaster; one *Bolton Evening News* report pointing out that Bolton suffered more casualties at Burnden Park in one afternoon than during six years of air raids on the town.[13] However, in retrospect the most tragic aspect of the Burnden disaster was that if it was quickly "Forgotten", so too were any lessons that might have been learned about crowd safety.

Despite the tragedy, huge crowds still regularly gathered at Burnden Park, a trend that continued unabated throughout the 1950s. To claim the paucity of any alternative entertainment during the dismal years of austerity as the reason for the gigantic attendance figures, does not sufficiently acknowledge the appeal of football during this era. Although from this "high watermark" football attendances across the country would go into steady decline for many years, those who went to Burnden Park during this period were privileged to watch players like Tom Finney, Stanley Matthews, Wilf Mannion, Jackie Milburn, Bobby Charlton and of course Bolton's most famous player, Nat Lofthouse, nicknamed "The Lion of Vienna" following an outstanding performance for England when they played Austria in 1952.

Captained by Lofthouse, the 1950s was arguably the most memorable decade in the club's history. In 1953, the Wanderers played in one of the most dramatic FA cup finals of all time against Blackpool. As the half-time whistle blew, Bolton were winning 2-1, one of the goals being scored by Lofthouse. As the players were leaving the pitch, Blackpool's Stan Mortensen shook Lofthouse's hand and congratulated him on scoring a goal in every round of the competition; a remarkably sportsmanlike gesture considering Mortensen and his team were facing a third cup final defeat on the run.[14] In the second half however, much to the dismay of Bolton's supporters, Blackpool came back eventually winning 4-3.

In 1958, Bolton reached another FA cup final where on an occasion tarnished by the horror of the Munich air tragedy in February, they triumphed beating the decimated remnants of the Manchester United team 2-0. Perhaps understandably, it was not the most popular of victories in the circumstances as most neutral football supporters were rooting for the team who had overcome such appalling adversity to even reach the final.

The bond between the town and team during this period was at its pinnacle especially as Bolton's players, as we have seen, did not earn much more than the supporters who watched them. Moreover, all of Bolton's players in the 1958 cup winning team were, without exception, the product of working class streets – another factor which strengthened their ties with people from a northern mill town. Five players alone were of Lancashire stock of whom two – Lofthouse and Banks – were Bolton born and bred. The other six players were from the Midlands, Yorkshire and County Durham. Even Bolton's goalkeeper Eddie Hopkinson, though born in the northeast, had moved with his family as a young boy to Royton near Oldham.

As well as coming from backgrounds that meant supporters could easily identify with them, many players often spent a significant proportion of their careers playing at Burnden Park. Moreover, they often lived in Bolton or at least close by; a pattern more prevalent at a time when footballers tended to be "one club" men typically only playing for a couple of seasons at a different club in the twilight years of their careers. Of the eleven Bolton players who won the cup in 1958, seven played in Bolton Wanderers colours for ten years or more; Lofthouse played for the club for sixteen years, Bryan Edwards fifteen, and Tommy Banks and Roy Hartle thirteen years each. Even Derek Hennin, the shortest serving player, still played for the Wanderers for some seven years. Little wonder supporters tend to remember players like these with great affection. In truth, this kind of loyalty may have only resulted from the fact that the movement of footballers between clubs was strictly controlled at the time but nevertheless supporters could more easily identify with players who had a long association with the club and the town.

In 1958, floodlights were installed at Burnden Park at a cost of £25,000. Supplemented by additional lighting around the grandstands, they created a special atmosphere at the ageing ground on dark winter nights. Not only did they shine brightly above Manchester Road beckoning the crowds like a beacon, but they could also be seen from the surrounding moorlands some distance away. With improvements to the ground, huge support, and First Division football, all crowned by the iconic Lofthouse clutching the FA Cup, the 1957–58 season was arguably the height of the club's success.

But it wasn't to last. In 1964, Bolton Wanderers were relegated from the First Division. Although they had experienced relegation before, the relegation that year inaugurated the longest period outside the top flight the club has experienced to date. As it turned out, the dismal season was about much more than the vagaries of footballing fortunes. It also brought the curtain down on the era when Burnden Park was essential to Worktown's identity. When the Wanderers' relegation was confirmed after a 4-0 beating by Wolverhampton Wanderers, working class players trudged off in front of working class supporters, in a traditional English ground in what was still a major industrial town. When Bolton Wanderers next enjoyed sustained success, the players, the social class of supporters, the cost of a ticket to the game and the club's communal ties had changed beyond recognition. Moreover, Burnden Park had completely vanished.

The economic prosperity of the post-war era affected football just as much as the cinema, the pubs and church attendances. The once magnetic draw of the terraces was competing with a host of other alternatives as Bolton's skilled working class, buoyed by the security of full employment, enjoyed a new affluence. Consequently they began to break with social patterns which had been established in Victorian Britain. Watching football at Burnden Park was one of them. Not only were Boltonians spending money on an ever-wider range of consumer products, but there was also a growth of alternative leisure pursuits and hobbies to be enjoyed in the home and beyond; all of which challenged the football matches' dominance of Saturday afternoons.

Despite the previously noted popularity of football in the immediate post-war era, attendances at Burnden Park – as well as other British football grounds – were in fact, slowly declining. Conversely, the numbers of home owners in Bolton was growing. Owning a house brought new responsibilities for the man of the household when it was still men who generally maintained the house while women mostly did the cleaning and cooking. As we have seen, watching football was an overwhelmingly masculine pursuit but in terms of preserving domestic harmony, what price the match which took up all of Saturday afternoon when the lawn required mowing, the lounge decorating and the car on the drive needed washing? These kinds of household responsibilities had been largely unknown to male Worktowners living in rented houses, most of them without gardens. As lifestyles changed there were fresh demands on peoples' time and one place where the impact could be seen was on the terraces of Burnden Park. Even without their new household responsibilities, the rising prosperity of the post-war years saw a generation of men getting more used to the kind of home comforts which had been largely unknown in Worktown. Hardly surprising then that the cold, windswept terraces of Burnden Park were not exactly the most attractive proposition compared with centrally heated "front rooms" complete with comfortable settees, carpets, and of course television sets with *Grandstand* and *World of Sport* filling the Saturday afternoon schedules.

Although attendances at football matches were falling overall, the decline was not experienced equally across the diverse spectrum of clubs who formed the leagues. Although statistics show that attendances tumbled generally from the 1960s, for the country's bigger more glamorous clubs, the downward trend was more sluggish. In reality, it was the less fashionable clubs in the lower leagues that bore the brunt of the game's declining popularity. Unfortunately by then, Bolton Wanderers were one of them, the team even being relegated to the Third Division in the 1970–71 season. The days when clubs like Bolton Wanderers could rely on generation after generation automatically supporting their home town team were passing.

Just as supporters became more prosperous in the post-war era, so did the players. The maximum wage for footballers was raised to £14 in 1951, £15 two years later, £17 in 1957 and in the year the Wanderers won the cup, £20. However, as some footballers pointed out, by then the gap between their wages and the earnings of industrial workers had narrowed to only £5, the average figures being £20 for footballers and £15 for a skilled worker. More importantly, only twenty-five per cent of footballers were actually earning the maximum wage in 1955 and of course, "it was only a short career" as disgruntled players were always quick to point out.

In January, 1961 following a campaign orchestrated by Jimmy Hill, the maximum wage was abolished. Two years later, George Eastham, an Arsenal midfielder, successfully challenged the football authorities over regulations which stopped players from negotiating new contracts with other clubs; restrictions that effectively prevented any player leaving a club for higher wages because their present club still retained their registration to play professionally even at the end of a contract. Although the FA argued this measure was necessary to stop the wealthier clubs signing all the best players, Eastham's victory finally brought the system to an end. Inevitably, it also brought an inflation in footballer's wages. Although nothing like the wages paid to footballers in the twenty-first century, footballers' ever rising wages began to distance them more and more from the people who watched them.

The growing cult of footballers as wealthy *celebrites du jour* was exemplified by Manchester United's George Best, the first British player to be as much of a star off the field as he was on it. During the late 1960s, where "the fifth Beatle" went, a lot of other footballers followed, usually to the nearest fashionably expensive and most exclusive nightclubs. Best's well publicised path of self- destruction via a succession of Miss Worlds, fast cars and fountains of champagne was the prototypical model for footballers enjoying glamorous, exorbitant lifestyles funded by astronomical salaries. Although arguably long overdue, the abolition of the maximum wage and Eastham's victory marked the beginning of the end of the time when players were the journeymen brethren of the supporters who watched them.

At the same time as footballers were breaking with a more proletarian past, there was a growing dislocation between football clubs and communities too. Working class communities – the lifeblood in football's traditional heartlands-started to change physically through slum clearances which undoubtedly affected communal spirit, and socially, when a better educated, more mobile society started to emerge. Although some supporters had travelled to watch football in the past, cars and motorways brought the glamorous, successful big city clubs within easier reach of ever-widening bases of support not necessarily rooted in the local area.

Over time, more young people started to go away to university too, often settling to work in the towns where they studied before moving to different parts of the country for better employment opportunities. Boltonians of all social backgrounds began to travel much further for holidays, not just going to Blackpool or other nearby resorts as was usually the case before. Consequently, the children and grandchildren of the original Worktowners gradually became more rootless, more cosmopolitan, and arguably more middle class than before. They did not always expect to grow up and raise their families in one town let alone on one street as their parents and grandparents had. As Boltonians tended to become less connected to the town they had been born in, they were not as inclined to celebrate communal identity altogether, nor all at the same time, and even less so in what was rapidly becoming a dilapidated Burnden Park. Significantly, the clubs in the north west most struggling to maintain attendances- clubs like Oldham, Rochdale, Bury, Blackpool, Stockport, Burnley, Blackburn, Preston and of course Bolton – had all by and large been products of an industrial society that was fast disappearing.

The advent of a more mobile, prosperous society also brought far more unwelcome effects. Social historian Dominic Sandbrook convincingly argues that it was prosperity not poverty, which fuelled the hooliganism that did so much damage to football's reputation during the 1970s. Younger supporters with more money to spare began to take advantage of the "football specials" – specially chartered coaches and trains – to have ugly confrontations with supporters of other teams.[15] When the carriages and coaches that took them to away games weren't being subjected to a barrage of bricks and bottles flung by opposition supporters, quite mystifyingly, they were also sometimes vandalised by those who actually depended on them to get home. For some twenty depressing years, self-styled "firms" of hooligans attached to clubs they notionally supported, revelled in notoriety. When firms following their team to other parts of the country- excursions which they viewed as sorties into opposition territory – they enhanced their status by "taking over" the ends behind the opposition's goal, usually because it was where the most fanatical, equally aggressive supporters of their opponents congregated.

Bolton's very own firm, the "Cuckoo Boys", was the collective name for a loose alliance of gangs drawn from all over the town and they were by all accounts (especially their own) a feared firm.[16] Their contribution to football related violence reached its sickening nadir on Saturday 24 August 1974, at Bloomfield Road in Blackpool's match against Bolton. Fittingly for the raucous seaside resort, the match day had begun in a carnival atmosphere with rather bizarrely, the parade of a camel from Blackpool Zoo. However, the holiday mood quickly evaporated after Bolton's Alan Waldron was carried off with a fractured leg midway through the first half. Shortly after, an announcement instructing all the supporters at the Bolton end of the ground to remain behind after the match to give their names and addresses was an indication that a fracas involving some Bolton supporters might be far more serious than just the usual skirmishing on the terraces.

News quickly spread that a supporter had been killed, the first ever murder recorded at an English football game. As if the senseless death of the "shy and unassuming" seventeen-year-old Kevin Olsson was not horrific enough, two more Bolton fans, neither of them the murderer, were also arrested for carrying knives (the *Bolton Evening News* with grim satisfaction reporting that one of the arrested youths described as a "hard man" by the police had wept in court).[17] As a homemade studded knuckle-duster and a sharpened wooden stake were just two of the other weapons recovered by the police, it is no exaggeration to suggest that the death toll might have been worse.

In the days which followed there was the usual hand-wringing, condemnation and demands for retribution. All the while Bolton's manager, Jimmy Armfield, himself a Blackpudlian by birth, sat at

Waldron's bedside. In a quiet moment he told his injured player "We can get you right but there is nothing that can be done for that lad." Unbeknownst to Waldron, Kevin Olsson had died in the adjacent hospital bed.[18] Only twenty-one years separated the repulsive murder and the handshake of Mortensen and Lofthouse in the most memorable of cup finals, but apart from the fact Bolton Wanderers and Blackpool were involved, the two events already seemed to come from completely different worlds.

In the same year, the owners of Manchester United, one of England's most charismatic and well supported clubs, were struggling to deal with problems caused by the hooligans of their own "Red Army" – reputedly the biggest firm in the country. Following a pitch invasion at Old Trafford after Manchester United's shock relegation, steel fences were erected at the Stretford End to prevent spectators getting onto the pitch; a draconian measure that rapidly appeared at other grounds all over the country too including Burnden Park.

In common with other British football grounds, by the early 1980s, Burnden Park was decrepit and intimidating in equal measure. For home supporters, crumbling, weed-strewn terraces awaited. For visiting supporters, there was a real threat to life and limb as the "Manni" Road became a forbidding Appian Way connecting the hostile territory of the town centre to the nasty brick strewn wasteland behind the Embankment; the part of the ground by then completely reserved for visiting supporters.

In the meantime, the silent majority of Bolton's supporters who actually enjoyed watching the football rather than fighting, were getting used to holidays on the continent, eating more regularly in restaurants, watching colour televisions in nicely decorated homes and washing their cars parked outside on the drive. In distinct contrast, even if they could make the time to go to Burnden Park, they were expected to spend a couple of hours virtually imprisoned in a cage, might be lucky if the Wagon Wheel biscuits and insipid tea hadn't run out before half time and had to visit disgusting lavatories with blocked drains and urine all over the floor. If all that wasn't bad enough, they watched the match in a vicious atmosphere with supporters of both teams routinely bellowing "You're going to get your fuckin' head kicked in" and other such threats at each other.

In this kind of atmosphere, little wonder that in the 1985–86 season, total attendances at all the nation's football grounds collectively were only

16.5 million, nearly two-thirds lower than the 1948-9 record breaking season.[19] Burnden Park was no exception to the overall trend but worse still for Bolton Wanderers, falling attendances went hand-in-hand with poor results on the pitch which brought a further downward spiral in support. After being relegated from the old First Division in 1980, the rest of the decade was a miserable one for Wanderers' supporters as their team tumbled down the leagues until in 1987 they found themselves in the old Fourth Division for the first time in their history. On 5 November 1985, only 2902 hardy souls could be bothered to drag themselves through the driving rain to watch an unappealing encounter with Darlington; the lowest recorded attendance ever for a league match at Burnden Park and incidentally, 100 supporters fewer than those who attended the reserve match Humphrey Spender had photographed in 1937. If the infamous rain sodden bonfire night was something of a damp squib, so was the performance on the pitch: Bolton lost 3-0.

But poor results were the least of the club's problems because by then, economic pressures were threatening its very survival. Faced with a desperate shortage of money, various fundraising schemes were introduced to try to fill the coffers of a club which only twenty-five years previously had regularly welcomed crowds of 40–50,000. Although the investment of the dyed-in-the-wool rump of supporters in the "Lifeline" and "Goldline" schemes – raffles by any other name – was laudable, it wasn't enough. In 1986, in a wretched bid to raise funds, part of the ageing Embankment terrace was sold and it was subsequently covered by a Normid supermarket, part of the Co-operative brand, which was actually built alongside the pitch over one half of the terraces. At a stroke, the capacity of the Embankment was halved but realistically it didn't matter. With average home gates of just 5000, the remaining portion of the Embankment could have easily accommodated all the supporters still wanting to get in without having to open the rest of the ground at all. Whilst the money was welcome, the ill-matched, red brick walls of the supermarket leering over the pitch jarred with the rest of the stadium. It would be fair to say, Burnden Park was never the same again.

In all probability, if it was any business other than football, Burnden Park would have been forced to close. It was however events at an FA Cup semi-final between Liverpool and Nottingham Forrest in 1989 that finally sealed its fate. On April 15, a crush at the Leppings Lane

End of Sheffield Wednesday's huge but outdated stadium resulted in the death of ninety-six Liverpool supporters. In terms of the cause and the outcome, the disaster was remarkably similar to the one at Burnden Park. The Hillsborough disaster made it obvious that attitudes towards the safety of football crowds were dangerously negligent; an institutionalised indifference rendered all the more shameful by the fact that sixty-six Scottish supporters had also been crushed to death at the Ibrox Stadium in Glasgow in 1971. Along with the Heysel Stadium tragedy which had led to the deaths of thirty-nine supporters in 1985 as well as the deaths of fifty-six supporters during a fire at Bradford City's Valley Parade ground in the same year, some 257 people had been killed at football grounds in just fifteen years.

Enough was enough, the violence, carnage and sheer ugliness that seemed to have engulfed football, could no longer be tolerated. In the aftermath of Hillsborough, Lord Justice Taylor was charged with leading the enquiry into the disaster whose remit went far beyond an explanation for the tragedy; the report's author was in fact, expected to make recommendations for the provision of safety at *all* sporting events in the future. Notwithstanding some concerns that it represented a Thatcherite attack on the most working class of sports, it was inarguable that something needed to be done to rid the national game of its rancid image, an image most savagely articulated in a *Sunday Times* article which declared that football "was a slum sport played in slum stadiums and increasingly watched by slum people who deter decent folk from turning up."[20] Even the most passionate lover of football's heritage found it hard to disagree when the miserable facilities routinely accepted at football grounds at the time were all the more unforgiveable considering many stadiums lacked even the most basic safety standards: an appalling situation confirmed at the Hillsborough enquiry in 2016 when it emerged that a major football ground hosting an FA cup semi-final didn't even have an up to date safety certificate.

Ultimately, it was Hillsborough that signalled the end for Burnden Park and many of Britain's other outdated football stadiums as well. The Taylor Report recommended the closure of standing terraces at all grounds, new safety measures on exits and entrances, and an advisory committee on new stadium design. Although it did not have the force of law, it was a significant turning point in the history of English football.

First and foremost, it brought to an end the kinds of terraces witnessed by Tom Harrisson in the 1930s, because henceforth, every stadium in the top two divisions was required to be "all seater". This arguably long overdue imperative kick started a wave of stadium building on a scale not seen since the early part of the twentieth century.

In the meantime, the way the game was administered, financed, packaged and sold was also changing fundamentally. Just two years after the Taylor Report was published, the Premier League was formed replacing the old First Division. The rationale behind the move was to reshape football to make it more commercially viable. As a result, unprecedented sums of money poured into the game after BSky secured the rights to televise the newly formed league for a whopping £262 million. With the prerequisite of an all seater stadium before a club could even join the bun fight at the top table of English football, many clubs with ambitions to punch above their weight in this changing football landscape found it made more economic sense to relocate rather than redevelop their existing stadiums.

Consequently, in the 1990s, football's roots in the Victorian age started to shrivel away as clubs as diverse as Millwall , Huddersfield Town, Middlesbrough and Derby County, all moved into new home grounds blazing a trail that would be followed in the twenty-first century by a whole gamut of other clubs ranging from the supremely glamorous Arsenal, to more workaday clubs like Doncaster and Rotherham; the latter's grandly named New York Stadium rather at odds with the dispiriting, anodyne "shoebox" architecture of many of the new stadia which were being built.

Rightly or wrongly, football was breaking its links with traditional working class supporters as it was reinvented to appeal to more middle class "consumers". Unlike the cross-generational masculinity found at Burnden Park, those responsible for marketing football aimed to attract supporters who drove to the match as a family and who expected to see cuddly mascots, fireworks, musical fanfares and American-style cheerleaders when they got there. Football clubs across Britain began to be torn from their communal roots as they moved to new grounds sited well away from town centres because of the space needed for the large car parks that usually surround them. Moreover, the growth in television coverage so essential to the Premier League's success would eventually lead to a time when those professing to support a particular club had never actually been to a match to watch their team, a quite striking contrast with the pre-television age when the only way to watch football was by paying money at the turnstiles, usually at the nearest club.

As might be expected, these changes have aroused much controversy. Harrisson's report and Spender's photographs of Burnden Park show why the disappearance of traditional grounds is often lamented by those supporters old enough to remember them. They argue, not without justification, that despite the more comfortable surroundings, new football grounds generate neither the passion nor the excitement that was produced by crowds of partisan supporters standing side-by-side on terraces. But perhaps far more importantly, supporters could at least afford to stand on them – as we have seen, an essential part of football's appeal to the Worktowners in the mid twentieth century. It barely needs saying that a more middle class sport carries a more middle class price tag and as the cost of admission began to rise rapidly, some Wanderers' supporters in common with football supporters throughout the country, found going to the Saturday afternoon football match was something they could no longer afford. Sadly for them, the spiralling cost of watching football has ended their association with a club that had been part of their family's lives for generations.

Despite reservations about the impact of the Premier League on the game overall, Bolton's supporters were overjoyed when the Wanderers reached football's promised land for the first time after a pulsating playoff win against Reading in 1995. Unfortunately, the next season the team were routinely outclassed and usually soundly beaten. For the masochists watching the thrashings, Burnden Park seemed to exist in a kind of time warp as the Wanderers played against Premier League clubs who had already enjoyed four years of the riches provided by the television deal. Somewhat predictably, the season ended with relegation, Bolton and their shabby ground being dumped out of the Premier League like an unwelcome runt in a litter of prize puppies. Happily, the following season, sustained success on the pitch saw them make an immediate return. As the Premier League beckoned for a second time it could hardly have been more different because during the 1996–97 season Bolton Wanderers Football Club was making preparations to leave Burnden Park.

Although discussions about relocating to a new stadium had taken place as early as 1986, it was the Taylor Report which was the catalyst for action. The official sod cutting ceremony for Bolton Wanderers' new home took place in November 1995 at the Middlebrook valley, an unprepossessing area of marshland in the green shadow of Winter Hill to the west of Bolton. For eighteen months the *Bolton Evening News*, breathlessly reported each stage of construction while amidst growing anticipation and excitement, supporters watched in awe as the spidery new stadium began to rise above the marshland.

For the time being though, it was all about the past rather than the future as the club prepared to leave a football stadium that for all its shortcomings, many supporters still felt deeply attached to. Fittingly, the last season at Burnden Park proved especially memorable with the team that gained promotion widely regarded as one of the best, most fluent sides in the club's history. Charlton Athletic were destined to be the last ever opponents at Burnden Park arriving to face a home side playing with an insouciant swagger having won promotion with five games to spare. As the game got underway Charlton scored the first goal briefly threatening to spoil the occasion but it was only a temporary setback. As Burnden Park became a cauldron of noise, Bolton's players hit their stride and eventually thrashed their opponents 4-1.

On an emotional night, Bolton's captain Alan Thompson admitted that he had been close to tears throughout the last few minutes of the match.[21] There were plenty of tears on the faces of those in the sell-out crowd as well for the final whistle severed once and for all, a link with Burnden Park that many of them had inherited from their parents and grandparents. As the supporters melted away, the ground staff locked the gates, and the floodlights were switched off for the last time. Mercifully, the ensuing shroud of darkness concealed the peeling paint, rusting iron and cracked bricks. Understandably, on a night when nostalgia and sentiment had taken precedence over reality, few people actually had the heart to admit the truth: Burnden Park was really just a sad, decaying remnant from another time.

Just two months later, it was demolished much earlier than scheduled to prevent the possibility of the crumbling site becoming a nuisance. The traditionalists mourning the end of the Burnden era were comforted by the fact they would soon see their team play in a stadium that not only befitted their Premier League status but was also the equal of any stadium in the country or for that matter, Europe.

Predictably, commercial sponsorship led to it being named the Reebok Stadium, scant comfort for those with an historical leaning, but at least Reebok was a Bolton based company. Unfortunately as the new season approached, the building of the stadium fell behind schedule and it wasn't quite finished. Consequently, the first three fixtures of the 1997–98 inaugural season had to be played away from home. As if to prolong the supporter's agonising wait, the first home fixture scheduled for August 30 was delayed for a further two days when the match was moved back to the Monday evening so it could be broadcast live on television. Before a ball had even been kicked in the new stadium, supporters were finding out that Worktown's totemic 3 p.m. Saturday kick offs had vanished along with Burnden Park.

With an unexpected free Saturday afternoon, the club's officials decided to use the time to allow the stewards and ground staff to sort out the logistics of running match days. Supporters were invited down to the Reebok for a "dry run" and a look around; a gesture that was marred a little by the club's somewhat short-sighted insistence that it was not an open day as such, as only those who had bought tickets for Monday's game were welcome. Nevertheless on Saturday 30 August 1997 the thousands milling around the concourse got their very first real look at the futuristic stadium. It was – and still is – a quite stunning architectural statement due to the way the superstructure is seamlessly integrated into the design.

On entering the stadium for the first time via their colour-coded turnstiles, supporters made their way under the stands to discover the much-vaunted television screens and modern catering facilities. Furthermore, as if to show just how far football had come, they were treated to toilets that were refreshing and clean, for both males and females. Still gawping in disbelief at the shiny surroundings the supporters made their way to the seats via their allocated "vomitory" – a word with rather unpleasant connotations that thankfully soon fell from use. On sitting down they were rewarded by ample legroom and a marvellous, uninterrupted view of the pitch; a luxury that even those sitting in the grandstands at Burnden Park never enjoyed due to the pylons supporting their roofs.

Although there was no game to watch, at 3 p.m. the old centre spot from Burnden Park was ceremoniously re-laid at the heart of the brand new pitch. One steward who had assisted at Bolton's matches for over a decade insists a groundsman told him that this was purely a symbolic gesture as the grass from the old pitch was incompatible with the new scientifically prepared surface.[22] Indeed the old centre spot appeared suspiciously healthy considering it had been hacked up and dumped in two plastic carrier bags five months before! Whatever the truth, the crowd enjoyed watching the nostalgic and sentimental gesture. However, despite the warm sunshine of the day there was just one niggling shadow: the home stadium of the team was no longer in the town that bears its name for Bolton Wanderers Football Club is now part of a retail park in Horwich – a small town several miles from Bolton.

If the club's roots in Worktown were vanishing, it was the same amongst the players. Of the eleven Bolton players Tom Harrisson saw, with the exception of one Welsh and one Scottish player, the rest of the team were English. Contrastingly, in the inaugural season at the Reebok the squad boasted players from England, Ireland, Scotland and Wales playing alongside two Icelanders, a South African, a couple of Danes, a Swiss and a Fin. Within five years, of nearly fifty players in the squad, only twenty-one were English and most of those weren't regulars in a first team that routinely featured Danish, Icelandic, German, French, Jamaican, Finnish, Greek and Norwegian players.[23] By then, Radhi Jaidi a Tunisian Muslim was playing in the Bolton defence alongside Tal Ben Haim a practising Jew. Black players like Bruno N'Gotty, Ricardo Gardner and Jay Jay Okocha were regulars in the side and thankfully no longer subject to the disgraceful racism that marred football when Afro-Caribbean footballers first made their names. Although the Abdoulaye's, El Hadji's and Khalilou's playing for the Wanderers were commendable role models for Bolton's multi-ethnicity, the more mercenary demands of the modern game made their links with the club more fleeting. Consequently, players no longer developed the kinds of long-term ties with the town that had once been so important in cementing relationships between players and supporters.

Bolton Wanderers' first match in their new home took place on Monday 1 September 1997 when they played in a sold out fixture against Everton (coincidentally, the same team who they had played at Burnden Park's inaugural match a century before). The match was very nearly cancelled due to Diana Spencer's death the day before and with the unprecedented wave of national mourning that followed, questions were raised whether it was right to play the match at all in the circumstances. Many (slightly guilty) supporters were relieved when it was announced the game would go ahead, although appropriately it was preceded by a minutes silence for the posthumously anointed "People's Princess". Amidst all the ballyhoo, the match didn't or couldn't live up to all the expectations and it ended in a pretty dull 0-0 draw. The only incident of note was a goal "scored" by Bolton's Gerry Taggart which the television replays clearly showed was disallowed in error by the referee who ruled that the ball had not crossed the line. The failure to get all three points that night came back to haunt Bolton at the end of the season when they were relegated again – a disappointment compounded by the fact that Everton of all teams survived at Bolton's expense by finishing one place above them.

Despite this setback, Bolton returned once again to the Premier League in 2001 under the guidance of an exceptional manager, Sam Allardyce, and subsequently enjoyed a long period in the top tier of English football which included two European campaigns, a remarkable achievement for any club outside of the big cities. Unfortunately, they were unable to sustain their success and at the time of writing they have been relegated to the second division – the old third division. Even worse, in an echo of the miserable 1980s, the club's very survival was again threatened in the winter of 2015–16 when catastrophic financial problems led to an unpaid tax bill, unpaid players and staff, and the very real threat the club would go into administration due to insolvency – a common problem affecting clubs who invest heavily in player's wages to compete in the Premier League and then struggle with the immense financial implications of relegation.

Whatever the team's fortunes on and off the pitch, as each new season dawns, Burnden Park recedes further into folk memory. At the time of writing, a twenty-five-year-old enjoying a visit to the Reebok (re-named the Macron Stadium in 2014) will have hardly any meaningful memories of Burnden Park even *if* they had been taken to it as a child. Also, just as the links to Burnden Park have been broken for a new generation of supporters, they have been broken in terms of the players who once played there too. Given that modern footballers tend to enjoy much longer careers than their predecessors, during the preparation of this book, it would not have been impossible for a current Bolton Wanderers player to have also played at Burnden Park. However, this was not the case because by the start of the 2013 season, a decade had already passed since the last Bolton player to have played at Burnden Park was part of the team. With dozens of foreign players having played for Bolton in recent years, predictably this significant milestone in the club's history in the end went to Per Frandsen, a Danish midfielder. Ryan Giggs, who enjoyed an extraordinarily long career at Manchester United, was in fact the last player still playing in the top flight of English football to have played in a competitive match at Burnden Park; when he eventually retired in 2014 this tangential milestone in Burnden Park's history slipped by largely unnoticed.

Memories of Burnden Park however are still kept alive by ex-players talking at sportsmen's dinners, nostalgia in the press, archive film on YouTube and of course when recalled in the conversations of supporters old enough to have watched matches there. Quite rightly, in 2016, there was significant media coverage of the seventieth anniversary of the Burnden Disaster which for a short while at least made the victims of the disaster a little less "forgotten". Occasionally, remnants of the old stadium come up for sale for anything of any value from Burnden Park was sold at an auction when it was demolished. Salvageable artefacts like the floodlights, corner flags, the turnstiles and even the boardroom carpet were bought by supporters ready to become novelty indoor decorations or quirky talking points when displayed on patios or in gardens. These scattered souvenirs are all that remain of Burnden Park. Today, anyone who goes in search of the spot where Humphrey Spender photographed Worktown's football supporters will find there is nothing left to see because the site of Burnden Park is completely buried beneath the car park of an Asda supermarket.

Five miles away, the Macron/Reebok Stadium is home to a new type of club employing players who might earn in a week what some supporters earn in a year. For generations, the workers of an industrial town had made their way through the cobbled streets to watch players with whom they shared an affinity and who often lived amongst them. Not anymore. Bolton Wanderers home stadium sparkles alongside a motorway junction surrounded by a huge car park. The adjoining retail park comes complete with shops, restaurants, a bowling alley and a multiplex cinema. On match days, the players emerge from their Ferraris and Bentleys distanced socially and economically from the crowds negotiating their way through thousands of cars parked in front of nondescript, hangar like retail stores.

As for the stadium itself, the commercialism central to the modern game can be found everywhere. To maximise profits, business consultants "sweat the asset" and the Macron/Reebok stadium inevitably boasts its own luxury hotel, conference facilities, offices, executive boxes and merchandising outlets. It not only makes money for the club on match days but also hosts concerts by major rock stars like Elton John, Oasis and Coldplay all of whom have played at the stadium in recent years as well as rather less well-remembered, fading pop stars of the 1980s in one of the first Rewind nostalgia shows. It is all a far cry from potato pies and cups of Bovril under the signal box of the old Embankment but these developments are simply unavoidable if the club is to survive at all in a more gluttonous footballing age. Ultimately, disconnected physically and socially from the town and community it once represented, it might be argued that Bolton Wanderers Football Club like other clubs up and down the country has become little more than a commercial brand.

In January, 2011, Nat Lofthouse, the man most associated with Burnden Park, died aged eighty-five. Nine days later, Bolton Wanderers played Chelsea at the Reebok Stadium. Before the match, black and white films showed the "Lion of Vienna" in his glory years before a warm minute's applause in his memory preceded the kick off. Outside, flowers and scarves from all over Britain had been laid on the concourse. The temporary cairn piled up under the memorial to the Burnden Disaster marked much more than the death of a footballer, it was the end of an era because Nat Lofthouse born in Bolton in 1925, the son of a coal-bagger, was the sporting embodiment of a Worktown that no longer exists. So was Burnden Park. When Bolton Wanderers relocated to a retail park in Horwich – a commercial enterprise devoid of community, tradition or history – the town lost a vital part of its identity, some might argue, even its soul. Worse still, as the first decade of the new millennium came to an end, the people of Bolton were fast realising that the development of the Middlebrook Retail Park had done more than recast their football club, it had changed the whole character of the town as well.

ARE YOU BEING SERVED?

A corner shop on Orm Street.
Humphrey Spender

On December 9 1960, all across Britain, people were settling down for a night in front of their black and white television sets. Over pictures of damp rooftops and smoking chimneys, a mournful tune announced the arrival of *Coronation Street*, a new drama set in the north of England. With its terraced houses, cobbles and working class people, "the street" was deeply rooted in the culture of Worktown; a town that still existed just outside the front doors of any Boltonians who happened to be watching it. As the opening titles faded away, the first conversation did not take place as might be thought in one of the street's nine houses, nor in the Rovers Return, its' soon-to-be-famous pub. In fact the very first words were spoken by Elsie Lappin over the counter of her corner shop.

A shop was so important to the fictional street from the outset for the simple reason that in real life, most people living in Britain's industrial towns were never far from one. Mass Observation reported that there were an extraordinary 3950 shops in total in Worktown. They included shops massed in Bolton town centre, others that stretched out in seemingly endless ribbons all along the roads, and the multitude of "corner shops" – so called because were often the last property in a row of houses on the corner of the gable end. Consequently, there was one shop to every twelve houses – an astonishing ratio of one for every forty-five Worktowners.

Because of their importance, shops, shoppers, shopkeepers and shopping patterns were of great interest to Tom Harrisson who directed his team of Observers to research them in some detail. Just as the football match was about more than which team won and cleaning routines had a deeper significance beyond hygiene, Mass Observation thought shops were much more than just places to buy things. They were right because until the later years of the twentieth century, besides selling everyday provisions, small local shops were an important part of the social fabric of working class communities.

In a different way but equally important, bigger prestigious retail businesses attracted people to a town centre where the shop names, their goods and produce, even the accent and speech patterns of the shopkeepers distinguished Bolton from other towns. Bolton's singular identity was further promoted by the fact that most shops were independently owned family businesses with local roots. These family owned shops with their canvas awnings thrusting out from under soot-smudged facades of terracotta, and black/red bricks, were the backbone of an unmistakeably northern town centre. And shoppers from far and wide came to it – in droves – leading Mass Observation to conclude that Worktown was an important subsidiary shopping centre for the whole of South Lancashire.

Deansgate, Bolton's premier high street running west to east across the town's northern edge, has always been at the heart of Bolton's shopping scene. Essential to trade since medieval times, Deansgate was – and still is – a barometer for the town's overall prosperity. For much of the twentieth century, it boasted handsome retail architecture, splendid banks and dozens of prospering businesses including two major department stores both dating from the Edwardian period. The first of them, Whitakers, opened for business in 1907. Housed in an attractive mock Tudor building, its location and the quality of its merchandise meant it soon established a reputation as one of the town's most upmarket shopping destinations. Just two years later, at the opposite end of Deansgate, Whiteheads department store opened housed in a handsome terracotta building modelled on the world famous Harrods in London. In 1913, Whiteheads' premises were extended to accommodate another illustrious business, Preston's jewellers; the only jewellery store outside of London which at that time offered its customers a lift to the top floors.

These important businesses drew crowds of shoppers to Deansgate and where crowds gathered Humphrey Spender followed. Secretly, he photographed them as they gossiped on corners, smoked cigarettes on the pavements, and looked in the shop windows. From Deansgate's main Post Office to the junction with Moor Lane and White Lion Brow, both of which Humphrey Spender photographed, it is a mere fifty-yard walk. Such was the concentration of shops between the two locations, had he been inclined Spender could have bought a roll of film from a chemist, cigarettes from a tobacconist, meat from a butcher and fresh vegetables from one of two greengrocers. He could have also had his shoes repaired in the cobblers, had his hair cut at the barbers and enjoyed a drink in a pub – and all this on just one side of the street.

Although the shops, banks and stores on Deansgate were the most imposing, the nearby streets, Bradshawgate, Howell Croft (north and south), Exchange Street, Oxford Street, Hotel Street and Newport Street – known colloquially as "shoe shop alley" because of the preponderance of shoe retailers – also had scores of shops. To investigate the role they played in Worktown, Tom Harrisson sent teams of Observers into the town centre to record how shops displayed goods, the prices of them, and the range of products for sale. Observers were also asked to undertake "follows"; an activity that simply required them to trail around following unsuspecting shoppers making notes about the kinds of purchases individual shoppers made, the length of time they took to make them, and the relationships that existed between shoppers and shopkeepers.

As well as all the thriving independent businesses in the town centre, Bolton Market Hall, a short walk off Deansgate, was another jewel in Bolton's shopping crown. When it first opened in December, 1855, it was proclaimed to be the largest covered market in the country and it soon became central to the town's commercial fortunes. The Market Hall's location right in the town centre naturally made it a focus for a number of Observers' reports which describe customers in abundance and shops aplenty in a thriving shopping destination. On the four outside walls alone, Mass Observation recorded no less than thirty-six independent retailers including wine dealers, watchmakers and two gramophone and radio dealers. Inside were a further 109 independently owned stalls arranged in seven aisles lettered A–G. To illustrate the breadth of provision, taking just one row of stalls – in this instance Avenue B – Mass Observation noted some seventeen traders including three drapers, four hardware dealers and five independent butchers. Next door to the Market Hall, Bolton's fish lovers were also well catered for by the eight suppliers of fresh fish trading from the similarly imposing fish market although sadly it was demolished to facilitate road widening shortly before the Worktown investigation began.

The Market Hall on the other hand was actually reopened in April 1938 following a substantial refurbishment, the kind of occasion that would naturally arouse Tom Harrisson's curiosity. A publicity booklet collected by the Observers describes the improvements made to the interior which included the installation of trading units of "modern design" containing two, three, four, or five units per block – stalls that remained virtually untouched for the next forty years.[1] These refurbished stalls were set out in such a way that taking a direct line from one side of the Market Hall to the other was impossible; a simple but clever device which forced shoppers to circulate around all the stalls increasing the potential custom for each business and in 1938 at least, the legwork of any Observers that happened to be following them.

The town's other major market, the open market based on Ashburner Street, was a very different proposition being a wholesale market in its early incarnation. With a total of twenty-six suppliers of fruit and vegetables, it kept Bolton's shops amply supplied with fresh produce. In 1924, an outdoor retail market in the same location was inaugurated opening on Tuesdays and Thursdays only. Humphrey Spender was drawn to it which resulted in a number of surreal images of the kinds of traders found there as well as shoppers milling about and examining the wares on the stalls. The activity on Ashburner Street market underlined one of

Mass Observation's preoccupations: the social importance of shopping. Describing the kind of hubbub seen there on busy days one Observer stated that it "cannot simply be regarded as a place for buying and selling any more than can the pub. People meet each other, chat, stroll about looking and fingering, and above all in the open market, they listen to the wonderful tales of the barkers, particularly those selling herbs, cures or dealing in magic."[2]

With so many prospering businesses in Bolton, the owners of Preston's jewellers were justified in claiming in the 1920s that "the enterprise and ideals of Bolton's retailers are indicative of the general character of the town. Boltonians visiting other towns feel justifiably proud of the fact that no other town of equal size has finer thoroughfares of handsome modern business premises."[3] This was more than just advertising rhetoric. Spender's photographs and the Observers' reports show that Worktown had a plentiful mixture of thriving independently owned shops; several renowned stores like Preston's, Whittakers, Whiteheads, and Gregory and Porritt's; and other retailers with national profiles like Burtons Tailors, Woolworths, and Marks and Spencer. It would be fair to say when the Worktown investigation was underway, Bolton's main shopping streets comfortably rivalled those of any other British town and indeed, many major cities too.

As well as the shops on Bolton's high streets, all the approach roads to the town had lengthy parades of them as well. Typically, the terraced rows abutting the pavements housed dozens of greengrocers, newsagents, general grocers, butchers, bakers and if not quite candlestick makers, at least the odd ironmongers.

Taking just one example, Derby Street, a main road leading south west from the town, the numbers and variety of shops found there in the 1930s was astounding. Starting with a wardrobe dealer, the next twenty shops on Derby Street comprised a fruiterer, a tripe dealer, two tobacconists and confectioners, a gent's outfitter, two drapers, an ironmonger, a garage, a pub (The Good Samaritan), an oatcake maker, two butchers, another furniture dealer, a building society, a pawnbrokers, a grocer and a fishmonger. Independent businesses like these continued virtually uninterrupted for its whole length – about half a mile – before finally the road's shops came to an end with a shoe shop, a grocers, a drapers, a builders, a cooked meat specialists, a physician and surgeon, a milliners, a furnishers, a motorcycle engineer, a pork butcher, and finally, a baker. In total, Derby Street had approaching 400 shops along its length.[4]

In addition to independent retailers, there were dozens of Co-operative stores serving each community as well. They were a particularly strong feature of retail life in the industrial towns of Lancashire and Yorkshire following the founding of the Co-op movement in Rochdale in 1844. The Co-ops were important in predominantly working class towns because their primary purpose was to help poorer people by selling food and other provisions at reasonable prices. Besides their competitive prices, Co-ops offered their customers a share of any profits via the "Divi" (dividend) paid out to them from the profits made. One Boltonian later recalled their importance saying: "The Co-op was almost a religion it had so many outlets, shops, halls, branches the country could have been the United Co-opdom"; a notion that was not so fanciful given the scores of Co-ops that were once spread across the town.[5]

As well as all the shops on the main roads, there were also dozens of "corner shops" amongst the regimented streets that led off them. They were no different to the rest of the adjoining houses in terms of size and construction but their bigger windows, advertising boards, and the forty-five degree angle of the door at the corner differentiated them from the houses. In most cases, they were very small businesses with no employees other than the family members who ran the shop between them. They were important in working class communities because as well as meeting the daily shopping needs of customers, they were valuable social hubs for the people living in the surrounding streets.

Most of Worktown's streets were able to support one or more shops like these because food was bought in much smaller quantities at a time when fridges were still unaffordable for working class people. Because of the problems of keeping it fresh, any food sold in shops was much more tied to the seasons: an annual rhythm noted by Mass Observation who recorded that one child said to an Observer that she knew when spring began because "the shops sell spring cabbage, new potatoes and lettuces which I like…" Apparently spring time was also a good time for the town's plentiful clothes shop owners as it was the time for buying new clothes an Observer being told that this partly happened because the "brighter weather" helped people realise that their clothes had got shabby.

As we have seen, Tom Harrisson thought that women were overwhelmingly responsible for domestic duties in Worktown, one of which was the daily visit to the shop. Observers' reports make clear how routine going to the local shop once was: "The working class housewife rarely makes a weekly order for her groceries for instance. She goes out for them during the time when her man is at work. Of housewives questioned, one said 'If I go out it's just to get something for the dinner, the butchers or some shop like that.'"[6] This kind of daily errand was quite normal in Worktown with thousands of housewives going to the nearest shop just to buy "something for tea". Indeed in more impoverished communities, buying one egg or a "penn'orth of bacon scraps" – barely enough for one meal – was a regular occurrence (as was buying other everyday items like single razor blades). Unsurprisingly, an Observer was told by several shopkeepers that teatimes tended to be their busiest times of day closely followed by midday when mill workers would often call in to corner shops to buy sweets and toffees during the dinner break.[7]

Before pre-packed goods became commonplace, shopkeepers were required to cut, weigh and measure out goods – all of which took time, therefore housewives had the opportunity for a chat with their neighbours or occasionally to hear some gossip while these tasks were being done – another incentive to go out to the shop every day. One Boltonian, Oliver Miller, recalled the importance of this particular aspect of shopping saying that visiting the Co-op was "a social occasion for many. All the ingredients were weighed out to order. Sugar in blue bags, butter patted up or curled up into balls. Loose biscuits weighed out into paper bags with broken ones put in for free."[8]

Whilst waiting for these tasks to be done, conversations occurred quite naturally, especially as the customers in any given shop were likely to be close neighbours or at least acquaintances. In a report entitled "Shopping as a Social Act", an Observer thought women shopped mainly because "The working class wife's activities outside her own home are not very many. She does not go out very much in the evening … So that when the wife does go out of the house, coming into contact with people outside the home-circle, represents a means of social intercourse for her…" before the report concludes that it was this daily social intercourse that gave shopping a much wider significance beyond just buying things.[9]

Occasionally of course, customers might be in a rush for one reason or another. One corner shop owner "new to the trade" told an Observer that she was surprised to find when she first opened her shop that sometimes "people took things out with them unwrapped, even butter and things like that."[10] Another shopkeeper on the other hand stressed the importance of chatting and gossiping to her shop's success telling an Observer "I think the main thing to do if you want to attract custom and to keep your present trade is to have a smile and a word for them all and treat them all alike. I have found that it pays."[11]

Besides their social function, having a range of shops nearby was much more important before the Second World War, as at that time, only middle class people were ever likely to own cars. Despite owning them however, Worktown's more prosperous families still had provisions delivered to their homes by scores of delivery boys who worked for the town's retailers. This was because cars were primarily viewed as vehicles to be used for business or for leisurely excursions, certainly not for routine shopping trips. It did not matter either way to working class people who had neither a car nor the money for errand boys leaving them with no choice but to walk for their daily provisions. Therefore, if shops were to prosper, they had to be in close proximity to people. This imperative was not only driven by the need to sell produce while it was still fresh to people who could walk to the shop but also because shopping in Worktown was restricted to what could fit in one shopping bag or basket when they got there – another limitation virtually forcing women to shop every day.

Although these factors partly determined shopping patterns, it was poverty more than anything else that dictated what kinds of things people bought and how they bought them, a fact of life all too apparent in Observers' reports:

The woman went on to list everything in her weekly shop and what it cost: tea coffee, sugar, soap and soap powder, salt, pepper and starch, a quart of milk every day, self-raising flour, lard and thirty pound of potatoes a week. All this came to £1 3/9d a week. At this point she sat down and said, "Eh I stop an' think I don't know how to carry on." The Observer asked about butter –"Oh we never see butter in this house. I get six pounds of marge at 5d" – she stopped. "Do you know when I went into Townleys (hospital) for this last un it's the first time I've tasted butter for three years" … When the Observer asked about meat, "Oh I don't buy meat-perhaps a bit of mince meat."[12]

Other reports suggest some families fared even worse. "Mrs D said they did not know how they were going to manage. 'Yesterday it was awful. The kids couldn't understand that there wasn't any butties. It's hard when the kids go hungry' Yesterday the D's only had six slices of bread and marge and some potatoes" recorded an Observer about one particular family experiencing hardship.[13] This sort of poverty could sear its way into the consciousness of working class people leaving mental scars that lasted a lifetime. Such was the fear of starvation in Worktown, my grandmother throughout her life always had a supply of potatoes and eggs in the house insisting that a meal of eggs and chips could at least be made should hard times occur.

The origins of these fears can be traced to the fact that any given household's money could completely run out. If it did, there was a very real risk of all kinds of privations including genuine hunger. In Worktown, the vast majority of people were paid their wages weekly, and always in cash. Credit was rarely available apart from that offered by the dreaded pawnshops; a harsh fact of life that was often reinforced by blunt signs in shops which "politely" requested customers to "refrain from asking for credit as a refusal often offends". Mass Observation did find some shops allowed a primitive form of credit on groceries (known as "tick") but tellingly, never on beer. The old adage "Neither a borrower nor lender be" characterised most relationships between shop owners and their customers which inevitably meant working class people only bought what they needed on a day-to-day basis: the origin of the colloquialism "living hand to mouth".

With so much everyday poverty it was normal to find tins containing different sums of money on the mantelpieces of homes or sometimes hidden in kitchen cupboards. This kind of basic budgeting for essentials – rent, gas, food, insurance – was necessary to ensure bills were paid, a way of life which has largely disappeared in contemporary Britain where, rightly or wrongly credit cards, payday loans and overdrafts are available to most people despite the risks of people amassing high levels of personal debt.

Given the numbers of shops servicing local communities, it may seem strange that Bolton's main shopping streets – Deansgate, Bradshawgate, Newport Street, Great Moor Street – also teemed with dozens of independent butchers, fishmongers, and greengrocers as well especially as on the surface, they merely replicated what was already available locally. However, they remained profitable partly because at that time more people lived in or close to the town centre and partly because town centre shops were generally sustained by a fierce customer loyalty based on a hard-earned reputation for quality and service. By delivering a slightly more gentrified shopping experience not necessarily found locally, the town centre's independent traders evidently made going into town worthwhile, otherwise their customers wouldn't have paid the extra bus or tram fare to get to them.

There was another important but rather less obvious reason to visit town centre shops. Generally speaking, there was more of a sense of occasion about a trip to town, which might seem strange given that most Worktowners lived within a couple of miles of it. This was particularly true whenever substantial purchases like furniture, carpets, domestic hardware and radios (later televisions) were being made. This "sense of occasion" was actively promoted in the department stores which provided a more personal, even deferential service and always in the most luxurious surroundings. As social historian Dr Sonia Ashmore observed, "The grand department stores provided city landmarks and labyrinthine environments that gave shoppers a sense of adventure and luxury." This certainly seems to have been the case in Bolton, as Whiteheads and Whittakers were two of the town centre's most popular shopping destinations for the best part of the twentieth century.

With the prospect of shopping in stores like Whiteheads and Whitakers, as well as in shops that were perceived to be more upmarket, the "sense of occasion" inherent in town centre shopping meant most Worktowners wore their best clothes to go shopping; a social pattern recorded by Spender as the people in his images of the town centre appear to be smarter and more formally dressed than in many of his other photographs. This contrast is most evident in the headwear with the vast majority of both men and women sporting a variety of hats (or at least flat caps!) when shopping in town. My mother, along with most women of her generation clung to the social conventions of Worktown throughout her life, never going into town unless well dressed and wearing some makeup for fear "of seeing someone" although who it might be or why it particularly mattered remained a mystery.

The distinction between town and local shopping was also apparent in peoples' shopping baskets an Observer noting that women usually had two: one for "everyday" and a better one for town centre shopping. Older Boltonians recall that it was common to see weavers carrying their "best" shopping baskets to the mills on Fridays because they often went shopping in the afternoon after work. This societal pressure to (at least) maintain appearances, explains why the all-too-apparent poverty in some of Spender's other Worktown photographs is less immediately obvious on the town's main shopping streets.

Whether they owned a large business or a back street corner shop, Bolton's independent shopkeepers merit separate discussion as they were part of a distinct social class in Worktown. Bolton's shopkeepers belonged by definition to the "shopocracy": a group generally considered –especially by the shopkeepers themselves – to be socially superior. This distancing from their working class customers is intriguing because shopkeepers were certainly not middle class as defined by educational qualifications, profession or income. In fact, most shops in industrial towns at best only supported a modest if comfortable lifestyle with many shopkeepers "living in the back" and above their businesses. However, despite many of them living on the same streets as their customers, shop owners enjoyed a standard of living known as "shopkeeper posh".

When times were good, it was shopkeepers who tended to acquire cars and televisions, and to go on continental holidays before anyone else due to their relative prosperity. One confectioner trading on Higher Bridge Street told an Observer that she was holidaying in Morecambe only so she could save up to go abroad for her next holiday having previously enjoyed trips to Switzerland; a telling response at a time when the nearest most of her customers got to holidaying in Switzerland was eating a Toblerone on Blackpool beach.[14] According to another Observer, a local man named Butterworth, the owner of a "rather prosperous looking shop" on the corner of Merehall Street and Leicester Street, only stood out from all his immediate neighbours because he had "quite a new car outside."[15]

These outward symbols of success were a crucial distinction between the shopocracy and the rest of the community because the acquisition of once fairly exclusive and expensive commodities showed everyone else that shopkeepers were upwardly mobile. In fact it was widely believed that owning even the most modest of shops was a step up from being a policeman, shop assistant or nurse because shop owners had the privilege of "being their own boss", an enviable status that was very rare in Worktown.

In general, shopkeepers tended to maintain an economic and social distance from local people even though they were happy enough to make their living from them. Consequently, they were often involved in civic life and charitable organisations most notably Freemasonry as well as what was perceived to be the "poor man's masons", the Royal Antediluvian Order of the Buffaloes (sometimes called "the Buffs"). Both of these organisations have traditionally attracted strong support in Bolton. Whilst the social pretensions of Bolton's more prosperous shopkeepers in forging an uneasy alliance with solicitors, accountants and bank managers in charitable bodies might appear to confirm the snobbery associated with the petit bourgeoisie, local charities undoubtedly benefitted from their generosity.

This particular aspect of Worktown's social strata persisted in *Coronation Street* long after it disappeared in real life. Fred Elliott, the hail-fellow-well-met butcher brilliantly played by John Savident was a superbly drawn character study of a member of the northern shopocracy. His blunt common sense, financial caution, puritanical morals and elevated position as Grand Master to the Square Dealers (a thinly disguised caricature of the Freemasons) meant Elliott was a respected pillar of the community and upholder of its somewhat conservative values.

Worryingly for any shopkeeper, fictional or otherwise, the profits on which they depended to elevate them above the mill and factory workers were always precarious. This goes some way to explaining why in political terms, Worktown's shopkeepers like most shopkeepers in Britain, were generally conservative by instinct and usually hostile towards the politics of the left especially the Labour Party, who they thought would take away everything that they had worked so hard for.[16]

Their innate conservatism was equally evident in their approach to business as well because shopkeepers were not entrepreneurial in the main. In fact, they were largely content to hold on to one single business which was in many cases a prudent option as businesses could fail just as much as succeed. As we have seen, some shops enjoyed a strong customer loyalty and consequently a sustained presence in the town for generations whilst others came and went seemingly before the "Closed" sign on the door was reversed to "Open". Indeed, advertisements in the *Bolton Evening News* and historic photographs confirm that it was normal for each generation of Boltonians to have its own familiar shops before they disappeared perhaps because of wider economic trends, occasionally poor management, but mostly, as a result of the vagaries of fashion.

For most of the twentieth century however, it was only a change in the type of business, or the owners within any particular premises that were affected, particularly in the town centre. Indeed, Tom Harrisson on returning to Bolton in 1959 noted just how little Bolton had changed physically since the original investigation. He found that Ye Olde Pastie Shoppe on Churchgate was doing "a roaring trade", a small milliners observed in the thirties had grown into one of the town's "biggest and brightest" stores, corner shop windows were bulging with goods "many new, many as before, all more expensive", and another "fairly typical" corner shop (with off-license) was thriving, still run by the same female proprietor he had met twenty years before. With Harrisson noting her new Ford Consul car outside and a deep-freezer inside, it would be fair to say that in the intervening years she had become a fully paid-up member of the shopocracy.[17]

With so many shops obviously still thriving in the early 1960s, no wonder a few years earlier Tillotson's, a trade directory for Bolton businesses, was trumpeting: "Shops! From the palatial town centre store to the tiny general grocery at the corner of the terraced street they play a notable part in Bolton's trading life." They soon wouldn't. Like other signature aspects of Worktown, before the century ended the corner shops, the Co-ops, and most of the town centre's shops and stores – palatial or otherwise – were not only struggling, they had all but vanished.

The decline of Worktown's shops can be detected in comments made to Tom Harrisson in 1960:

The multiple stores have long played a part in moulding local taste- notably Marks & Spencer, expansive and enterprising even in the drearier thirties. Their position has distinctly strengthened since. Some small shopkeepers complain. The operator of a small local newspaper remarked: "The multiple stores are taking over, and the small man can't compete."[18]

The struggle to stay in business the "small man" would eventually face could scarcely have been imagined when the London Co-operative Society first began to experiment with self-service stores during the Second World War – a radical break with tradition caused by wartime staff shortages. What was originally an expedient driven by necessity was retained after the war ended with the Co-operative society opening a further ten self-service supermarkets in 1947. Each brought the novelty of "Q less" shopping to at first tentative, somewhat bemused, shoppers.[19] The new shopping pattern began to take hold and four years later, the first British supermarket to have three checkout lanes was opened by Express Dairies. Encouraged by the success of self-service, the Co-op, ironically the society that placed the highest possible value on the social role of shops, went on to introduce it whenever possible so that by 1950, ninety per cent of all Britain's self-service stores were Co-ops.[20]

Serving oneself before paying at a checkout was at first a novel experience but it rapidly grew in popularity encouraging more and more shops all across the country to introduce self-service shopping. These early supermarkets grew in scale and numbers during the 1950s buoyed by aggressive marketing strategies like money off coupons, on pack promotions, price reductions, and in the case of the bigger stores, television advertising after ITV was launched.[21] By the mid-1960s, supermarkets were starting to affect when, where and how people shopped. Ultimately, it was locally based, independent shops that would prove most vulnerable to the changing shopping patterns which step-by-step were beginning to favour the growing supermarkets.

Despite their proliferation and the potential threat to independent shopkeepers, the impact of supermarkets on other shops was at first more subtle. Because pre-wrapped goods, brightly packaged to stand out on shelves where customers were expected to browse were essential to the success of self-service stores, their introduction ended the need for shopkeepers to count out, cut, weigh and measure goods.[22] At the same time, processed foods like Birds Eye Beef Burgers, first launched in 1950, and their Fish Fingers introduced five years later, started to undermine specialist butchers and fishmongers even if the new products might be an inferior substitute for fresh meat and fish.

Similarly, products like Tetley's Tea Bags, Maxwell House Instant Coffee, Nesquik milk shake, and Dairylea Cheese Spread, which all arrived on the shelves in the 1950s, all came pre-packaged too. Because of this changing pattern, Bolton's general grocers were no longer required to weigh and wrap tea and coffee or to cut cheese and butter from a block. Sweets once sold from a tempting array of glass jars – the staple of many a corner shop and a magnetic draw for children – increasingly came pre-packed too, again ending the need to weigh and bag them. Although pre-packed goods brought convenience, they heralded a move away from personal service as people over time got used to shopping for themselves. Even the department stores found the need for shop assistants declined as people simply became less inclined to be advised what to buy.[23] The social aspect of shopping once considered so important by Mass Observation was starting to diminish.

Despite the growing challenge they posed to local businesses, it is worth remembering that supermarkets were generally welcomed at first, especially as in the 1960s and 1970s they were only one part of a more balanced retail offering. One of Bolton's first supermarkets, a relatively small Spar, was originally at the centre of Harwood Shopping Precinct, built two miles from the town centre in 1965. Initially the supermarket benefitted local shoppers and more crucially, other surrounding shops too, by bringing shoppers to the precinct from further afield. When it first opened, the Spar traded alongside amongst others, a furniture showroom, an electrical goods store, a gentleman's outfitters, a cafe, a newsagent, two banks, a bakery, a launderette and the Black Swan pub; all of which were located in the precinct's rows of shop units. To a large extent, the planners succeeded in preserving the social role of shops by placing the precinct at the heart of the suburb of Harwood with the flow of shops, the pub, the cafe and the adjacent library, all helping to promote social interaction as unintentionally did its launderette where in time-honoured fashion, bored adolescents gathered to gossip on the step.

Over time however, the shops struggled to remain profitable and the idealistic, functional precinct became a dilapidated eyesore. In 1983, it was branded "an utter disgrace" by one local politician who demanded to know "why the 18 year old precinct had been allowed to deteriorate".[24] It seemed no one had a simple answer although it can be safely assumed that most of the shoppers who once went there were driving their cars to the much larger supermarkets which had opened in considerable numbers across Bolton in the intervening years. The Harwood precinct was eventually demolished and tellingly, when the site was redeveloped in the late 1990s, it provided space for just *one* Morrisons supermarket with, inevitably, a much larger car park.

The story of Harwood Precinct simply reflected what was happening all across Bolton because the brutal reality is that major supermarkets have grown by putting other shops out of business whether located on precincts, streets or in the town centre. In turn too, smaller supermarket groups like Spar and Supasave along with other long forgotten independent supermarkets once found in Bolton like Hanbury's and Lennon's also succumbed to the dominance of just four major chains – Tesco, Morrisons, Sainsburys and Asda – a development central to the history of shopping in the last twenty years.

The grip of the biggest four supermarket groups on shopping habits began in 1964, when GEM opened Britain's first superstore in Nottingham. Two years later, it was bought by a group of farmers trading under the name of Associated Dairies. After being rebranded as Asda, their concept of satisfying all the needs of their customers under one roof began to be rolled out across the country. Boltonians got their first taste of this "one stop shopping" in May, 1970 when Asda opened what was Bolton's first superstore in Astley Bridge, just over a mile from the town centre. Although at first it only opened between 10 a.m. and 6 p.m. for three days of the week and closed on Sundays, Asda advertised somewhat disingenuously that Fridays was the day for a "family shopping experience". The phenomenon of the once a week "big shop", rather than the once a day visit to the local shop was gathering momentum.

Changing habits notwithstanding, other shops remained viable when supermarkets first opened as they could at least open at times when the supermarkets didn't, a pattern that was sustainable for a while as people were prepared (or had) to pay a little more when buying at unsociable times. However, consumers naturally tend to buy where it is cheapest and different shopping patterns emerged with people buying in bigger quantities and using their local shops as little as they could to avoid the extra cost. This trend accelerated year after year because the major supermarket chains were attracting customers with distinctly cheaper prices as their enormous buying power enabled them to sell goods to their customers at the same price as it was costing local shopkeepers to buy them wholesale.

For those who value the communal role of shops, the statistics make for grim reading. In 1950, Britain's supermarkets could only muster twenty per cent of the country's grocery market between them whilst small shops and Co-ops still serviced the other eighty per cent. By 1990, this situation had been totally reversed. Furthermore, between 1961 and 1997, the number of independent grocers in Britain fell from 116,000 to only 20,900 whilst in the same period, the number of independent butchers declined from 25,300 to 8344. The visual transformation alone of Worktown's shopping streets confirms that Bolton was no exception to what was widely considered a growing national problem.

As the end of the twentieth century approached, the major supermarkets only continued to increase their share of the British market by building ever-bigger superstores, some of them – the so called "hyperstores" – were of extraordinary size, their numbers growing from 457 in 1986 to well over a thousand by 1997.[25] Unsurprisingly, the people of Bolton – a densely populated town – got their fair share of superstores and hyperstores along with plenty of time to shop in them after The Sunday Trading Act introduced in 1994 allowed supermarkets to open on Sundays. When further legislation permitting 24-hour opening followed, the last meagre advantage enjoyed by local shopkeepers was destroyed as many had only been able to survive by opening at inconvenient times and usually only by selling alcohol as well. As Bolton's independent bakers, butchers and grocers continued to close with monotonous regularity, people were left with little choice but to shop in the town's supermarkets.

In spite of the criticisms levelled at supermarkets in terms of their impact on other shops, superstores and hyperstores have been embraced willingly. This can partly be explained by the fact that after Boltonians embraced the car owning revolution of the mid twentieth century, a single car ride to a destination where everything is in one place and can be paid for all at once saves both petrol and time; the latter a precious commodity especially in families where both adults work full time – it bears repeating, a social pattern that was almost unknown amongst working class families in Worktown but which became common as the century progressed.

Despite any nostalgic yearning for the shopping streets of the past, in reality, few contemporary Boltonians have the time to visit several shops in different parts of the town to buy what happily fits into one supermarket trolley. Also it should be remembered too that during Worktown's peak years, its town centre shops closed at 5.30 p.m. each day except for Wednesdays when they actually closed at lunchtime. Moreover, they did not open at all on Sundays. Therefore it not only took the Worktowners much longer to shop, but the times when they could go shopping were far more restricted too; limitations which would be unacceptable to today's consumers who have become accustomed to shopping in ways that fit around what are arguably much busier and more stressful lifestyles.

In spite of the advantages supermarkets offer to "time poor" families, reservations about "one stop" supermarket shopping and its potential long-term impact on other independently owned shops were apparent from the start. In 1981, after an Asda was built in the centre of nearby Farnworth (part of the borough of Bolton until 1946) one disgruntled resident wrote to the *Bolton Evening News*: "the planning department at Bolton suggested the opening of the Asda store and extended Co-op store would bring trade to the town. Instead the reverse has happened. Now everyone drives to Asda where they buy almost everything they need, then drive straight home again."[26]

This problem was mirrored in Bolton itself and it was if anything even worse because not only were supermarkets offering everything under one roof, many were located well away from the town centre due to the space needed for their car parks. In this respect, the supermarket giants were fortunate when they built stores in the town because Bolton's industrial decline meant there were numerous redundant, dilapidated mills ripe for redevelopment; an opportunity never going to be missed by the big chains because building on "brown field" sites generally attracts less opposition. Consequently, where Worktowners once laboured in Hesketh's mill, Atlas mill, and Hick Hargreaves Engineering works, their grandchildren park on giant car parks, and push trolleys around the supermarket aisles of Asda, Morrisons and Sainsburys. With so many of Bolton's supermarkets offering ample free parking, people had even less reason to visit the town's traditional shopping streets which unfortunately over time also gained an unwelcome reputation for being full of parking meters, yellow lines and overzealous traffic wardens.

Unsurprisingly, the major supermarkets have used their commercial power to exploit the wider societal changes of the last thirty years. Now they routinely offer Bolton's busy, car owning people, an extraordinary range of goods from paint, electrical goods, music, hardware, furnishings, clothing and cigarettes to medical prescriptions, mortgages, insurance and birth registrations; all products and services which were once the preserve of the town's high streets.[27] By becoming all-encompassing shopping destinations, supermarkets – most successfully it should be added – can now meet all the needs of their customers in one place; customers who as one historian of British high streets put it, have simply "left behind the traditional world of greengrocers with their poorly spelled price tickets, of fishmongers with their produce brought fresh from the coast each day or of butchers with their ready advice on how to cook the various cuts of meat."[28] Indeed, by the end of the twentieth century, Worktown's housewives going to the corner shop to buy "a little bit of somethin' for tea" already belonged to urban folklore . Moreover, by then, a weekly – even monthly – "big shop" was a well-established national institution as Bolton born comic Peter Kay's jokes about it showed.

Even without the impact of supermarkets, Worktown's shops were already disappearing. As we have seen, slum clearance programmes in Bolton were concentrated on the oldest streets closest to the town centre. When the bathroom-less rows of terraced houses were reduced to rubble, so too were any shops on their corners. As new housing estates covered the old streets of Worktown, any new shops that were built to replace the old corner shops tended to be concentrated on utilitarian concrete parades with people expected to walk much further to them from the more dispersed housing; a change which inevitably affected the idea of the shop as a communal hub at the end of the street. Indeed figures in 2016 show that of Lancashire's remaining "convenience " stores i.e. locally based independent shops, one in three of their customers actually drive to them. Moreover, unlike in Worktown where women shopped each day, one in four people were found to visit their local shop only once-a-week with as much as a fifth of local people visiting them even less frequently.

Just as corner shops on Bolton's side streets have largely disappeared, so too the old shopping parades on Bolton's arterial roads. Closest to the town centre, whole rows of shops have been demolished mainly to ease the growing traffic congestion. In particular, wider roads, re-routing of traffic and the imperatives of town planning and regeneration have necessitated the demolition of much of the previously noted Derby Street as well as the eastern end of Deane Road. On Bolton's north-eastern rim, Kay Street, Higher Bridge Street and Folds Road have all been substantially redeveloped. As a consequence, on the main approaches to Bolton, there is a barren, more soulless townscape of dual carriage ways, car parks, petrol stations, and as we shall see, huge retail parks, with virtually no local shops to be seen.

Even in those parades of shops that survive on main roads, they bear little resemblance to those that characterised Worktown. In fact they reflect the structural social changes that have affected Bolton, shops now being more ethnically diverse and also generally speaking, offering goods and services that appeal to people with more disposable income. As early as 1960 Tom Harrisson wrote:

> Down at the bottom of Davenport Street what had once been an ordinary corner grocer's now had smart new wooden slat-panelling over the front and a big notice:

CONTINENTAL AND DELICATESSEN SHOP

> This reflected what we soon found to be one of the more important lesser changes in Worktown outlook: a wider acceptance of the world... Unthinkable in the thirties, successful now, were two Chinese, Spanish and Greek restaurants, an Indian one (often open after midnight). It used to be impossible to get anything except fish and chips after 7.30 p.m.

Harrisson wouldn't have any problem buying his supper today. In a remarkable visual transformation, dozens of Indian takeaways, Chinese takeaways, Kebab houses, and Turkish grills provide food until the early hours of the morning in the shop premises where Worktown's greengrocers, grocers, butchers, and fishmongers once prospered. In the shops that aren't selling fast food, tattoo parlours, tanning salons, beauty salons, false nail boutiques, mobile phone repair shops, e-cigarette suppliers and dog grooming salons reflect a society with very different priorities and of course more money to spend on what would have been considered non-essentials only two generations previously.

As the twentieth century came to an end, the kinds of local shops once considered so important by Mass Observation had become increasingly hard to find; a decline that has only continued in subsequent years. Indeed, by 2016, figures show that there were only 5425 convenience shops in the whole of the northwest region: not much more than the number of shops once found in Bolton alone. The same statistical analysis showed there was a ratio of one "convenience" shop to every 1309 people. As we have noted, there had been one shop to every forty-five people in Worktown.

Given their more prestigious location, it might be thought Bolton's town centre shops would have been better placed to survive or redefine themselves for the twenty-first century. However, they have proved as vulnerable as any others because it has been town centre shops that have been most affected by the contemporary British (and indeed worldwide) love affair with shopping in malls. Bolton's first retail mall, an Arndale Centre, was built in 1969 somewhat predictably replacing a Victorian arcade of shops at the heart of the town. The inclusion of a water fountain and more bizarrely, a large aviary with live budgerigars inside it, did little to dispel the feeling that Bolton's mill town heritage had been surrendered to a fairly uninspiring development. Over time the units in the Arndale Centre became increasingly dominated by national retailers with few local connections, the precursor to the disappearance of the local businesses that had once given Worktown's shopping streets such a distinctive flavour.

Despite any reservations about its rather bland, functional appearance, at least the Arndale Centre brought people to the town centre whereas the malls which have followed are a very different proposition. Brent Cross Shopping Centre, Britain's first retail park, became an immediate success following its opening in north London in 1976. Crucially, in a distinct break with the past, it was envisaged from the outset as an *alternative* to shopping in a town centre. Boasting eighty-six shops and 5000 car parking spaces – later extended to a massive 8000 spaces – Brent Cross provided a blueprint for scores of similar out-of-town shopping destinations. The Metro Centre in Gateshead which opened in 1986 dwarfed Brent Cross in its scale and ambition by amassing 342 shops under one roof – Europe's largest shopping centre at the time. Due to its novelty, it at first attracted excursions from all over the north of England including tellingly, Bolton bus station.

With out-of-town retail centres proving a huge success in other parts of the country, it was not long before similar plans were made for the northwest. In due course, construction began on the Trafford Centre, a gargantuan two-storey mall situated to the west of Manchester alongside the M62 motorway. Taking twenty-seven months to build at a cost of 600 million pounds it eventually opened in September 1998 and is the largest centre of its kind in Europe to date. It rapidly became an irresistible magnet for the growing numbers enthusiastically embracing the twenty-first century culture of "shop till you drop." Unfortunately, with the Trafford Centre on their doorstep, Boltonians were neither shopping nor dropping in their own town centre any more.

From the outset, the plans had been controversial with opponents expressing fears about the Trafford Centre's impact on the high streets of surrounding towns. It seems the concerns were entirely justified when a government survey in 2014 recorded that one-in-five of Bolton's shops were unoccupied. Just three years later another government survey confirmed that Bolton had the sixth highest percentage of empty shop units in the country: a bleaker contrast with the bustling shopping streets of Worktown would be hard to imagine.

As if the challenge of the Trafford Centre wasn't enough, the opening and expansion of several retail parks located much closer to Bolton have brought yet more problems for Bolton's beleaguered town centre shops. As we have seen, the Middlebrook Retail and Leisure Park in Horwich, by far and away the biggest in Bolton was opened in 1997, the same time as the Macron/Reebok Stadium. It has been followed in recent years by the Trinity Retail Park just off St Peters Way; Bolton Gate Retail Park on Turton Street, and latterly Bolton Shopping Park on Trinity Street; all out-of-town shopping destinations of some considerable scale. In addition, the redevelopment of Manchester Road with its rash of large prefabricated stores culminating in yet another retail park (Burnden) has piled on the agony for the owners of Bolton's remaining independently owned shops as prospective shoppers have been enticed *away from* rather than *to* the town centre.

Not surprisingly, there was considerable opposition to the expansion of retail parks so close to Bolton from the outset. When Bolton Council gave permission for the building of a further fifteen factory shops at Middlebrook in 1999 just two years after it opened, Peter Hope, the Chairman of the Planning Committee of Bolton and District Civic Trust, expressed the anger felt by many about the year-on-year decline of the town centre's shops. With depressingly accurate foresight he wrote:

It must be obvious that such a development and it would be enormous – 8000 sq.meters – would knock the stuffing out of the remaining privately owned shops in the town. Do the council live in the same world as we do? Do they not walk down Oxford Street, Bradshawgate, Great Moor Street etc. Do they not see the boarded up shops, some for months or even years and the rows of charity shops where prosperous businesses used to be?[29]

They can't have done because in subsequent years the Middlebrook has only continued to expand. Indeed it might be argued that Bolton town centre is in fact still prospering but just like its football team, its shopping streets have been relocated five miles away.

The challenges Bolton's town centre shopkeepers face are in reality a national issue. In 2014, the government, alarmed by the decline of British high streets, appointed the retail specialist and television presenter, Mary Portas, to prepare a report with recommendations on how they might be revived. She concluded that to thrive again, high streets need an engaging character, unique places to eat, and local shops catering for niche markets. Ironically, just the kind of streets that characterised Worktown.

Unfortunately, in common with most British towns, multinational franchises like McDonald's, KFC, Burger King, Coffee Republic, Cafe Nero, Starbucks and Subway restaurants now dominate Bolton's shopping streets. Similarly multinational retailers like Carphone Warehouse (which as one wag pointed out, didn't sell phones for cars and neither was it a warehouse), Claire's Accessories, Zara, Next, Top Shop and Primark – to name but a few – have squeezed out the local traders. Although on the one hand they provide familiarity for consumers who clearly like what they offer, their presence creates "clone towns". Consequently, over time Bolton's shopping streets have become hard to distinguish from any others: something that could never have been said about Worktown's independent retailers.

For the town centre's few remaining independent shops, the extraordinary growth of internet shopping in the last twenty years has only added to the formidable challenges they face. Amazon, the staggeringly successful online retail giant, has become a dominant force in shopping patterns even having a significant impact on Christmas – the one time of year retailers could traditionally look forward to with confidence. For a generation that has grown up with the worldwide web and indeed for older people who have also embraced it, the convenience of internet shopping as well as the competitive prices found on the internet have fundamentally changed when, where, and how people buy things. As we have seen, in Worktown only the middle class had goods delivered to their doors but with the advent of online shopping, fleets of vans deliver goods bought on the internet to homes across Bolton every day. In this respect, perhaps "we are all middle class now" but more problematically of course, internet shopping does little to promote vibrant town centre shops.

Where high streets still thrive in Britain, it is usually because they have become leisure destinations with an emphasis on restaurants and bars as much as shopping. In Bolton, this pattern has been most evident on Bradshawgate – traditionally one of the town's busiest shopping streets. Bradshawgate began to develop more of a "night time" economy in the early 1980s after Corks Wine Bar first opened blurring the distinction between pub and nightclub. The success of Corks brought a slew of other bars with dance floors, flashing lights and music blaring out onto the street from the doors of what had been some of Worktown's most prestigious banks and shops. Over time, Bradshawgate's function was changed to such an extent that it was deemed necessary to appoint a "night time manager" to monitor the area – a role that would have been incomprehensible to a shopping basket carrying Worktowner.

By embracing the potential offered by a night-time economy, Bradshawgate's business fortunes were saved for a while. Unfortunately, in this instance it came at a hefty price because by definition most businesses in Bradshawgate don't open until early evening making one of the town's most important thoroughfares a lifeless shadow of its former self during the day. Worse still, it can be a raucous and intimidating place at night. With its function so fundamentally changed many affectionately remembered shops like Hilary Anns boutique, Wardrobe and Small's Army Stores were converted into fast food outlets providing cheap suppers for intoxicated revellers. Bradshawgate's utter collapse as a shopping destination was finally complete when the Arndale shopping centre (re-named Crompton Place) was severed from the street after a budget clothing store took over one whole side of the mall. In doing so, it obliterated the original entrance doors; a planning decision that ensured any would-be shoppers wanting to enter or exit from Bradshawgate couldn't, and they had to walk a further 200 yards or more to actually get in to the shopping centre.

In all probability, it didn't matter by then, as in common with many other post-industrial towns, few shoppers were visiting Bolton town centre anyway. This spiral of decline has been further exacerbated by the massive private and public investment in Manchester, just a short train ride away. In the last ten years, the "rainy city" has shrugged off its dour industrial image to emerge as a dynamic, cosmopolitan destination for an upmarket shopping experience or a more sophisticated evening out. Unfortunately, as Manchester city centre has boomed, many consider Bolton has become its contracting, shabby poor relation; a perception not without foundation if the palpable sense of decline across Bolton's shopping streets in the twenty-first century is anything to go by.

Only seventy years ago Humphrey Spender recorded dozens of Worktowners browsing the windows of prosperous shops on Deansgate. At the time of writing, in one terrace of seven shops adjoining the Post Office that Spender photographed, three shops are closed. In another row, a charity shop, an advice centre for the unemployed and a fly-blown, derelict Chinese takeaway occupy the original shops. Equally dispiriting, all around, stores emphasising budget goods and price cutting alongside myriad charity shops bear witness to the fall from grace of Worktown's shopocracy.

It is the same story on the adjacent Churchgate, historically one of the town's busiest thoroughfares. When surveyed in 2014, in Churchgate House, all five shop units were unrented as was the large retail premises which once housed a Safeway supermarket. The quirky little gift shop, Ye Olde Wench and Trinkets, had been long closed in common with the Originals boutique facing it (with breath-taking irony, after the shop closed it was briefly home to the "Be Strong Have Hope Training and Enterprise Centre"). Only the indomitable Walsh's bakery (Ye Olde Pastie Shoppe) and Booth's music store serve as reminders that this was once one of the busiest streets in Worktown.

Fifty yards away, Bolton's glorious market hall has also become a shadow of its former self. In 2005, councillors took the puzzling decision to remove all the stalls in order to redevelop it as a shopping mall; a decision all the more baffling as a couple of years before it had garnered special praise in a government survey which described it as "an attractive shopping space full of small traders within a traditional market hall."[30] The move caused considerable anger with 80,000 people signing a petition opposing the plan. However the redevelopment went ahead transforming the Market Hall into a shopping arcade dominated by multinational chains. Tony Brown, the manager of Beales Department Store (previously Whittakers) articulated the resentment over what many saw as a poor man's Trafford Centre (but without the free parking) when he told the local press: "The town centre has been systematically overlooked over the years. The town centre has enough competition with the Trafford Centre and Middlebrook. Closing the old market as part of the Market Place redevelopment was insanity."[31] Despite the furore, petition, and alleged madness, in the end, the Market Hall's famous old stalls went the same way as other salient aspects of Worktown: they vanished.*

In the meantime, nationally renowned retailers trading in Bolton were also disappearing. Almost unnoticed, Woolworths closed in 2009 after trading on Deansgate for nearly a century. Major retailers that once prospered in Bolton like MFI (furniture) and Comet electrical stores have also gone out of business. 2016 proved to be an especially calamitous year. Nationally, the British Home Stores group went into administration, the shutting of their Bolton store punching a gaping hole in the shopping provision right opposite the town hall. Beales department store – often still called Whittakers by older Boltonians despite the name change – announced it was to close thus bringing the town's love affair with department stores to an inglorious end, its contemporary, Whiteheads, already having been closed for some twenty years. But perhaps most shocking of all, in August, Preston's jewellers on Deansgate announced it was to close after serving the people of Bolton and beyond for nearly 150 years. Despite claims that it couldn't respond to the changed retail climate, it is revealing that their other branches – one each in Wilmslow, Guildford and Leeds – remain open for business. Whether the company will still retain the iconic name, Preston's *of Bolton*, remains to be seen.

Despite all the doom and gloom and the seemingly insurmountable problems, there may yet be a glimmer of hope for Bolton's last few independent town centre shops. The extraordinary growth of small supermarkets like Aldi and Lidl in recent years is perhaps an early

---

*   In 2016, the Market Hall became the Market Place after an impressive, award winning re-development.

indication of growing disenchantment with superstores and the generally joyless, perfunctory nature of shopping in them; a dissatisfaction that can also be discerned in the upturn in the fortunes of the Co-ops which have latterly reversed their decline by re branding themselves as more ethically sound as well as being smaller and based in local communities which increases their appeal to the consciences of many twenty first century consumers.

These developments suggest that rising customer expectations may yet lead to a revival of shops which emphasise service and quality. Should it happen, Bolton still has a handful of traditional shops. They include Arthur Morris tobacconists on Bradshawgate, with its original Edwardian interior; Booth's musical instrument shop on Churchgate, reputedly one of the oldest music shops in the world; Ault's men's outfitters on Newport Street which was established in 1891; and R. Allen's shoe shop on Great Moor Street, once a saddlery in Victorian Bolton. Remarkably, all of them were serving customers when Tom Harrisson was typing his reports in Davenport Street. Similarly, other shops like X Records- a rare independent vinyl record store on Bridge Street; Harker and Howarth, and HW Audio-both musical instrument stores; and the Modern Radio electrical repairs shop located on Derby Street which opened in the 1940's, are all unique Bolton based businesses offering customers niche products and the kind of bespoke services which have endeared them to Boltonians for generations.

Such shops garner affection and loyalty because they are connected to Bolton in a way national and international businesses aren't, and perhaps more importantly, never will be. Indeed small, independent shops evoke such strong feelings of nostalgia, with jaw dropping irony some supermarkets strive to recreate them with kitsch market stalls manned by "bakers" and "butchers" sporting aprons and straw hats; sterile, ridiculous versions of the real shopping streets supermarkets helped to destroy. In much the same way, the current vogue for Christmas street markets and the obsession with recreating "Victorian Christmases" is partly because the London "town" of Scrooge, with its brightly lit, bow windowed shops as it is portrayed in the numerous film versions of *A Christmas Carol*, is an idealised version of what people would like their shopping experience to be again.

Although Bolton's shops were rarely bow windowed never mind picturesque or quaint, they were unstintingly part of the town's character whether on one of its high streets or on the corner of a dingy back street. Most nostalgic yearnings for the shops of a not-too-distant past stem from the belief that local shops and businesses were "the social glue" which bound communities together: the very reason Mass Observation thought shops mattered.[32] Clearly the writers of *Coronation Street* think so too. No character does a "big shop", buys things on the internet or drives their car to a retail park. They scarcely need to, because when they aren't being set on fire or destroyed in train crashes, a kebab shop, a cafe, a florist, a bistro, a newsagent, and a traditional corner shop at the gable end all still flourish. Back in the real world though, Worktown's dozens of long vanished shops only highlight that *Coronation Street's* original gritty realism has morphed into an anachronistic fantasy. But *Coronation Street's* biggest implausibility is in fact reserved for another gable end in the cobbled street for the scriptwriters insist that the residents still have a local pub to drink in.

SPIT AND SAWDUST

The Grapes Hotel, Water Street.
Humphrey Spender

The Grapes Hotel was an unprepossessing, dingy looking pub just outside Bolton town centre. In September 1937, Humphrey Spender left Davenport Street, made the short walk across town and took two photographs of it. At around the same time – most likely the same day – Spender also photographed the Tonge railway viaduct. The quickest route from the Grapes Hotel to the viaduct would be along Folds Road, a journey of less than 300 yards. Walking between the two locations, Spender would have passed no less than five other similar pubs: the Eagle and Vulcan, the Church Inn, the Lord Clyde, the Dog and Snipe, and the Waterloo Tavern. In the unlikely event these pubs weren't enough to satisfy any thirsty beer drinkers, there were also another fourteen pubs in the warren of streets surrounding Folds Road.[1]

Pubs in extraordinary numbers so close to one another were found all over Worktown. Being so numerous and so integral to communities, Tom Harrisson considered pubs to be of immense significance. He came to the conclusion that "more people spend more time in public houses than they do in any other buildings except private houses and work-places".[2] The Worktown archive contains dozens of documents about pubs, what people did when drinking in them, the types of customers they attracted, the facilities on offer, and not least, the everyday conversations of the Worktowners recorded by the Observers drinking secretly besides them.

When charged with making reports on pubs, the Observers living in Davenport Street did not need to walk far to find one. The Howcroft – a red brick, ordinary looking pub – was about thirty yards away in the adjacent street while the more ornate Royal Hotel was almost the first thing any Observer would see on leaving their house. Turning right at the Royal, they would have only a short walk down Vernon Street, before they reached another pub, the Caledonian Inn, a type of pub found in monumental numbers throughout Lancashire's industrial towns and the prototype for the Rovers Return at the heart of *Coronation Street*.

In appearance, these kinds of side street pubs looked much the same as the adjoining houses apart from the gas lamps which hung over their doors which were usually at a forty-five degree angle to the pavement. In addition, their ground floor windows were often framed by fake columns with words like "vault" and "parlour" etched into the frosted glass. On the inside, most pubs of this sort were unadorned and functional. This was especially true of their vaults and taprooms in which pub-goers were usually confronted by a straight bar counter painted with thick yellow imitation graining and worn, scrubbed wooden floors, often "spit littered and strewn with match ends and crumbled [sic] cigarette packets".[3]

Tom Harrisson thought the vaults in pubs like the Caledonian had an anthropological significance in both their visual appearance and the behaviour of those who went in them. With their spittoons (receptacles for gobs of saliva and phlegm) "some with sawdust some without" he believed "there is something of the gent's lavatory and structure in a vault which is almost always long and thin, and stone floored (in the older pubs). It is nothing like home. It is an exclusively male gathering."[4] With men being the dominant presence, the language in vaults was likely to be earthier, the tobacco smoke more impenetrable, and beer swigged more enthusiastically than in the pub's other rooms. One customer bluntly summed up their atmosphere telling an Observer "You may spit on the floor or burn the bar with a cigarette, and the barmaid won't rebuke you. You can do almost anything you bloody well like in the vault, short of shitting on the place."[5]

Given the brutish atmosphere of vaults, most women were probably glad they were banned from them. In fact, the only females that were ever seen in vaults were the landlord's wife or barmaids, who might be subjected to bawdy innuendo, mild insults and drunken flirtatious approaches although according to an Observer's account, one landlord's wife gave as good as she got being observed to swear just as much as her customers.

At the time of the Worktown investigation, it was common for drinkers to have a few drinks in a local pub like the Royal or Howcroft before heading off into town – especially at weekends. This was partly because there was a marked difference between grander town centre pubs which attracted customers from a wider area, and the more workaday side street pubs or beerhouses which tended to serve local communities. Although both types of pub were very different, they were collectively a direct product of the 1830 Beerhouse Act. This legislation had been introduced to address the social problems caused by the consumption of cheaply manufactured spirits, especially gin. Besides the unruly, drunken behaviour associated with drinking it – the infamous "gin fever" that once blighted British towns and cities – it was believed that the availability of cheap spirits contributed to the appalling poverty found in the most deprived households. By licensing premises to brew and sell only beer, the Beerhouse Act was intended to wean people off more potent spirits by encouraging them to drink beer which in Britain at least, has always enjoyed a reputation of being a wholesome, even nutritious drink.

In spite of the good intentions, the Beerhouse Act simply resulted in a rash of licensed beerhouses. In their early incarnation, they were little more than a front parlour in a house where beer was served by the householder paying two guineas for a license to brew beer. Opponents of the Act believed it did little to discourage the consumption of alcohol arguing that it simply promoted a different type of drunkenness; a view not without some justification if the number of beerhouses once found in Bolton was anything to go by. Worse still for those who advocated temperance, the effects of the legislation simply encouraged the bigger breweries to search for new ways to attract customers to their pubs.

In the late nineteenth century, powerful brewing concerns alarmed by the explosion of beerhouses invested in ever more opulent pubs which aimed to draw people into town centres by offering drinkers magnificently appointed rooms complete with mahogany bars, mirrored backboards and yard upon yard of etched glass – the latter installed to reflect the light from the gas lamps. Ironically, they became known as gin palaces although in truth the term referred to a much earlier manifestation of elaborately decorated licensed premises mostly found in London. Although no genuine gin palaces survived beyond the end of the nineteenth century in London or indeed anywhere else, the name persisted and tended to became synonymous with any large urban pub with more elaborate decorative features. Bolton's best examples, the Balmoral Hotel, the Fleece Hotel (presently the Flying Flute), the Prince William, and Yates's Wine Lodge at the time of writing are still operating as pubs although their interiors have all changed drastically.

Of course not all town centre pubs were of this type, nor were they all a product of the late Victorian age. The Swan at the junction of Churchgate and Bradshawgate, the Commercial Hotel on Victoria Square, and The Three Crowns on Deansgate had been licensed premises in Georgian times. Most of them were observed as part of the Worktown project and with the exception of the Commercial Hotel, they still operate as pubs today. Other pubs like the Man and Scythe with its origins in medieval Bolton; the Pack Horse (currently called the Dragonfly, previously Barracuda's), more of an upmarket hotel at one time; and the Star and Garter and the Hen and Chickens- two typical examples of Bolton's Victorian pubs – were also observed and at the time of writing are still part of the town centre's drinking scene. However, many other town centre pubs reported on by the Observers like the Saddle and the Nag's Head have long since disappeared.

In the 1920s, another kind of pub made an appearance in Britain, a few of which could be seen in Worktown. Appalled by the drunkenness witnessed in pubs, some people demanded a more genteel, refined type of establishment to enjoy a drink in. The campaign for "improved pubs" that could offer refreshments as well as intoxicating liquors, also called for environments that were "airy, commodious and comfortable..." Furthermore, their proponents argued these new types of licensed premises ought to offer "proper seating and sanitary accommodation and (should) contain provision of suitable recreation."[6]

This resulted, especially in the south of England, in the building of much larger pubs located outside town centres. They were intended to attract both the middle classes living in the suburbs and also the embryonic motorist trade, and were very different in tone to side street pubs and rowdier town centre establishments. In principle, rather than there being a pub on every street, one large pub would serve a wider geographical area; a reflection of the belief that middle class people didn't mind a stroll or even a drive to the pub. Clearly, this was very different to working class men (or women for that matter) who preferred a pub they could walk to on their own street or at the very least, the next one. Indeed Mass Observation recorded that ninety per cent of drinkers didn't walk more than 300 yards to their usual pubs, a figure that was only to be expected in Bolton at a time when although there were some 180,000 people living in the town, there were only 3998 private cars in total.

Predictably for a predominantly working class town, Worktown had few "improved pubs" but as most of them were built in the much maligned "brewer's Tudor", their scarcity was probably considered a blessing in disguise when they first appeared. With vernacular architecture, fake half-timbered facades and interiors that came complete with oak panelling and false beams, the more discerning patrons they aimed to attract were usually treated to a mythical version of the coaching inns of "Merrie England". This yearning for a supposedly gentler, bygone age is even suggested in the names of the two best examples in the Bolton area: the Shakespeare in nearby Farnworth, and the excruciatingly named, Ye Jolly Crofters just outside Horwich. Quite what Shakespeare or the rural crofters of medieval England – jolly or otherwise – had in common with a smoky mill town let alone the middle class car owners they were meant to attract remains a mystery but with a subsequent change in taste, their panelled interiors and impressive external details means both pubs are now rightly appreciated as superb examples of the genre.

Like "improved pubs", genuine country pubs tended to be few and far between in Worktown mainly due to Bolton's industrialisation and rapid expansion in the nineteenth century. Some parts of the borough, especially to the north, were however surprisingly rural before the housing estates built in the 1960s and 1970s swallowed up the fields and the farms. Further afield, there were several pubs in the nearby villages of Edgworth, Egerton, Affetside and Belmont ready to serve the few car owners, village mill workers, farm labourers or even those prepared to walk several miles for refreshment in a different kind of pub. Observers recorded in some detail their impressions of the House Without a Name in Harwood – the beer at the tiny pub being described as "excellent with some 'body' in it".[7] Favourable impressions were also recorded of another rural pub, the larger White Horse on Stitch-Mi- Lane which was completely surrounded by farmer's fields at the time of the Worktown investigation.

The variety and numbers of pubs in Worktown in the mid twentieth century was far from unusual in any of Britain's major towns. In Bolton's case – as in most manufacturing towns – their proliferation simply resulted from the fact that factory workers have always drunk a lot of beer. Indeed in 1937, in a list of the top twenty towns in the country with the highest density of pubs per inhabitant, sixteen were in the northwest; a proportion that reflected the fact that Lancashire was one of the country's most industrialised regions. Indeed Northampton – a shoemaking centre – was the only town from the south of the country to feature on the list at all.[8]

To meet the demand for beer from thirsty workers doing labour intensive work, there were 149 hotels, inns or taverns massed in the centre of Bolton in 1900. Although, their numbers did fall in the early part of the twentieth century, there were still 87 pubs in the town centre proper in 1936. In addition to these, the Chief Constable's Report to the General Licensing Meeting in 1937, noted a further 465 premises licensed for the sale of intoxicating liquor throughout the town. As well as all the pubs, there were another sixty-five licensed social and recreational clubs of which just over half had some political affiliations. The report shows inns accounted for 126 of the total number of licensed premises with an additional 144 beerhouses licensed only to sell beer for drinking "on" or "off" the premises. The rest of the licenses were accounted for by various outlets granted to sell beer, wine, spirits and cider for consumption "off" the premises.[9] With a ratio of one pub for every 381 inhabitants, Bolton was only exceeded in pub density per person by Halifax, Dewsbury, Oldham, Rochdale and Preston – tellingly, all of them manufacturing towns with their share of mills and factories too.

The evidence gathered by Mass Observation about Worktown's pub culture provides a fascinating record of when, where, and why people went out drinking in pubs in the mid twentieth century. One aspect explored in some detail was the way town centre pubs differed from others in terms of the gender of those frequenting them. Side street pubs were mainly patronised by males during the week because of the belief that a woman's principle responsibility was looking after the home and children. Happily for men, this left them free to go to the pub whenever they could afford it (or not as was often the case). It was only at weekends when female customers were seen in greater numbers in pubs – and predominantly those in the town centre.

However, despite more women being in pubs overall at weekends, vaults still remained an all-male preserve with men congregating in them even when they were out drinking with their wives. Whilst enjoying manly communion in the vault, husbands bought drinks for their partners who sat separately with other women in the pub's lounge or parlour. According to Harrisson, when men eventually joined their wives they became quieter "women's men with collar studs." He also went on to note they had to pay more to drink the same beer in the lounge as in the vault which might go some way to explaining the change in their behaviour.[10]

The Observers also recorded the types of women frequenting pubs and what they got up to whilst in them. One count of customers in Yates's Wine Lodge revealed that at 8.40 p.m. there were 150 females present, a number never likely to be found in any side street pub even if they could have fitted in one. The author of the report hardly disguised his disapproval of women drinking in pubs saying that the wine lodge was "reeking with prostitution."[11] Similar allegations were made about the Prince William just across the road where one man happily pointed out the different types of prostitutes to an Observer – one pair of prostitutes apparently a mother and daughter. Rather bluntly, the man ended the conversation by telling the Observer "and there's Ginger over there you can do her on the doorstep for 2/6."[12] At the same time, Tom Harrisson recorded there were "about 24 prostitutes" in Bolton but quite how he arrived at such a precise figure remains a mystery.

As well as the disdain shown towards alleged prostitutes, Observers' comments were generally disrespectful towards any women they saw drinking in pubs. Some Observers believed women drinkers were "tarts" and "whores" with one report describing how women encouraged men to "come onto them."[13] Another Observer investigating the Grapes Hotel wrote "some of the women were young, not exactly whores but getting on for it."[14] Whether such pejorative comments resulted from different cultural norms at the time or simply reflected the prejudice of the Observers is difficult to determine but it is perhaps not too surprising that young, middle class academics out and about in the alien environment of a mill town tended to describe the drunken women they encountered with thinly disguised contempt.

In fairness to the Observers, disrespect towards females in pubs was also in evidence amongst local people too. In a report about the Dog and Partridge on Bank Street, an Observer describes how one man took a live tortoise out of his coat pocket before threatening a terrified woman with it. After much laughter at the woman's expense, a conversation followed about the food it ate. On the other hand, a description of an old Irish woman hobbling into the One Horseshoe pub covering her head with a black shawl is rather less humorous – an Observer recording that she "only had half of her face, the rest had gone for syphilis".[15]

The pub going habits of Worktowners during midday opening hours were also explored by Mass Observation. In shocking contrast to contemporary health and safety regulations, a number of pubs were found to do a roaring trade serving factory workers during the "dinner" break. The landlord of the Globe on Higher Bridge Street, a small pub close to two huge engineering firms, Dobson and Barlow, and Musgraves – the latter employing some 10,000 workers – told an Observer that he drew 100 pints of beer in readiness for the lunchtime rush before explaining he did so because: "Engineers are thirsty people."[16] Another Observer was of the opinion that a large, nearby pub, the Falcon on Kay Street, had been built specifically to cater for the workers of Dobson and Barlows and other local mills. At the Falcon, Observers again recorded 100 pints being pulled in readiness for the midday break although it was noted that "The landlord reckoned he would lose about ten pints in hundred, the rush was so great."[17]

After the dinner break was over, or in pubs further away from mills and factories, the Observers noted pubs tended to be very quiet at midday. "No one in lounge, no one in passage bar. Two men in vault" ran one report before continuing that "This is an average of the activity in any Worktown pub during its weekday/midday opening hours." There were generally so few daytime drinkers for them to spy on that in the end, Observers abandoned their activities concluding that it was "unprofitable to work the pubs except in the evenings, firstly because there was no chance to observe without being oneself observed, secondly because (being so few people about) every visit meant having a drink, and that never helped the afternoon's work."[18]

Even with a midday lull, drinking was part and parcel of daily life for many Worktowners. Inevitably, there were problems associated with it. The Chief Constable's report of 1936 preserved by Mass Observation provides compelling evidence of the Worktowners' propensity for drinking alcohol and more disturbingly, the effects of overindulgence. In his report ranking British towns in order for the most number of convictions for drunkenness per thousand people, Bolton registered the fifth worst in the whole country only being superseded by Rochdale, Huddersfield and Lancaster. Rather surprisingly, the genteel resort of Southport had the unenviable distinction of topping the list. In that year alone, 143 Boltonians had proceedings for drunkenness taken against them. Somewhat predictably, 123 of those convicted were men with just over a third of the offences occurring on a Saturday night which the chief constable stated was "of course, only to be expected."[19]

The chief constable went on to note that Bolton's licensed premises "on the whole have been well conducted, and I have received very few complaints." Although this may have been true in an official capacity, my grandmother who lived in one of the town's most impoverished areas insisted that there was a fight in the streets at closing time *every* Saturday night, with children running from one street to another to watch the best one. According to her recollections one notorious drinker – the gloriously named Caractacus Waterworth – would even delay the start of a fight just so an acquaintance could fetch his clogs which he then used to inflict even more damage on the shins of anyone who had the temerity to provoke him.

In spite of the threat of alcohol-fuelled aggression, it was quite common for young children to go into pubs carrying jugs in order to fetch beer for the adult members of the household wanting to drink in the house; an errand known as going for "t'llowance" (the allowance). This phrase along with the shared memory of many older Boltonians who recall carrying jugs to and from pubs, strongly suggests that money was reserved for the purchase of beer as part of an essential weekly or even daily cycle in spite of any other pressures on often very meagre household budgets.

To ensure that people could procure "t'allowance", Worktown's pubs, like those in most British towns, were supplied by an extraordinary number of breweries. In 1932, there were eleven breweries in Bolton producing beer for consumption in their own licensed premises as well as supplying it to other local pubs. These included the Cornbrook Brewery based at the Britannia Hotel on Pikes Lane, William Greene brewing at the Colliers Arms on Chorley Old Road, William Smith operating at the Bay Horse in Horwich, John Hamer brewing at the Volunteer in Bromley Cross and what turned out to be Worktown's last surviving independent brewery, Howarth's Model Brewery located on Spa Road. In addition, there were also a number of beerhouses brewing their own beer but not selling it wholesale like the previously noted House Without a Name and the Lord Raglan on Halliwell Road.

Of all Bolton's breweries, Magee Marshall Brewery was not only the biggest, but also the one that became most associated with Worktown. David Magee began brewing beer in 1866 after establishing the Crown Brewery just off Derby Street. The premises were soon extended and it became Magee Marshall following the acquisition of Marshall's brewery in 1888. Five years later, the Crown Brewery was further extended and shortly after the company expanded their operations beyond Bolton by first buying the Wigan Brewery, then building several new pubs and purchasing existing outlets in Blackpool and Southport; a sound business strategy at a time when Blackpool was the most likely holiday destination for the vast majority of Boltonians.

In spite of Magee's dominance, Mass Observation discovered that the quality of their beer was not always appreciated. One publican told an Observer that "a man who can drink Magee's Mild must be able to feed on rats" whilst another customer said dismissively: "Magee's – it's only bloody sugar and water."[20] Magee's directors might have taken some comfort in knowing their beer's reputation was marginally better than that reserved for a rival brewery's beer served in a pub on Great Moor Street. According to one Observer's report it was widely known as "cricket's piss". Curiously in a town where drinking beer was a way of life for many people, one customer in a vault told an Observer that "you get no good beer in the town locally."[21]

Opinions about beer however rarely affected drinking patterns because pubs have always represented much more than just places to drink. If nothing else, pubs provided a welcome change from routine and a time to relax in the company of friends or at least drinking companions. This wider social aspect of pub going reached its zenith in the mid years of the twentieth century when the notion of the pub as a "local" really took hold.[22] What led a man – and it was generally men who adopted "locals" – to choose a particular "local" as *his* pub was variable including his relationship with other regulars, the preferences of his workmates, the taste of the beer, the personality of the landlord and, on occasion, even the pianist who played there.

However, one reason above all others influenced people to adopt a particular pub as a "local": proximity. In Worktown, pubs depended on the local community for their custom and it was essential as we have noted that working class people could walk to them. Therefore first and foremost, a side street pub functioned as a gathering place for the local community that surrounded it. It was in the "local" that working men and on occasion, their wives, enjoyed warmth and a gossip with their neighbours, even though the great majority of drinkers were often only a couple of streets away from their own front doors. One report about an evening in the Waterloo Tavern reveals much about the attraction of "locals": "19 drinkers of whom 15 are women; obvious that the majority are friends or neighbours of each other. At 9.30 p.m. the place is a hubbub, not overnoisy, but everyone seems to be talking at once. The waitress is having difficulty in fulfilling orders and is looking desperate and bewildered. It is remarkable how the pub atmosphere plus the drink, creates a spirit of bonhomie that can be found nowhere else…"[23]

As well as a place for neighbourly conviviality, Worktown's men in particular regarded their local pub as a bolthole from domestic strife. In the pub they drank, grumbled and often hid from their wives amongst others who were also usually doing much the same. One man drinking in the Bark Street Tavern when asked why he went to this particular pub replied "I only live across the road and I pass a couple of hours in here out road of wife." Another made similar remarks but was rather more scathing about his fellow drinkers: "I come here to have a drink and a game of dominoes, or darts, or ow't as is going on. I'm not the same as some buggers, henpecked."[24]

Because of this role, the pub-as-refuge became a staple comic device in films, television sitcoms and stand up comedians' routines, with pub landlords helping to conceal male customers' whereabouts from their wives. Lazy "lummox" Stan Ogden and the equally work-shy Jack Duckworth in *Coronation Street* were often skulking in the Rovers Return when they wanted to avoid domestic responsibilities only to be harangued by their wives when they were discovered or returned home. Although the shenanigans of male pub-goers hiding away in pubs were probably overexaggerated by scriptwriters, the pub-as-refuge was clearly rooted in some reality which might explain why on one notable occasion Humphrey Spender was threatened with violence when his camera posed a threat to the privacy of some drinkers in one town centre pub.

As well as providing sanctuaries, pubs were places to play games like darts, dominoes and cards. In addition, less familiar pursuits like quoits, "shove ha'penny" and skittles were also popular. Although formal gambling was strictly illegal, pub games at the time of Mass Observation usually involved stakes of some kind, an Observer investigating card games being told by a landlord that "Nobody wants to play cards for love."[25] Unlike card games, gambling machines had yet to become commonplace in Worktown's pubs although they were appearing in some social clubs by the end of the 1930s – one Observer on seeing a fruit machine located inside the West Ward Labour Club on John Brown Street stating that it was the first he had seen in Bolton.[26]

Besides the social aspects of pub going, some Worktowners claimed they drank beer partly for health reasons. Unsurprisingly, these beliefs were promoted vigorously by the brewers. Magee's Family Ale was pronounced a "very wholesome and nutritious beverage" in a national survey of brewing companies in 1891. Forty years later, the brewers of Findleter's "nourishing" Stout were promoting their beer's medicinal properties by advertising rather bizarrely that it was "specially recommended for invalids". For those suffering with mental rather than physical symptoms, the brewers of Guinness boasted that their stout had a most soothing effect on the nerves for "such patients" who are "most on edge" – claims supported by a doctor according to their advertisements.[27]

Wholly predictably, the brewers' claims that beer promoted good health were enthusiastically embraced by those drinking it. One Worktowner when asked why he drank beer responded: "Why I drink beer is there is hops in which is good for you, also Barm which keeps your body in good health." One man told Tom Harrisson: "Why I drink beer, because it is food, drink and medicine to me, my bowels work regular as clockwork and I think that is the key to health." Similarly, another forty-year-old man told an Observer: "I drink beer because I think it does more good than doctor's medicine, it keeps my bowels in good working order."[28]

Beer drinking in Worktown apparently had other benefits beyond its impact on daily ablutions. Dutton's brewery based in nearby Blackburn, advertised in Bolton's newspaper that their OBJ ale (Oh Be Joyful) was an ideal pick-me-up if the football game should be called off due to bad weather. As well as lifting the spirits of woebegone match goers, drinking lots of beer could also lift sexual performance- or at least that's what some would-be Lotharios claimed. One twenty-five-year-old man told an Observer: "This stuff (beer) gives me a good appetite and puts plenty of lead in my pencil." Another aged about thirty-five boasted about the improvement in his sexual performance although on this occasion the Observer was reluctant to record his precise words:

> "If I get three pints down me I can…" What he said is the sort of thing considered "unprintable". It amounted to the fact that when he went home he was able to have sexual intercourse with his wife with the maximum of efficiency, and when he woke up in the morning he was able to repeat the process with the utmost satisfaction.

The gratitude of wives in the bedroom aside, overindulgence of alcohol was widely regarded as one of the main pitfalls for working men in the mid twentieth century. Unfortunately, those with least money to spare were often the ones who drank the most. If gin was "the quickest way out of Salford" as was often said, it seems beer was a more ponderous but equally intoxicating route out of the hard life of Worktown. In 1937, the *Bolton Evening News* reported how one well-known drinker, Richard Ryan, found himself in court over arrears that had accrued under a wife maintenance order. The court was told he "was said to 'sub' his wage and to 'sup' it even faster." The police inspector informed the magistrates "If he has ten shillings, eight shillings go on drink" before telling the court that Ryan "had not a single redeeming feature if the public houses were open." [29] It would be fair to assume that such cases were far from unusual. Indeed both my grandparents insisted that despite the poverty they witnessed in the 1930s, people somehow *always* found enough money to drink.

It is hardly surprising that advocates of temperance cited the drain on already tight household budgets, the problem of absenteeism from the home, and the prospect of more severe alcoholism as arguments against drinking. Seemingly, the latter concern was not without foundation as the chief constable reported in 1936 three cases of drunkenness in Bolton caused by the consumption of methylated spirits. The national Temperance Movement which had its origins in the industrial heartlands of the northwest did its best to discourage drinking alcohol although an Observer witnessing the pleas for abstinence from one activist on Bolton Town Hall steps concluded that there was "little interest in most of the few people who listen."

Besides the financial and health implications, one of the worst problems was the domestic violence that sometimes accompanied drunkenness. Although cultural norms change over time along with the boundaries of what is considered acceptable behaviour, women behind closed doors could all too often be the victims of aggressive, drunken husbands. In one appalling incident in my own family history, my great-grandmother sent her son to tell her husband to come home from the pub because she needed money for food. For her troubles, she was rewarded with a vicious punch to the face, a permanently damaged nose and a warning from her enraged husband that he was never to be disturbed in the pub again.

In 1939, the advent of the Second World War signalled the end of the Worktown project. It also marked the beginning of the end for the pub-going experience they had witnessed just before it – as we have seen, a more masculine, unpretentious, earthier drinking culture mostly centred around local pubs that functioned as hubs of communal life. With hindsight, the war may be seen as something of a swansong for those kinds of pubs when they provided a welcome distraction to a beleaguered people facing an uncertain future.

In the somewhat anticlimactic years that followed the end of the war, pubs retained their dominance in Bolton's social life. If it is true that "misery loves company", it is not difficult to see why people continued to embrace pub-going during the grey, drab years of austerity; a seemingly never-ending misery typified in 1946 by an acute shortage of glass that forced the Whitbread Brewery to threaten: "You don't deserve a Whitbread unless you bring those empty bottles back."[30] Fortunately for Bolton's bottle-less drinkers, rationing finally ended in July 1954 but when the British economy at last recovered, many pubs started to struggle in the face of the challenges presented by a town that was rapidly evolving.

Buoyed by the post-war economic recovery, the Conservative government relaxed restrictions on mortgages and hire-purchase credit in the mid-1950s allowing millions of British families to acquire both more easily for the first time. Consequently, over the next few years, home ownership increased significantly. In 1951, only thirty-one per cent of British people were owner occupiers but this rose to some forty-four per cent in the next decade.[31] After obtaining a mortgage, Bolton's new young house owners tended to spend any spare money they might have on a widening range of labour saving appliances, furnishings and domestic comforts.

Their acquisition often went hand-in-hand with a passion for home improvement as DIY (do-it-yourself) became something of a national craze. The appearance of *Practical Householder* magazine for aspiring home handymen, Polycell wallpaper paste, and Polyfilla plaster in quick succession in the mid-1950s, were indications that in common with people all over Britain, "house proud" Boltonians were transforming their homes. Profitt's store – amongst others in Bolton – was happy to help them do so with "Do it Yourself Kits"and "Ideal Home" kits which came complete with drills for £13 – both products demonstrating that the tradition of working class self-improvement was by then finding expression in conspicuous displays of home improvement. In Bolton's terraced houses, wooden cupboards began to be replaced by Formica units in an ever-widening range of colours as "fitted" kitchens became something to aspire to. More significantly, the Formica used in kitchens brought "clean-at-a-wipe" efficiency to young housewives as did a growing range of accessories like butter dishes, toast racks and modish sputnik-shaped jam dishes which were all manufactured in easily washed plastic.[32]

With "contemporary" design emphasising the virtues of cleanliness as much as comfort and style, Bolton's dingy Victorian side street pubs, became a less attractive proposition for a night out, especially to any women who might have gone in them. Tom Harrisson had recorded that "the woman's place in the pub is in that part of it which is a home from home, a better home from ordinary worker's home... And as usual, the woman's part (of the pub) is the one of cleanness, ashtrays, no random saliva, few or no spittoons."[33] With growing affluence, the front rooms of even modest homes were as comfortable and more importantly, far cleaner, than pub lounges, let alone their filthy vaults. Over time, people became less inclined to spend their time in a dismal, smoky room even if the spittoons were emptied regularly and the sawdust swept away every day.

Other wider social influences were affecting Bolton's pubs too. As we have seen, pubs had always been to some degree, bastions of masculinity. During the original investigation, Mass Observation had noted that women accounted for only sixteen per cent of all Worktown's pub-goers. However, in the 1950s, a range of drinks were marketed specifically to appeal to women. Cherry B, Pony and perhaps the most enduring, Babycham – all introduced around the same time – were the genesis of a wider acceptance of women drinking in pubs. In 1960, on Tom Harrisson's return to Bolton he noted "younger women on Babycham (unknown 1937) and Cherry Wine especially."[34] Another Observer was told "Women, they come in much more than they used to, they drink Babycham… The girls have their Cherry Babycham and usually a gin and lemon."[35] With new drinks aimed at women, along with a growing familiarity with wine, Britain's drinking patterns were beginning to change. Of course the beerhouses were not licensed to sell anything other than beer which made them increasingly unattractive to approximately half of Bolton's drinkers. Although it is difficult to pinpoint precisely when cultural norms regarding women going out for a drink transformed pub going habits, the social acceptability of women drinking in pubs undoubtedly had an adverse effect on those pubs that remained unapologetically masculine in tone and clientele.

The beerhouses and side street pubs were the foremost casualties of these changing patterns and they began to slip quietly into history. Their decline was further exacerbated by the root and branch transformation of the communities they were anchored in. As we have seen previously, in the late 1950s, national slum clearance programmes commenced in earnest across Bolton. Just as they affected corner shops, they also affected the beerhouses and side street "locals" too, mainly because most of them were situated in the grim girdle of nineteenth century expansion closest to the town centre. During the 1960s and 1970s, whole swathes of the oldest, most enduringly working class streets of Bolton were reduced to rubble. Of course this meant the pubs on the gable ends of terraced rows disappeared too.

As these streets gave way to high rise blocks of flats or new social housing estates, pubs were no longer interwoven in communities in the same way. Arguably, in this respect alone, tower blocks and new housing estates could never have the same communal spirit as the streets they replaced. Even when new, bigger pubs like the Cotton Tree on Prince Street were built in the 1960s and 1970s, they were intended to serve people from a much wider area. As a result, they appeared unable to recreate the social role of locals like the Caledonian Inn which had served people from the surrounding streets and the workers from Mossfield Mill. Whatever the "pros" and "cons" of the town planning of the mid twentieth century one thing can be said for certain: the side street pubs vanished because of it.

The changing nature of working class communities was also seen to have an effect on people's behaviour. When moving to corporation housing estates, Mass Observation found there was a tendency for people, especially men, to leave their pub-going habits behind. A report about Top O' th' Brow, a corporation estate to the east of the town found that men settling into their new houses went to the pub less frequently than before, even those known to have visited pubs five, six or even seven nights a week. The Observer making the report suggests several reasons for this change in behaviour including reduced economic circumstances, the fact that there were less pubs on or around new estates, gardens creating fresh incentives to stay at home and finally a feeling that the authorities' renting the houses were somehow the "distant guardians" of their tenants' behaviour.

Even without the social change, Bolton's beerhouses had started to disappear partly because over time most were granted full licenses, and also because a sizeable number were extended taking over neighbouring properties to become bigger multi-roomed pubs. By 1980, the Lodge Bank Tavern on Bridgeman Street was Bolton's only surviving beerhouse. When it too was granted a full license, the town's last link with the act of Parliament that had created beerhouses 150 years before was finally broken.[36]

At the same time Bolton was losing its beerhouses, it was losing its breweries. Most of the pubs that had their own breweries like the previously noted Lord Raglan and the House Without a Name found it no longer made economic sense to brew their own beer but like others across

Britain which gave up on brewing, they continued as pubs. One by one Bolton's independent brewers ceased production or were amalgamated into larger regional and national concerns; part of a pattern which was leading to the decline of regional brewers all over the country. In 1969, Howarth's Model Brewery – the last independent brewery in Bolton – ceased production bringing Bolton's ancient tradition of brewing to an end (at least for the time being as we shall see). The Model Brewery was however briefly outlasted by Magee Marshall but by then Worktown's biggest brewery had been part of the Greenall Whitley concern for over ten years. In spite of Greenall's national profile, Magee Marshall closed in 1970, the brewery buildings being demolished fourteen years later.[37]

While beerhouses were closing largely unlamented, some other pubs closed in more controversial and arguably more unforgivable circumstances. In 1972, a proposal to demolish the Commercial Hotel, a handsome Regency pub on Victoria Square, led to fierce opposition from some quarters; an emotive issue not helped when at a meeting in Bolton Town Hall a councillor told those opposing the proposal "not to be silly and sentimental." In the end the views of the town planners prevailed and the pub was demolished and replaced by a Mothercare store. Various redevelopments in the town centre in the 1960s and 1970s put paid to other equally historic pubs like the Red Cross facing Nelson Square. Similarly, the Legs of Man, the Star Inn, the Boar's Head (colloquially known as the "whore's bed") and the Derby Arms were also all demolished after various somewhat insensitive developments were foisted on Churchgate, Bolton's oldest street.

Some of Bolton's traditional pubs were able to survive this first cull because of their more favoured position on main roads. But for many, it would prove only a temporary respite. Just as increasing car ownership fundamentally affected shops, it had an impact on pubs in a number of different ways. In the first instance, road-widening schemes necessitated the demolition of some older buildings; planning decisions which went largely unopposed as most of them were considered with some justification to be unworthy of preservation. With many larger pubs being focal points on the town's busier road junctions, they were the most vulnerable when the year-on-year increase in road traffic created several frustrating bottlenecks for drivers. In the 1980s, the previously noted Falcon Hotel and the more workaday Peel Hotel on Higher Bridge Street were both demolished to ease the traffic congestion when the Topp Way bypass was constructed.

The growth in car ownership was also affecting pubs in more subtle ways. In 1961, a milestone in the growth of British car ownership was reached when the millionth Morris Minor was sold. By the mid-1960s there were well over eight million car owners in Britain and as we have seen Boltonians were no exception to the motoring revolution. [38] Consequently, pubs started to offer car parks to attract car owning customers although they often came at the cost of tarmacking over bowling greens which had once been attractions outside a lot of pubs. For car owners, going for a drink in the evening became a different proposition as they could now enjoy a pleasant drive *en route* to the pub. This was of course not without its hazards in terms of the law and in 1967 over one million breathalyser units were issued to police forces all over the country to combat the dangers posed by drinking and driving; reckless behaviour that was not entirely a modern phenomenon as rather surprisingly twelve people had been convicted for the offence in Bolton in 1936. [39]

The risk of breaking the law notwithstanding, driving out to pubs became something of a trend for a while and was oddly enough, more socially acceptable. Almost by definition, the sort of pubs people drove to were very different in tone and clientele to those witnessed by Mass Observation; less rowdy and more comfortable but more significantly, they lacked the working class homogeneity of Worktown's pubs because they were in quieter suburbs or in country villages. Ironically, what the advocates for improved pubs had urged through parliamentary means in the 1920s was in the end achieved through the rising prosperity of the post-war period. Because of this, for a while at least, pubs further away from Bolton town centre were helped to survive by both the new car owners and also the embourgeoisement of the areas that surrounded them. On the other hand, any resolutely working class pubs that had survived the first wave of demolition were edging closer to oblivion.

In the latter half of the twentieth century pub numbers were declining all across Britain. Between 1951 and 1971, the number of licenses in England and Wales fell by thirteen per cent. This latter figure represented one "on license" for every 761 persons. In contrast, in 1928, there had been one "on license" for every 458 people. [40] To a large extent, the loss of Bolton's pubs simply reflected the national pattern. Whilst slum clearances destroyed many of the side street pubs in one fell swoop, demographic and social change began to slowly and surely affect the surviving pubs on St Helen's Road, Deane Road, Halliwell Road, Blackburn Road, Chorley Old Road and Bury Road: all major routes into and out of the town with more substantial buildings on either side of them including several long-established pubs.

The terraced houses surrounding many of Bolton's main roads – of which thousands still remain – on the surface, shared much in common with those being demolished in the slum clearances. They were however, bigger and more substantially built which helped them survive in greater numbers. From the late 1950s, the town's better terraced houses – many with miniscule front gardens, something the first houses built for Bolton's mill workers never had – were a rung on the ladder of home ownership for young aspirant Boltonians. After starting their own families, as soon as they could afford to, they left their first homes and bought semi-detached houses on the new estates mushrooming on the greener fringes of the town. In the meantime, the relatively cheaper and to some extent less fashionable houses they left behind became increasingly populated by the first waves of immigrants who had been encouraged to come to Bolton to work in the ailing cotton industry.

Within half a century, Bolton became home to a large immigrant community. By 2013, nearly eight per cent of the total population of the town was of Asian heritage and significantly, they have their deepest roots in those areas nearest to the town centre – the areas where pubs had been most densely concentrated. As well as immigrants with Indian heritage, Bolton has a sizeable Pakistani population with the biggest communities found in just three areas: Great Lever where the Pakistani community represents just over twenty-one per cent of the population, Halliwell where it is nearly sixteen per cent, and Rumworth with ten per cent: all three wards previously some of Bolton's most working class areas with more than their fair share of pubs.[41] Unlike Worktown's mill workers however, the immigrants' religion and culture for the most part precluded the drinking of alcohol leaving the pubs marooned in these transformed communities living on borrowed time.

They teetered on in the 1980s and 1990s, largely buffered from closure by older people who had not embraced the social and geographical mobility of their children and equally importantly, by their proximity to one another. This latter factor ensured that for more reckless drinkers – usually young men – there were still a number of legendary "pub crawls" up the "Halliwell mile", Blackburn Road, Deane Road and Derby Street. But a once-a-week Friday or Saturday night pub crawl was not enough to sustain them in the long term as for most of the week their huge rooms lacked atmosphere and conviviality with only one or two customers drinking in them. To try and stay open, some pubs were refurbished, others provided live music or karaoke "music" but all began to struggle as sadly their remaining ageing clientele died or were no longer capable of going to the pub.

As pubs on main roads tended to be bigger, they at least offered prime locations for redevelopment when they were struggling. As the new millennium dawned, many closed their doors for the final time as property developers took advantage of their size to convert them into offices or residential flats. Some pubs became Polish or Indian supermarkets while others like the Albert, the Pilkington Arms and the Derby Arms, all on Derby Street, were converted into takeaway cafes or restaurants serving ethnic food to the predominantly multicultural population living in the streets around them. In an extraordinary transformation, where the Observers had once recorded Worktowners drinking pints of mild, it was not unusual to find chicken biryani and lamb madras being served to the multi-ethnic people of a very different sort of town.

Inevitably, gaps where pubs used to be started to puncture the old pub crawls. To illustrate, Derby Street and St Helen's Road – two roads which go through some of the town's most densely populated areas – lost a total of five pubs in just eight years. The closure of the Farmers Arms in 2001 was followed by the previously noted Albert Inn and Pilkington Arms which both closed a year later. The Pike View became an ethnic supermarket in 2007 and the Stag's Head closed two years later despite a publicity campaign to try and save it which was enthusiastically reported in the local press. From the Derby Arms (which became briefly an Indian restaurant but at the time of writing is trading as a pub again!) heading away from the town centre, it is now nearly a mile to the next pub, the Oddfellows Arms: not much of a pub crawl there.

Similarly, the eastern end of Deane Road which runs parallel to Derby Street- another well-renowned pub crawl – was losing its pubs too. The Gibraltar Rock, where Spender took several photographs of

Worktowners competing on its bowling green, closed in 2009 becoming a Spar supermarket and the Cross Guns, just a little further up the road, closed in the winter of 2015. Tellingly, a mere 400 yards away, the minaret of the Zakariyya Jaam'e Masjid (mosque) now dominates the skyline; ironically, just across the road from the site of the demolished Magee's brewery.

For the remaining pubs at the southern end of Halliwell Road and Blackburn Road, two other major roads, it was a similar story. The New Inn closed its doors for the final time in 2007, the Bowling Green in 2009, the Victoria British Queen in 2011 and the similarly named Original Queen Victoria also closed in 2013 before its eventual demolition three years later. These four pubs were situated within yards of each other but far more significantly, they were within yards of two busy and thriving mosques: further evidence of the fundamental societal changes that have helped seal the fate of so many of Worktown's pubs.

Meanwhile, the growth of Bolton's immigrant communities was having more indirect consequences on pub-going habits. For many Boltonians, eating out in the 1960s and 1970s mainly involved restaurants serving food that, rather oddly, could easily be cooked at home – tinned tomato soup, steak and chips, apple pie and so on: fare epitomised by the Berni Inn restaurant on Churchgate or the Lamplighter restaurant under the market hall. For what was on offer, restaurants were relatively expensive, so people tended to go infrequently or only on special occasions. Due to the growth of more affordable continental holidays and the influence of immigration, the British people in general began developing a more adventurous palate. To cater for it, Italian, Chinese, Greek and Indian restaurants began to open in greater numbers offering a very different, more casual dining experience. More crucially, they were more affordable. Consequently, younger Boltonians began to eat in restaurants regularly in a way their parents hadn't. Indeed going for a curry in particular became part of the British way of life for the generation who grew up in the 1970s. Although people often had a drink on the way to a restaurant (especially curry houses!) this meant people going out were less inclined to spend the whole evening drinking in a pub like they once did.

Other lifestyle changes were also affecting pubs. As previously noted, one of the most loathsome aspects of the Davenport Street headquarters according to the Observers who lived there was the constant smell of fish and chips; the only takeaway meal available to them. It would be a fair bet that if the experiment was conducted now, the aromas of kebabs, pizza, burgers, curry, crispy duck, Pad Thai and fried chicken would be just as likely. In 2002, *Ant and Dec's Saturday Night Takeaway* – a long running light entertainment television programme – was first broadcast : its title alone confirming that by then a takeaway meal enjoyed at home often accompanied by a bottle of wine or some beer had become something of a national institution. And moreover, on what had once been the busiest night in Worktown's pubs.

Somewhat ironically, the trend for "eating out" rather than just "going for a drink" was actually providing a lifeline for some pubs because they proved ideal for conversion into restaurants especially when they were close to prosperous suburbs or in Bolton's surrounding villages. The Spread Eagle in Turton Bottoms was one of the first of the town's pubs to be converted to a restaurant and it was already a well-established pizzeria by the early 1980s, a fundamental change of function that was soon followed by others. The King William in Egerton, the Royal Oak in Bradshaw, the Nab Gate on Hardy Mill Road and the Wrights Arms near Belmont all became Italian restaurants (Ciao Baby, Erico's, Baci and San Marino respectively). Similarly, the Volunteer in Bromley Cross (demolished in 2015), the Crofters on St George's Road, the Willows on Bradshaw Road, the Crofters in Bradshaw, and the Sally up Steps on Chorley Old Road have all enjoyed varying fortunes after being converted to Indian or Thai restaurants.

Other pubs in the meantime were becoming something of a hybrid. By offering a range of "pub food" of bewildering sophistication, the old distinction between pub and restaurant became virtually meaningless as Boltonians embraced the national trend for eating regularly in "gastro" pubs. Pubs like the Wilton Arms on Belmont Road, the Rose and Crown, the White Horse and the Black Bull – all in Edgworth, the Thomas Egerton (previously the Globe) and the Brewhouse (previously the Cheetham) both on Blackburn Road – amongst numerous other examples – are all pubs where the food is as much an attraction as the beer. Although they were once part of Worktown's network of pubs, the availability of alcoholic drinks on the premises is usually the only thing they have left in common with them. Moreover "ladies who lunch", parents eating with children, and Bolton's more prosperous pensioners wielding the much coveted "grey pound" means unlike what the Observers witnessed in Worktown, many pubs are now busier at lunchtime than in the evening and moreover they thrive by serving a very different age, gender and type of clientele.

Like cinemas, the story of what happened to Bolton's pubs cannot be divorced from the history of television. In the 1960s, *Dr. Kildare*, *Till Death Us Do Part*, *Z Cars*, *The Man From U.N.C.L.E.*, *Dixon of Dock Green*, *Steptoe and Son* and of course *Coronation Street* – ironically featuring the kind of local pub people were no longer frequenting because they were at home watching a fictional one – all garnered huge audiences which started to challenge the hegemony of the pub over people's evening recreation. It is no coincidence to find that the first decade when televisions had become virtually a staple in every British home was in fact one of the most dismal for Bolton's pubs with significant numbers of them closing their doors for the last time.

In the decade that followed, rather than going to the pub Boltonians could be found in record numbers watching *Top of the Pops*, *The Two Ronnies*, *Some Mothers Do 'Av 'Em*, *The Morecambe and Wise Show* and *Parkinson* on their new colour televisions; programmes which have acquired in retrospect, a legendary status in the memories of those old enough to remember them. This enduring success is not entirely explained by their indisputable quality or even the power of nostalgia. In the days before video recorders, if a programme was missed, there was an uncertain wait for a "repeat" showing. This had two effects. First, it brought massive viewing figures for popular programmes and second, it often stopped people from going out for a drink. A pint down the pub or *Fawlty Towers*? No contest.

These changes meant having a drink at home became much more of a social habit than previously. This difference in where people often drink alcohol can partly be traced to 1936 when the stewards of East Sheen Tennis Club near Richmond complained about beer going off as they only opened their bar at weekends. Their suppliers responded with an offer to experiment with a new pasteurised keg beer, the soon-to-be-infamous Watney's Red Barrel. This new keg beer enjoyed two advantages over cask beer: it kept longer and it could be more easily transported. Red Barrel – and in fairness to the much maligned Watney's, other keg beers as well – soon became symbols of the declining quality of British beer as keg beer influenced the tastes of those who knew no different. It would be fair to say, over time people simply got used to pretty much flavourless beer and consequently were happier to drink bottled/canned beer or lager at home because it hardly differed in quality from the keg beers commonly served in pubs.

As a result, brewers specifically made beer meant to be enjoyed *at home*. In 1966, Watney Mann produced a World Cup Ale to accompany the televised football and four years later the Party Seven and Party Four were launched; enormous, unwieldy tin cans of beer that soon became a prerequisite at every "groovy" 1970s party despite the substandard taste and the challenge of pouring a pint of beer without splashing it all over the host's cheesecloth shirt and flared trousers. Over time, drinking at home as much as the pub became integral to the British way of life, so much so, supermarket aisles have gigantic displays of cans and bottles to cater for the demand. Worse still for pub landlords, they can sell alcoholic drinks at such low prices that dozens of pubs have simply been unable to compete and have been all but forced out of business.

With more adventurous palates, the availability of cheap alcoholic drinks and increasingly comfortable homes to drink it in, entertaining friends at home rather than meeting in the pub became more popular; a relatively recent social habit immortalised in Mike Leigh's excruciating comedy of manners, *Abigail's Party*, first broadcast in 1977. Drinks parties let alone dinner parties, were concepts that would have mystified most Worktowners to whom dinner was a meal eaten at midday. From a contemporary perspective it is easy to mock nervous hosts for offering schooners of sweet sherry and glasses of Liebfraumilch to their guests before serving them prawn cocktails, Steak Dianes and Black Forest gateau, but these changes exemplified the way working class Boltonians were breaking bonds with a mill town whose way of life was being transformed by middle class tastes.

As the end of the twentieth century approached, the landlords of those few pubs still anchored in a rapidly vanishing Worktown, found they were caught in a time warp. Their potential customers had been eating regularly in restaurants, watching colour televisions, entertaining guests in their homes and drinking outside whilst holidaying abroad for some twenty-five years. No wonder any surviving smoky pubs with their bench seats and frosted windows were looking decidedly shabby, old fashioned and ultimately second rate.

In the end, it was government legislation that finished them off. In the late 1980s, changes to the licensing laws permitted pubs to open all day ending the hiatus between afternoon and evening drinking which had characterised Worktown's drinking patterns; a change to British lifestyles that brought a more continental ambience to pubs (but unfortunately not the weather). Moreover, further legislation in 2005 virtually abolished any restraints at all on pub opening hours. As a consequence, before the first decade of the new millennium had ended, the grandchildren of the original Worktowners could enjoy drinking round the clock in pubs or just as likely, in sophisticated wine bars catering for the very different tastes of a more demanding clientele. In many of them, they could do so while eating breakfast, lunch, dinner or late night supper if they wished. In July 2007, amid considerable controversy and lobbying from camps on both sides of the debate, smoking in British pubs was banned completely. Whatever the rights and wrongs of the legislation, metaphorically and literally, it was the last gasp of Worktown's pub culture.

Ironically, it is the emergence of more middle class tastes that may yet provide a more secure future for Bolton's remaining pubs. The Campaign for Real Ale (CAMRA) – a pressure group founded in 1971 –has been vigorously defending local variation and quality cask ales for forty years. This has led to a wider regard for the nation's brewing heritage and moreover, a welcome renaissance in regional breweries and the more recent phenomenon of microbreweries. Paradoxically, there are at present more breweries in Bolton than any time in the town's recent history. The first to open, the Bank Top Brewery began brewing in 1995. It has been followed in recent years by the Dunscar Brewery and the Black Edge Brewery. The Bank Top Brewery's flagship pub, the Brewery Tap which opened in 2010, has proved an especially welcome success story. Focusing on serving quality cask ales, its success is testament to the determination of the brewery's directors to recreate the type of pub that seemed to have become unfashionable and anachronistic: namely the old side street local. Significantly, this unpretentious but friendly local is busy every day of the week; equally significant, in 2014, the Bank Top Brewery's owners opened a second pub in Horwich.

The Brewery Tap's success story however, is rare – a cursory journey around the pub-less roads and streets of Bolton will confirm that. Indeed, of all the nineteen pubs on or around Folds Road when Spender photographed the Grapes Hotel, only one, the Lord Clyde has survived. Inside, a tiny bar still services the main rooms and the last pub vault in Bolton that bears any resemblance to those found in Worktown. Standing in this tiny, fragmentary reminder of Worktown's legion of lost pubs – complete with wood partition, curved bar, bench seats, frosted windows and all – it is just possible to imagine that beyond the front door nothing much has changed. Stepping outside however, the reality shatters any such illusions because the cobbled streets, terraced houses and factories where the Lord Clyde's customers once lived and worked, have all completely disappeared.

COBBLES TO CARPET

Children playing street games near Snowden Street.
Humphrey Spender

Holt's Hosiery Mill was an unexceptional mill just to the west of Bolton town centre. In the summer of 2014 it was demolished – yet another fragment of Worktown gone forever, this time to make way for Bolton University's expanding campus. At least Holt's Mill survived for much longer than all the streets that once surrounded it; they were demolished fifty years ago. With names redolent of Worktown – James Street, Kirk Street, Ebenezer Street, Roundcroft Street, Bethel Street, Liptrot Street, Ardwick Street – streets like these were once the beating heart of working class communities. But over time Worktown's heart stopped beating and like so many other vanished streets all across Bolton, there is not a single brick, gas lamp, kerbstone or cobble left to mark where they once were.

When Worktown's streets disappeared, so did a type of childhood peculiar to the urban north. At the height of Bolton's industrial might, children played outside on streets which skulked in the shadows of the mills that would bring their childhoods to an end at fourteen years of age – the age most young people left secondary school. Although the majority of Worktown childhoods passed largely unrecorded, fortunately for social historians, the Observers documented children's hopes and aspirations, what they did in their spare time and at school, and in a rare break with the secretive methods usually employed, children were asked to write essays about their lives for Mass Observation.

In addition to the written reports, Humphrey Spender took several photographs of children at play, many taken within yards of Davenport Street. Spender recorded them running around the walls of Union Mill, playing amongst the grime on Snowden Street, riding a rocking horse in a park, loitering by the gable ends on Horatio Street and Marsh Fold Lane, rummaging in the dirt of a wasteland and perhaps the most memorable of all, two children urinating together to make a puddle in the dirt. Astonishingly, although the activities, clothes, and the environment in the photographs appear to belong to a completely different age, at the time of writing, some of the children in them are known to be still alive.[1]

Although the kind of children's activities Spender photographed are within living memory, there is an enormous gulf between contemporary childhood experience and this particular aspect of Worktown, not least because a young man in a mackintosh was able to wander around taking photographs of children apparently without any suspicion or accusation being levelled at him. Also, the children in the photographs are roaming abroad in the streets without any obvious adult supervision and moreover at a frighteningly young age. But above all else, what separates the contemporary viewer from the not-too-distant past, is the searing sense of poverty in the images.

It was the pervasive, grinding poverty of Worktown perhaps more than anything else that shaped the lives of its youngest citizens. Mass Observation found the spectre of hunger, even starvation, haunted children. In essays about the importance of money written specially for the Observers, food or lack of it – was a recurring theme. "If we did not have money we would not be able to have bread butter tea and sugar…" Florence Bentley wrote whilst her classmate, Alice Read stated: "The chief use for us having money is that we should buy good food." Another boy, Thomas Robinson describing what he would buy if he had money wrote: "Every day I would have beef." For the Observers' benefit, Thomas's teacher attached note to his essay explaining "This boy has free meals. So meat is evidently a luxury to him." Another schoolgirl, Joyce Norris, summarised the poverty experienced by many working class children when she wrote: "Without money everyone would be down and out and more than that people would starve for if there is no money they can't buy food…"[2]

Another survey conducted by Mass Observation, this time into the weekly spending money of forty-two children aged eight and nine, suggests just how poor many families were. Seventeen children had only 1d pocket money a week, ten had 2d, nine had 3d, one had 7 and 1/2d, four had a shilling and one comparatively fortunate youngster, was given 1/– and 3d each week. To put these figures into context, when the survey was conducted, with their weekly spending money, a significant portion of the children could afford only half a Mars Bar or half a small Cadbury's chocolate bar.[3]

Adolescents did not have it that much better. Of thirty-six children surveyed aged between eleven and fourteen, Observers recorded that one youngster got 3d spending money each week, seventeen had 6d and the others had an unspecified 6d plus. Therefore, Worktown's young citizens – who it should be remembered were soon about to become wage earning adults – could maybe buy a Mars Bar, a comic and if they were lucky a cinema ticket too with their weekly allowance. Given the relative lack of treats it should come as no surprise that in another bunch of essays asking children how they might like to spend a large sum of money one girl simply wrote: "I would buy a box of chocolate milk every day, bickets tofy [sic]."[4]

Poverty's grip on working class households inevitably shaped where children played, how they played, what they played and when they played. As large families living in gardenless, two-up, two-down houses were common, it is little wonder children were eager to go out to play no doubt equally "encouraged" to do so by parents sharing the same cramped space. Living cheek-by-jowl in houses which afforded very little privacy, children probably spent most of their free time outside simply because they didn't want to be inside. Moreover, Bolton's densely packed streets meant there always was an army of playmates to call upon living close by. Once children had ganged together, they were able to roam freely because trusted adults – in many cases their own aunts, uncles and grandparents – usually lived in the same neighbourhood as well. The presence of extended family members as well as the custom of adopting unrelated "aunts" and "uncles" enabled children to play safely due to a web of informal, passive supervision provided by familiar adult faces living on the same streets.

Although ingrained in mill town folklore, it is no mythology that doors *were* left open and unlocked during daylight hours. My grandmother, who lived in Villiers Street, Halliwell – a typical Worktown street – insisted that the doors of the houses were rarely if ever locked during the day although she also pointed out somewhat drily that this was because nobody had anything worth stealing anyway. Because this kind of trust was so normal, children often wandered between houses "calling" for friends to go out to play often without even knocking on the door.

When they got together, the town's major parks, Moss Bank Park, Queen's Park, Haslam Park and Leverhulme Park along with many smaller local parks were always popular destinations for children but their daily playground was first and foremost just beyond their doorsteps where gable ends, gas lamps, railway bridges, canal paths, alleys and ginnels awaited them. For generations of children, playing out amongst the gloomy, sooty streets at all hours of the day and night was completely natural.

One report, "A day in the life of the street" (in this instance, Davenport Street), shows just how universal outside play once was. The Observers recorded that when children arrived home from school there were always several of them outside until late at night. One child – a boy called Colin – was seen by an Observer to play out continuously for over three hours after school finished.[5] Even on winter nights, children would often congregate on the door steps of houses or shops, but mostly they gathered under the sullen light of the flickering gas lamps before the lateness of the hour, rather than the darkness, forced them to go home.

With so little money to spare, necessity was the mother of invention as far as street games went which led children to weave their own rich tapestry of imaginative, communal play. Notwithstanding the uninspiring surroundings, the games that were played on the streets are usually remembered with great fondness by older Boltonians. Alice Foley later recalled: "Our street games were simple and traditional but we found them wholly captivating".[6] Another Worktowner, Arnold Harrison, born in 1933, reflecting on his childhood, said it's "sad to think that all these magical pastimes are now gone forever."

This sort of nostalgia is most likely rooted in a longing for a return to the shared values, spirit of nurture, and sense of belonging that were at the heart of what were once close-knit communities. Living alongside neighbours in rows of terraced houses, there was a collective ownership of each street most evident in the annual Rose Queen processions and the street parties held to celebrate royal occasions and of course the end of the Second World War. This sense of ownership was articulated by children in the oft used phrase "our street" even though each "our street" was virtually indistinguishable from any other. These strong attachments to particular neighbourhoods meant that in all weathers, all year round, children were usually found playing on or around their own street. Some activities came and went with the seasons like cricket in summer, conkers in autumn and sledging in winter, but others like football were played throughout the year.

The influence of seasons and the ritualistic elements of children's play inevitably interested Tom Harrisson who found a tendency for fads in children's' pastimes and games although why this should happen was not immediately apparent. A newsagent told one Observer:

> "Three weeks ago it was all catapults. You never can tell: last week
> we sold out of tops and whips in fact I went and got another gross.
> Yet we have hardly sold one since then." The shopkeeper explained
> that sales tended to follow fads. Piggy was a fad. Spring skipping
> comes back in. Observer tries to ascertain how kids know, to be
> told the weather changes they have been penned up then the "older
> ones who have played the year before start: and the others follow."[7]

In spite of the best efforts of shopkeepers to make money from fads or crazes, in most households, if there was any money left over from the tight, weekly budgets, it is unlikely much of it would be spent directly on children's recreation. Therefore, it was essential that most street games should cost nothing to play. Accordingly, there were dozens of popular games that required no equipment at all. Competitive games like "Thrust",

"Jump-a-backs" or "Finger, thumb or icky" were usually enjoyed by boys being ritualistic tests of strength involving teams of players being jumped on by others to make them collapse under the increasing weight. "British Bulldog" was another boisterous game, again generally played by boys who charged across the street to the opposite pavement without being wrestled down by opponents in the no man's land in between. "Leap Frog", a jumping game, and chasing games such as "Tig" or "Tag", "Stick in the Mud", "What time is it Mr Wolf?" and "Hare and Hounds" were equally boisterous and energetic. Other games like "Hide and Seek", "Kick-a-ball-run" and "Kick out Ball" – all variations of hiding games – were regularly played especially as the labyrinthine nature of the back streets, ginnels and alleys provided plenty of good places to hide.

Ball games were also staples of street play. "Catch" was one of the simplest as was "Queenio Queenio" – generally regarded as more of a girl's game – which involved the players hiding a ball until it was discovered. Other games were enjoyed by both boys and girls, one such simple game, "May I?" involved children granting their playmates permission to cross the street in a number of different ways. Another street crossing game, "Creeping up on London", involved children freezing like statues, so that a child designated to be "on" didn't see them move. Along with other noisy favourites like "I Spy" and "Piggy in the Middle", popular memory suggests there was always a cacophony of excited shrieks and shouts across Worktown's streets.

Naturally "children will be children" in every generation and occasionally they were involved in some mischief. "Knock-a-door run" and "Caplatch" both involved knocking on doors then running away; the protagonists enjoying the thrill of remaining unseen by the irritated house owners who found an empty doorstep. In the more homogenous communities of the 1930s however, it appears children rarely tormented more vulnerable residents most probably because they knew which particular house they lived in on any given street. More cynically of course, everyone knew where the children lived too, and in an era when adults were more likely to ally with one another against the younger generation, this shared knowledge of the local community was in itself a very effective deterrent to potential mischief makers.

Games involving rhyming, clapping and singing were always popular and were perhaps enjoyed by girls rather more than boys with the simple rhymes providing a rhythm for the clapping that accompanied them. All of them were part of an oral tradition passed generation to generation, variations of which are found throughout the world. "Pat-a-cake, Pat-a-cake", "A sailor went to sea" (to see what he could see, see, see), "Mary, Mary quite contrary" (believed to have originated in Tudor times) and "Ring-a-ring-o-roses" – a rhyming game that reputedly started during the Great Plague, were all familiar to Worktown's children.

Skipping games played with ropes of varying lengths shared similarities and were just as popular –again, particularly amongst girls – and could be enjoyed as a solo activity, or by children in groups. Skipping could be either competitive or collaborative and involved dozens of different chants and rhymes, some of which were very simple. An Observer on seeing a group of five girls skipping in Derbyshire Park found that they were simply skipping in time to the letters of the alphabet.[8] Another report highlights rather more developed skipping rhymes:

"Soldier Soldier stand at attention
Soldier Soldier stand at ease
Soldier Soldier salute to the officer
Soldier Soldier bend your knees."[9]

Another rhyme recorded by Observers was more localized referencing Daubhill train station to the west of Bolton:

"Mrs Mason broke a basin
On the way to Dobble Station [sic]
How much did it cost her 1d, 2d, 3d, etc."[10]

Although the rhymes were nonsensical, Tom Harrisson considered them "very important" leading him to investigate in some detail other popular rhymes which were not associated with skipping. A handwritten report about Mere Hall Park, a short walk from Davenport Street, records one such rhyme told by a boy aged fourteen to another younger boy:

"The Boy stood on the burning deck
And (indecipherable) he blew his hooter

And who do you think came riding by?

Gandhi on a scooter"

In the same vein, the report records another boy reciting an equally silly rhyme:

"The boy stood on the burning deck

Shelling peas by the peck

Did he wash his dirty neck?

Did he? – heck!"[11]

Other popular children's activities did require some money to play them, but all were still relatively inexpensive. As we have seen, Tom Harrisson noted the importance of Bolton Wanderers to the people of the town and football was extremely popular amongst boys of all ages, many of whom harboured ambitions to one day play professionally. Obviously, a football was necessary to play and when keen young footballers had one, matches took place in the streets, on wastelands and in nearby parks whenever it was light with children using their jumpers for the goal posts. Other football related games like "Kerby" or "Beat the goalie" could be played in groups or in the case of the former just for individual practice.

Cricket was also popular although in Worktown it bore little resemblance to matches contested in the dappled shade of a quintessential English village green. Generally there was no grass to put stumps in so gas lamps became somewhat thin (and tall!) wickets. For young cricketers wanting more realistically proportioned wickets, chalk or stones were used to draw them on the gable ends of houses, and the walls of mills and factories. Somewhat inevitably, the problem presented by two-dimensional bails which didn't fall off when struck by the ball led to arguments about whether a batsman was actually "in" or "out". Sticks of chalk were also useful for drawing "hopscotch" grids on pavements – a simple but engaging game that involved throwing a stone into a square before skipping or hopping to retrieve it without falling over.

When there was some spare pocket money and after Christmas or birthdays especially, there were other popular pastimes involving simple toys. Marbles were collected or swapped and were used for games like

"Wally" and "Ringy". Rubber balls, toy soldiers and yo-yos featured in a variety of games which occupied children for hours for an investment of just a few pennies. Although Mass Observation noted that most Worktowners hardly went to the surrounding moors and seemed to have little interest in nature, fishing was popular with youngsters able to take advantage of Worktown's many canals, lodges, ponds, and streams. Children who didn't have fishing equipment could still join in by washing jam jars to be used as makeshift keepnets for fish or to collect tadpoles: a rather naive example of eco-awareness long before it entered the mainstream conscience. One Observer summed up this particular aspect of childhood writing "4 boys going down Moore Lane towards St George's Road. All have tadpole nets. One has a jam jar with a string handle."[12]

Just as cinema was popular amongst adults, it was an important pastime for children as well. Being relatively inexpensive, cinemas were somewhere for children to go with their friends unaccompanied by adults, depending on the film's classification of course. Many cinemas had regular matinees featuring films with a specific appeal to children whilst others had Saturday morning children's clubs although they were notoriously rowdy with children shrieking throughout the film and more surprisingly given their scarcity, throwing sweets at each other. One respondent to Mass Observation's survey of cinemas emphasised its importance to young people writing: "First of all cinema is a place mostly to entertain youngish people and I myself think it keeps young people from loitering on the streets."[13] Another twelve-year-old film lover, Constance Thomas, told Mass Observation that she went to the cinema four times a month adding rather charmingly that "The organ is very beautiful and when I get settled into one of the seats listening to the music, I feel that I could stay there forever."[14]

Swimming was enjoyed by most children whenever they could afford the relatively cheap price of admission to Bolton's public pools. Until the later years of the twentieth century, the town catered for young swimmers splendidly with excellent facilities on offer in the neo-Georgian splendour of Bridgeman Street Baths which first opened in 1845, Moss Street Baths in Halliwell which opened in 1924 and High Street Baths in Daubhill which first welcomed swimmers in 1903 – none of which survive today (although being a listed building, the facade of Bridgeman Street baths has been preserved). There was also a much smaller swimming pool located some distance from the town centre in the unimaginatively named Water Street in Egerton. This pool – part of the Deakin family's ambitions for a model industrial settlement around their mill – has also been demolished although anyone (like the author) who is old enough to recall the icy water and the cockroaches is unlikely to lament its passing. On the hottest summer days, cool water was as tempting to the children of Worktown as it is to children today and canals and mill lodges were popular places to swim in spite of the inherent dangers and occasional tragedy.

Trainspotting was another pastime that was very popular – especially amongst schoolboys. The publication of Ian Allan's first locomotive book in 1942 formalised the hobby by printing the serial numbers of every British locomotive. These pocket-sized books were an important milestone in the development of a hobby that cost very little to enjoy. For many years, Worktown's bonanza of stations, railway sidings, bridges and goods' yards were a magnetic attraction to children before flask carrying, anorak wearing, Roy Cropper type figures gave train spotting an unshakeable image problem – an image it ought to be said, that is both unfair and patronising because the sound, smell and appearance of steam locomotives in full flight was utterly intoxicating which goes a long way to explain their extraordinary appeal during the mid-years of the twentieth century. Tellingly, the decline of this once popular hobby began with the disappearance of steam trains in the 1960s although thankfully for the nation's heritage, many ex-trainspotters went on to become the mainstays of preservation groups like the nearby East Lancs Railway Society.

Although this sketch of childhood in Worktown has mainly focused on outdoor activities, there were indoor pastimes to occupy children who for one reason or other couldn't play outside. Building up stamp collections and compiling autograph books were popular hobbies amongst young people. Similarly, cigarette cards, given away with packets of cigarettes, were also collected and they have enjoyed a lasting popularity amongst ephemera enthusiasts. These tiny coloured cards introduced as a promotional gimmick, featured a wide range of subjects from exotic birds and animals to famous battles and explorers, but film stars and football players of the time were generally the most sought after (in the case of the latter, just like their modern equivalent the enormously successful Match Attax cards). Whatever subject was illustrated on them, all cards were useful currency when children swapped them amongst themselves in order to complete a full set although the incentive to buy more cigarettes to find an elusive card can hardly have promoted the health of Worktown's many smokers.

Board games enjoyed something of a surge in popularity in the mid twentieth century and were excellent standbys on rainy days. As they were relatively more expensive they were often given as birthday or Christmas presents. The word game Lexicon was found in many of Worktown's terraced houses as was Monopoly – "the rage of America" – which arrived in Britain in 1936 to delight and torment in equal measure as the most brutal aspects of capitalism were inflicted with the toss of the dice. Totopoly, a horse racing game, appeared in 1938, the same year as Scrabble, however it was the early 1950s before the latter became more widely played and appreciated.

Despite the time-honoured concerns of the older generation that young people don't read enough, reading was an important recreation for many children especially at a time when there was a strong emphasis in education on the "three R's" –*"Reading, (w)Riting and (a)Rithmetic"*. In addition to Bolton's magnificent Central Library which opened just before the Worktown investigation began, there were several other libraries spread around town, all encouraging children to enjoy a wide range of literature.

In the early 1930s, of Bolton's libraries, the High Street Branch boasted over 12,000 volumes for loan, the Mere Hall branch 7000, the Astley Bridge branch nearly 10,000 volumes, the Halliwell branch another 10,000 volumes, the Great Lever branch some 11,000 and the Tonge Moor branch 8000 volumes. Of course not all of these books were for children but Tillotson's Directory preserved by the Observers highlights that four of the branch libraries had Reading and Writing rooms specifically "for boys and girls."[15] Moreover, all were open every day from 9.30 a.m. until 8 p.m with the exception of Sundays and Wednesday afternoons when they closed.

Supplementing book reading, comics of all kinds were collected, swapped and read and re-read until they were falling apart. The comics of the 1930s appealed principally to boys mainly because they featured masculine heroes and often had stories about football and the First World War. Some of the most memorable included *Knock Out, The Gem, The*

Wizard, *The Hotspur*, *The Triumph* and *The Modern Boy*; the latter clearly making no attempt to disguise its blatant gender bias. All these comics had roots in a more working class society, all disappeared long ago.

On the other hand, *The Dandy* launched in 1937 and *The Beano* which was launched in the following year proved extraordinarily durable. When they first appeared, characters like Dennis the Menace, The Bash Street Kids, Minnie the Minx, Desperate Dan and Roger the Dodger played pranks and poked fun at stereotypical authority figures in a world that was instantly familiar to the children laughing at their antics. However, they inevitably became more anachronistic with each passing decade. Sales of *The Dandy* fell from a peak of two million a week in the 1950s to a dismal 8000 in 2012. With such poor sales, publication was eventually discontinued although its legacy continued briefly with an electronic version of the comic appearing online. However cyberspace and catapults were always going to be uncomfortable bedfellows and even this stab at modernity couldn't save it: in 2013 *The Dandy* disappeared completely. At the time of writing *The Beano* still entertains children due as much to its web presence as the printed version and for now at least, it is the sole survivor from the generation of comics inspired by the proletarian townscapes of the 1930s.

In contrast to the popular comics, many of the books that appealed to young Worktowners featured characters enjoying adventures in a world completely at odds with the soot-peppered townscape which was their daily experience. For younger readers, Rupert the Bear – who had first sauntered through a soporific English village in 1920 – maintained his popularity with his Christmas books even surviving war time rationing. Thomas the Tank Engine made his first appearance in 1945, the adventures of the celebrated engine also taking place in a rural idyll a long way from the industrial north which might go some way to explaining why the little steam engine became so extraordinarily popular.

Similarly, Enid Blyton's first Famous Five book published in 1942 was the start of a series of books which proved so successful there was even a national fan club where for a shilling (5p) children got to wear an "FF" badge so they would "know each other at once". Unlike a lot of the working class characters who appeared in comics, Blyton's four children along with Timmy the dog were steadfastly middle class. Even their names – Julian, Dick, Georgina and Anne – emphasised their superior social standing to the young Brians, Ronnies, Maureens, Shirleys and Sandras who read them. The adventures of the Famous Five took place in a rural paradise overflowing with homemade marmalade, cured hams, lemonade and of course ginger beer which was totally alien to the children of Worktown more used to potato pies, jam butties, and Tizer "pop", which probably explains the immense appeal of the books.

Even those children who were reluctant to read were encouraged to get their head in a book at least once each year by the printed "Annuals" that appeared every December; larger format books which usually featured popular cartoon characters of the time. Annuals had been around since the 1920s, but they became something of a Christmas institution in the mid twentieth century. The *Mickey Mouse Annual* first appeared in 1931, reflecting the growing influence of the Disney brand which was joined as the decade progressed by long forgotten characters such as Teddy Tail, Bobby Bear and Uncle Oojah the Elephant.

In the 1950s and 1960s, as Christmas approached, Annuals devoted to film stars, pop singers and groups, television programmes and all kinds of sports and sportsmen appeared in the shops, the examples from each era reflecting the changing interests and tastes of the children who enjoyed them. Such was their enduring popularity, they became a staple Christmas gift supplementing the "big present", a selection box, and a token piece of fruit before the post-austerity generation more familiar with exotic fruits from around the world could no longer feign delight at finding a clementine in their stocking and the fruit-as-a-present disappeared.

As might be expected, Tom Harrisson searching for parallels between the things that mattered to the Dayak head-hunters and those that mattered to the "savages" of Bolton was especially interested in the totemic rituals and the numerous religious festivals celebrated in Worktown each year. St George's Day, St Patrick's Day, Shrove Tuesday, April Fool's Day, Bonfire Night, nearby Westhoughton's Keaw Yed celebrations, and of course Easter and Christmas were all investigated. Whether the differences in content about each reflects more interest in some than others or simply results from the resources Harrisson could deploy is hard to ascertain, but most of them involved children in some way or other.

At St George's Parish Church on 23 April 1938, the vicar told the 260-plus boys and girls who were being counted by an Observer that "St George's Day is your day" before continuing to say "how proud they should be – you have got a King who is called George and this is St George church." Seemingly, appealing to their patriotic and parochial instincts did not arouse the interest of the younger members of his congregation too much; the Observer noted that "The kids fidgeted" throughout the service.[16]

Children had rather more enthusiasm for pancake day with Observers recording that all but one of the local shops reported increased demand for pancake ingredients, before stating that the vast majority of children had enjoyed them for tea. One boy aged ten confirmed this was an eagerly anticipated annual treat saying "Yes I could eat them till I burst." Another boy however was somewhat less fortunate; on being asked whether he would be having the treats he replied "No I wish we wer [sic] but my mother says it's too much trouble to make them."[17]

Although April Fool's Day and May Day pass by largely unmarked in contemporary Britain, both days were important to Worktown's children with Observers noting that children were "very keen" on April Fool's in particular. On the day, children mostly played harmless, silly tricks on their parents, friends and teachers. In one rather cruel instance however, a nine-year-old boy told an Observer how his father said he had bought him a new bike. Unfortunately for him, on going downstairs to ride it the boy discovered it was an April Fool's prank.

May Day was a special, symbolic day for children. One Observer found a group out and about playing at being Queen of the May, a "dressing up game" that on this occasion saw "the queen" wearing a homemade outfit of curtains and crepe paper. As the little procession made its way through the streets the girls were singing:

"I'm the Queen of the May – I'm the Queen of the May
The flowers, the flowers grow everywhere, I am the Queen of the May."

When questioned by an Observer about their activities the group couldn't tell him what it was all about, nor could they give a reason for dressing up although they did at least know they were doing it to collect money so they could host a tea party in a back yard. However, after the observer gave them a generous 4d for their funds it appears the planned party was soon forgotten. After taking the money the children told him they "might go to the pictures now."[18]

In addition to informal activities, May Day was also marked by more communal, organised events. A leaflet for the 1937 celebration at St Barnabas' School preserved in the Mass Observation archive announces a "Special Coronation Maypole Festival" will be held. The highlight of the day's festivities was the crowning of a child as the May Queen, a ceremony which would be carried out by the "ex-queen attended by King and ex-King." In addition, attendees could look forward to up to sixty children taking part in a number of activities which included Maypole dances with intriguing names like "The Barber's Pole", "The Ropes" and "The Spider's Web".[19]

For children used to spending so much of their time outside, unsurprisingly, Bonfire Night was also a special night. As 5 November approached, bonfires were built on virtually every back street or patch of open ground. Building them took weeks with children collecting wood from early October so they could brag about having the biggest fire. One Boltonian, Allan Burrows, recalled that the size and density of a "blaze was a status symbol among the young 'uns" on any given street; another illustration of the strong bonds children had to particular "our streets".[20]

To celebrate the night, companies like Brock, Standard and Wessex manufactured fireworks which were bought by children who had often put money away in savings clubs run by local shopkeepers. Others might be specially treated to fireworks by their parents, while some children got money from the custom of "Penny for the Guy", a thinly disguised form of begging which tended to be most successful outside pubs where customers leaving fuelled with beer were more likely to treat children. The Observers found gender differences on bonfire night – girls being more attracted to sparklers and the fountain or cascade types of fireworks, boys on the other hand favouring noisy bangers. One Observer reported that a shop on Higher Bridge Street had sold an astonishing 2000 bangers in the run-up to Bonfire Night.[21]

Easter was another time of year eagerly anticipated by children. Mass Observation concluded that enthusiasm for it was partly because it heralded the return of spring and the time for playing out again. At the request of the Observers, a number of schoolchildren wrote essays about what they had done in the Easter Holidays. Some describe going out walking, others about getting new clothes-a very strong Easter tradition in Worktown – and of course, most had enjoyed gifts of chocolate eggs.

When the essays were written, it was an unusually cold Easter with many essays describing how the snow fell on Good Friday. Consequently the essays reveal that many children went to the cinemas which presumably did unexpectedly good trade, but tellingly several children still stated they had been disappointed that they had not been able to play out. Interestingly, two children wrote they had helped their mothers do the laundry on the holiday Monday which can't have been the most enjoyable way to spend a day off school. When the weather brightened over the holiday, a lot of children described visiting local parks or their relatives. Several children wrote about Easter eggs being collected and distributed to the sick in hospital ("Nowadays that is the custom," wrote Vera Makin) although pitifully one child wrote "The only thing wrong was that there was no Easter egg for me, all the others had one."[22]

As might be expected, of all the annual rhythms, Christmas was the most eagerly awaited time of the year however it was the time when poverty was perhaps most keenly felt by children. In December 1937, the *Bolton Evening News* opened an appeal to provide presents with the editor pleading: "Many children are placed in unfortunate circumstances, and their Christmas will be joyless and comfortless unless our fund can assist. We are daily receiving batches of heart-rending letters, telling of dire distress, but we can only help them if you help us." To encourage people to help, the newspaper reported that one woman told its reporter her husband had given her ten shillings (50p) to buy Christmas presents for their children before adding that the family were not well off. When the reporter expressed surprise at the seemingly generous amount he was shocked to find that the sum was meant to buy presents for seven children.

The fund's progress was conveyed to readers each day; reports which in themselves demonstrate the kind of poverty being experienced in some households. On 6 December, a child's heartrending letter in spidery handwriting was reproduced in full:

Dear Father Christmas

Will you please bring my little sister _____ and myself_____ a doll. My daddy has not been working for two years he has had an accident at work. I am 8 years old and _____ 5 years old. So please don't pass our house at Christmas if I don't see you we both wish you a very Merry Christmas.[23]

Another letter from two young girls was an appeal for a donation of money to buy a dog license for a "dog given us and my dad is not working yet and can't buy one."[24] Happily for the girls, the next day, the newspaper was able to reveal that several donations had been received in order to buy a dog license.

Although the newspaper featured advertisements for Meccano sets "for the mechanically minded boy" and another for toy prams "just like Mammas" presumably for Bolton's maternally minded girls, it is interesting to note that most advertisements in the newspaper in the run-up to Christmas in 1937 predominantly featured gifts for adults. These included ties, pens, furniture, whisky, socks and even a home movie projector. Somewhat surprisingly in contrast with contemporary Christmas preparations, few advertisements were directly aimed at children.

The importance of both Easter and Christmas in the annual cycle illustrate the wider influence of religion in children's lives. In 1932, Bolton had no less than fifty-two churches, chapels and mission rooms, fifteen Roman catholic churches, twenty-one congregational churches, two Presbyterian churches, six Unitarian churches, fourteen Methodist churches, one New Jerusalem Church, a first Church of Christ Scientist, one Catholic Apostolic Church, one Welsh Tabernacle, one Breightmet Free Church (photographed by Spender), one Salvation Army Citadel, one Spiritual Hall and one Jewish Synagogue.[25]

With such numbers, it would be fair to state Bolton's young were spoiled for choice in terms of spiritual succour and moral guidance. Indeed, one of the striking features of the essays children wrote about religious beliefs for Mass Observation is not only the extent of their faith, but also the knowledge they had of the Christian narrative; the inevitable result of the influence of Sunday schools and more widespread church attendance. If nothing else, lots of children enjoyed the processions organised by religious organisations through the year as well as the parties provided by Sunday schools and churches in the run up to Christmas.

As the Second World War began, the mood in Worktown darkened with the fear of air raids and the miseries of rationing. At the same time, children's board games with names like ARP (Air Raid Protection) and Bomber Command provided topical if uninspiring pastimes in blackout Britain. Thankfully for young people enduring the privations of the Home

Front, comics like *Boy's Own* and books featuring Biggles the pilot proved more engaging. Both described exciting wartime adventures; a theme which retained its popularity especially amongst young boys long after the war ended. On the other hand it's safe to presume that anthropomorphic characters like Boo Boo the Barrage Balloon and Wimpy the Wellington (bomber) were forgotten almost as soon as the VE Day celebrations ended.

In spite of the trials and tribulations, the Second World War had little or no lasting impact on the way children played in Bolton in the post-war years apart from providing the odd derelict bomb site to play on. Indeed, after the conclusion of hostilities in 1945, the street scenes witnessed by the Observers remained virtually unchanged well into the 1960s as Bolton's children continued to play on the streets. But just as it was poverty that determined most children's lives in Worktown, it was growing prosperity that characterised their childhoods in the years which followed. The period of full employment which accompanied the post-war economic boom brought a growth in the relative affluence enjoyed by many families. This inevitably began to shape a very different experience of childhood. The changes were so profound, by the time Davenport Street was being demolished in the early 1980s, the kind of activities, festivals and children's street play recorded there belonged to a type of childhood that had vanished.

Perhaps no commodity symbolises the growing prosperity that marked the post-war era than the car. As we have seen, cars changed other aspects of Worktown life but their impact was perhaps most keenly felt by children. Worktown's streets were considered safe havens for play, mainly due to the absence of traffic. Indeed, Spender's photographs confirm there were hardly any cars on Bolton's streets although he did photograph the aftermath of a traffic accident on Vernon Street in January 1938 – fortunately on this particular occasion there do not appear to have been any casualties. However, the extraordinary growth in the volume of cars on Britain's roads after the Second World War meant Bolton's youngest citizens, like others all over the country, were about to pay a high price for the British obsession with car ownership.

From the very beginning of popular motoring there had been fatalities on British roads. Indeed, between 1924 and 1933, some 12,000 children were killed in road traffic accidents. In the late 1920s, the launch of Safety

First! – a children's board game designed to improve road awareness-suggests there were growing concerns about the mounting death toll amongst Britain's children. Within ten years, traffic safety information was being printed on the back covers of some exercise books used in Bolton's schools. This included advice for children to always cross the road safely accompanied by other warnings like "Don't play at being 'last across the road'" and "Don't follow a rolling ball into the road or street while there is traffic about."[26]

In spite of such efforts, the carnage continued. In 1934 alone, there were 7343 deaths on Britain's roads and 231,603 injuries. Half of the casualties were pedestrians and equally worrying, seventy-five per cent of the collisions occurred in built-up areas. In that year, Leslie Hoare Belisha, the Minister for Transport, responded by introducing the Road Traffic Act. This legislation imposed a 30 mph speed limit in built up areas, rewrote the highway Code, introduced a driving test for aspiring motorists and instigated the eponymous Belisha Beacons to provide safe passing points for pedestrians. An analysis of accident statistics in 1937 however found those most at risk of being involved in accidents were children aged between three and seven. In the same year, a letter in the *Bolton Evening News* submitted with no shortage of irony by a concerned "Motorist father", warned of the dangers to children posed by the increasing number of cars on Bolton's roads. The headline accompanying the letter "Road Perils to Children" said it all.[27]

Clearly some action was needed and with admirable foresight, the government introduced the Street Playgrounds Act in 1938, which allowed local authorities to close some residential streets to traffic between 8 a.m. and sunset.[28] This was followed in 1940 by the kerb drill introduced specifically to improve children's roads safety:

At the kerb halt!

Eyes right

Eyes left, if the road is clear

Quick march!

Although the strident tone reflected the military mood of the time, both measures were laudable efforts to address a problem which has blighted British childhood for the last seventy years. Moreover, they were indications of the way the notion of streets-as-playgrounds was beginning to change.

The government's best efforts notwithstanding, during the war when the Blackout was in full force, Britain's road casualties were at their worst – 9000 in 1940 alone. Even when the war ended, a warning in the *Bolton Evening News* in 1946 issued by the still extant Ministry of War Transport (it became the Ministry of Transport a month later) highlights the continuing concerns:

> 15 people who leave their homes each day cheerful and full of plans never come back alive. The roads claim them. And each day 364 more, although escaping death are maimed or injured. Pedestrians follow the road drill. Drivers be cautious and alert![29]

Tragically, neither pedestrians nor drivers were it seems sufficiently cautious or alert in the years that followed for casualties on British roads continued to rise peaking (in peacetime) in 1966 with 8000 casualties.

The upward trend simply resulted from the year-on-year growth of cars on British roads. Throughout the 1950s, British factories were producing more cars than ever before, second only in production totals to the USA. When Parliament approved the new Highway Code in 1954, half a million booklets were printed in readiness for those holding provisional licences. In Bolton, those applying for their first licences were being encouraged by institutions like the East Yorkshire Driving School whose Bolton based branch was informing would be drivers "that you must pass your Driving Test urgently" without saying quite what the urgency was all about.[30] At the same time, the attractions of car ownership were being actively promoted with growing numbers of newspaper advertisements encouraging people to buy the latest models of cars, garages advertising their services and driving lessons being offered at 10/– an hour (50p) – a significant change from the pre-war period when such advertisements were rare for the obvious reason that most people couldn't afford cars.

To illustrate the seemingly unstoppable momentum of car ownership, at the time of the Worktown investigation, there were only 7545 cars, buses, taxis and motorcycles on Bolton's roads of which 4538 were privately owned cars. According to the Marketing Survey of the United Kingdom in 1937, only one family in eleven in the town had a motor car.

Given that they would be the better off, the chances are, there were none to be seen on most terraced streets. Within ten years however, the number of vehicles in Bolton had grown to 10,307, by 1960 Tom Harrison was recording that the number had reached 19,337. Most significantly private cars on or around the town's streets numbered some 10,642, twice the number found at the time of the original Worktown investigation.[31]

As a result, the idea that streets were safe places to play began to change. Apart from the risks of accidents, cars affected children's play in other ways too because when they weren't actually being driven, they had to be parked somewhere. Consequently, children were discouraged from playing outside when their ball games in particular threatened to damage cars parked on narrow streets. Ironically, in the 1960s Matchbox, Corgi and Dinky toy cars became immensely popular as children played *inside* with replicas of the vehicles which were stopping them playing *outside*.

But a far darker shadow was about to be cast over the presumed safety of children when playing outside. When Leslie Halliwell began visiting Bolton's cinemas as a young boy in the 1930s, in spite of travelling through badly lit streets alone he recalled "nobody ever suggested that it might be dangerous for a small boy to explore back street routes through areas totally unknown to him, skipping at night from one pool of lamplight to another. 'He'll come to no harm' said mum once when the subject came up. 'Why Bolton's as safe as houses'."[32] Twenty-five years later, after events unfolded in Manchester people no longer believed it was.

In October 1965, Ian Brady and Myra Hindley were arrested for the murder of Edward Evans. Although there was mounting evidence pointing to their involvement in several other murders, the pair refused to confess. In the end, dogged detective work led to the discovery of two children's graves on the moors above Manchester, both victims of the depraved couple (although two other children, Pauline Reade and Keith Bennett were missing as well, they were not confirmed as victims until later). The murdered children, John Kilbride and Keith Bennett both aged twelve; Leslie Ann Downey, just ten years old; and sixteen-year-old Pauline Reade were all abducted when they were out alone, which might suggest that their families had in some ways neglected their children's safety. Nothing could be further from the truth. The parents of the victims would simply not have considered their children could be in any danger when they were out and about in their own familiar neighbourhoods. The very nature of the abductions – John was lured from Ashton Market, Keith whilst walking to visit his grandmother, Leslie Anne from a fairground, and Pauline on her way to a dance – is evidence of the unshakeable belief that children were safe on the streets.

One of those most involved in the horrific case, David Smith, who was married to Myra Hindley's younger sister, confirmed this ingrained assumption saying: "The streets were innocent ... kids could come home from school (and) if mum and dad were out at work it didn't matter, neighbours were there; they could have a jam sandwich and disappear for a couple of hours."[33] Appallingly, his sister-in-law and her boyfriend made five children disappear forever.

While these were by no means Britain's first child murders – nor sadly the last – there were two factors which made the case especially shocking. First, the complicity of Myra Hindley in the murders was deeply disturbing because she was a typical young "aunty" figure who would have been expected to look out for children in the community where she lived – indeed Hindley had known Pauline Reade for a long time. Secondly, the abduction of children from precisely the type of streets hitherto deemed safe seemed to shatter old certainties forever. Although cases of abduction are still thankfully very rare, from this date parents tended to be more wary of letting children play outside following the widely reported, sickening details of the crimes. Arguably, it was the Moors Murders which brought to an end a more innocent era of childhood. By the twenty first century a gaping chasm in experience had developed between Worktown children having "kickabouts" and playing hide and seek on backstreets, and their modern counterparts being driven in cars by parents to organised activities, sporting clubs and the more recent phenomenon of children's "play dates".

In truth, things were already changing before the Moors Murders. It was Worktown's Victorian streets which had fostered a particular type of children's outdoor play and those were the ones that were mostly swept away by the slum clearances. It has been estimated that between 1955 and 1985, one and a half million British properties were demolished affecting nearly fifteen per cent of the population; the latter figure excluding people who moved away voluntarily. As we have seen, Bolton got its fair share of these demolition programmes. Whatever the rights and wrongs of the town planning of the 1960s, the social housing that was integral to it – especially the building of high rise blocks of flats – broke the link with Worktown's traditional streets which had functioned naturally, if unintentionally, as children's playgrounds. Although communal play areas were often provided around high-rise flats, children might be separated from their uneasy parents by a lift and several flights of stairs.

In cases where houses rather than flats replaced the old streets, they often had small gardens surrounded by fences which made it more difficult to monitor what was happening on the street outside. This change was apparent as early as the 1930s when some families first moved to corporation housing estates where property was rented from the council. Mass Observation noted although "the general tone of the estate is harmonious as regards social relations, there are two points where sharp breaks occur. These points are children and gardens. In regards to the children they appear more quarrelsome, which as a consequence, results in more sharp exchanges between the mothers. The children on the whole, are wilder, more unruly and more disobedient to their parents than is normal."[34] The reasons for this are not immediately apparent neither does the Observer suggest any, but it would be fair to say that the inherent supervision created by rows of houses in close proximity to each other was lost when a garden separated the house from the pavements. While it is important to acknowledge that many families were happy to move from the old terraced streets to enjoy the benefits of indoor lavatories, running hot water and gardens there was however one undeniably negative result: children could no longer roam freely within earshot of their own front doors.

The kind of houses people aspired to live in continued to change childhood experience. In the mid-years of the twentieth century, many young couples still clung to social patterns ingrained in Worktown choosing to get married and have children at a relatively young age. However, after buying their first house – usually on a terraced street like the ones their parents lived in – many moved their young families to better houses boasting front and back gardens as soon as they could afford to. Just like adults had to walk further to pubs and shops when they moved to housing estates, children were more dispersed too and now walked much further to call for friends. As more women were working full time and grandparents rarely followed their more aspirant offspring onto estates, the communal supervision of children was less immediately apparent than before. Over time, parents became more inclined to let children play inside their homes or in the privacy of back gardens; a luxury which had of course been unattainable and unknown for most Worktowners.

This change in where children spent their time was also helped by the decrease in the average size of British families. Large families had been common in Worktown which of course meant houses were usually crowded and by definition, less comfortable. Indeed, it was not unusual for children to share bedrooms with their parents well into adolescence. Over time, British families tended to be smaller than before due to the more widespread use of contraception although sharing a bedroom with a teenager must have been as good a "contraception" as any for a lot of parents. As many of the new houses being built in Bolton in the post-war years had at least two double and one single bedroom, children living in smaller families often enjoyed the luxury of their own room: a distinct break with the past and a particularly welcome boon for adolescents who now had their very own door to slam. With more space and privacy, children were inclined to spend time in their own rooms painting Airfix models, engineering things from Meccano or listening to records on their Dansette players. If it was true that the parents of the mid-years of the twentieth century had "never had it so good" neither had their children.

With many children living in bigger and more comfortable houses, it stands to reason they would want to spend more time in them. There was nothing new about the appeal of home comforts. Indeed, well furnished, attractive homes had featured widely in advertisements in Worktown too. Typically they showed clean children playing on carpets in front of raging fires whilst their mothers —always smiling with the joys of domesticity – knitted or darned on the settee in the background. By the end of the 1960s, that kind of middle class, comfortable domesticity was becoming increasingly normal for what had previously been working class families who once lived in two-up, two-down houses.

As the century progressed more children were brought up in houses which had entrance halls, lounges *and* separate dining rooms, fitted kitchens, inside bathrooms, central heating, three bedrooms or more and utility rooms – all of which made them more suitable for playing inside as family members were no longer on top of one another. In Bolton's affluent suburban strongholds – Lostock, Bradshaw, Egerton, Heaton, Bromley Cross, Dunscar, Sharples, Harwood, Smithills – children went from the cobbles to the carpet in two generations. In doing so, they became like the idealised families in the advertisements of the 1930s –although by then their mothers were more likely to be watching *The Liver Birds* on television instead of knitting.

As we have seen, watching television was by far and away the most significant addition to the nation's leisure habits from the mid twentieth century. Just as adults abandoned cinemas, pubs and football in favour of watching more television, children inevitably also began to watch it in preference to playing outside. This became especially so after the number of hours of broadcasting increased in the 1950s bringing an ever-wider choice of programmes to the nation, including those especially aimed at children. As early as 1955 – even before the launch of ITV and BBC2 – the BBC was reporting that eighty-five per cent of British children were watching television every day.[35]

The launch of two new channels and then colour broadcasting could only increase television's appeal to children even though for most of the 1970s daytime television largely consisted of a photograph of Carole Hersee, a young girl in a headband, sitting by a blackboard surrounded by her rag dolls. Although the picture was essential for television engineers, the nation's children gave a collective sigh of relief in the late afternoon when it gave way to fondly remembered programmes like *Jackanory*, *Basil Brush*, *The Magic Roundabout*, a memorable – if badly dubbed – *Robinson Crusoe* and two long-running magazine shows, *Blue Peter* and its rival, ITV's funkier though somewhat plagiaristic *Magpie*. These engaging programmes began to clear the streets of children an hour before teatime so that mothers no longer had to call reluctant children in to eat because most were already sat in the "front room" gawping at the teak-encased television set.

Television started to affect children's lives in other ways too not least because of its impact on the toys and games that appealed to them. From the early years of the medium, toys modelled on television characters proved immensely popular. In the 1950s, a proliferation of puppet shows like *Andy Pandy*, *Bill and Ben the Flower Pot Men*, *Rag Tag and Bobtail*, *Pinky and Perky*, *Muffin the Mule* and *The Woodentops* appealed to the nation's youngest audiences principally because they were enchanting, and to the television producers because they were cheap to make. Toy manufacturers were quick to cash in launching *Andy Pandy* rag dolls,

Pinky and Perky painting sets, *Muffin the Mule* puppets and an easily cloned *Sooty*, as the expressionless little glove puppet was not exactly sophisticated in the first place. For older children, there were models of *The Lone Ranger* and games based on *Rawhide*, *Hopalong Cassidy*, *Wyatt Earp* and *Champion the Wonder Horse*; all of which reflected an obsession with the American Wild West on television. Other games and toys for children were launched based on successful British programmes like *Take Your Pick*, *Double Your Money*, *Dixon of Dock Green* and *Emergency-Ward 10*.

The success of merchandise linked to iconic programmes encouraged an avalanche of similar themed toys and games in the years that followed. After *Doctor Who* first terrified the nation's children in 1963, model Daleks and a miniature Tardis were launched for children brave enough to come out from behind the sofa long enough to play with them. Toys, jigsaws, games and books associated with the *Man from U.N.C.L.E.*, *Z cars*, *The Avengers* and *Coronation Street* also appeared. In the slipstream of earlier space heroes like Dan Dare and Buck Rogers, Gerry Anderson took puppetry to a new level of sophistication in the mid 1960s, the resulting models of *Captain Scarlet*, *Joe 90*, *Fireball XL5* and the most enduringly popular of all, *Thunderbirds*, helping define the decade which first saw their appearance.

Equally era defining were the board (bored?) games that reflected the 1970s "golden age" of television. *Dad's Army*, *On the Buses*, *It's a Knockout*, *Kojak* and bizarrely Esther Rantzen's *That's Life* consumer awareness programme were all made into board games – most surviving examples of these rarely played games now cluttering the shelves of Bolton's charity shops. When Mass Observation was first established, the children of Worktown had never seen a television set, just thirty years later, when they weren't actually watching television, they were often found playing with toys associated with it.

But above all else, it was television that was crucial in turning children into consumers from a very early age. Toy manufacturers were never likely to miss the fact parents had more disposable income than any time before and they began promoting their products by investing in ever more expensive advertisements aimed directly at children. "When we are thinking about writing advertising ... we always think of children as well ... because children are much easier to reach with advertising.

We can exploit that relationship and get them actually pestering their parents for products," said the marketing director of Saatchi and Saatchi international advertising agency in 1999; a comment that left no doubt as to how important this demographic had become before the twentieth century had ended. Moreover, many of the toys they were getting children to pester for required an expenditure a world away from the money once spent on marbles, skipping ropes and yo-yos in Worktown.

The increased spending on children's toys symbolised the way affluence changed children's lives – a phenomenon that simply grew year-on-year. In the 1950s and 1960s, Subbuteo table top football and the less popular Subbuteo cricket, Chad Valley and Casdon football games, and Peter Pan's Test Match Cricket were all relatively costly indoor versions of what were in essence, inexpensive outdoor activities. Other games like Crossfire where players fired ball bearings from plastic guns across a table top, and KerPlunk with its marbles in a plastic cone, were to all intents and purposes variations of marbles games but of course, more expensive. Similarly, the old Ludo board game was re-invented as Frustration with the additional novelty of a die in a plastic dome instead of a cup; a simple change which meant the manufacturers could charge substantially more for what was in essence the same cheap board game. In 1971, even the humble pastime of conkers which cost *nothing* was reinvented to cost *something* with the launch of Klackers before the plastic exploding "conkers" caused numerous injuries which led to a ban in some schools.

Tom Harrisson on returning to Bolton in 1960, thought children's toys demonstrated the growing affluence in the town. He wrote "Worktown children still play largely or wholly on the streets. But today they often play with plastic ducks, expensive tri-cycles, balloons and rubber balls, seldom seen in the thirties".[36] Quite what he would have made of Raleigh's iconic Chopper bi-cycle launched ten years later remains unknown but its success was a potent symbol of the way children were by then potentially lucrative consumers. With forked handlebars, small front wheels and an elongated saddle the radical design of the bike aped the Harley Davidson motorbikes of the film *Easy Rider*, and became a must-have for any youngster "Born to be Wild" in the town's more prosperous suburbs. The Chopper was originally priced at £32, at a conservative estimate, £600 at today's prices. This eye-watering expense would have been unthinkable only thirty years before when boys in Worktown had coveted a trolley made from a plank, recycled pram wheels and a steerable axle lubricated with margarine.

But the most seismic shift in the way children played – especially boys – was not so much to do with affluence as new technology. In the mid-1970s, the "Interstate" television game arrived without too much fanfare; a laughably poor simulation of a tennis match. Nonetheless, for many children it was their first encounter with games played on a television screen. With only primitive electronic bleeps and oblong "bats" striking square (!) balls, it was nevertheless infuriatingly addictive. Games like Space Invaders, Asteroids, Battle Zone, Inter Galactic Invaders, Pac-Man, Donkey Kong, Bandido and Frogger followed in its wake but at first they could only be played in Bolton's pubs, or gaming arcades like Space City (previously Va Va's/Pips nightclubs) in the town centre.

Video games in pubs and arcades however, began to disappear after the Sinclair ZX, introduced in the early 1980s, opened the flood gates for a new breed of gaming consoles which meant that sophisticated arcade games could now be enjoyed on a television set at home. In the early 1990s, Nintendo's Super Mario and Sega's Sonic the Hedgehog became the iconic torchbearers of a generation of mesmerising, colourful and highly addictive "platform games". Sony's hugely successful PlayStation arrived in 1994 making the first person genre of "shoot em up" games like Call of Duty and other similar gore fests accessible without a high speed PC system. Microsoft later entered the market with the rival Xbox and soon games were developed – then launched – with promotional budgets that rivalled Hollywood blockbusters.

Manufacturers of computer games, noting that blood drenched, dystopian landscapes did not appeal to girls quite as much as boys, responded by launching the Wii console in 2006. With dancing, music and games they believed were more in tune with girls' interests, the grip of virtual reality on the nation's young people was complete. Xboxes, PlayStations and Wii consoles, along with iPhones, laptops, computers, tablets and kindles define the childhoods of Bolton's millennials; a greater contrast with the poverty saturated photographs of Worktown's children taken by Spender would be hard to imagine.

Ultimately, it may be argued this kind of change is all perfectly normal – after all, throughout history, each generation of children has experienced childhood differently; and usually, in more prosperous, comfortable ways than their predecessors. But to older people whose young lives were spent playing boisterous games in the fresh air, seeing their bug-eyed grandchildren engrossed in their screens, the rupture between generations is disturbing, even alarming, not least because of the health implications for children who are inactive for most of the day.

In spite of the growing concerns around children's physical health, it is unlikely that the days of playing out will ever return. In the unlikely event children wanted to spend time on "our street" again they would find them few and far between not least because on modern housing developments there aren't any. Houses today are as likely to be found on "Ways", "Groves", "Drives" ,"Walks", "Gardens", "Courts", "Closes" and "Crescents" – anything but "Street" as if in some ways streets were inferior. They weren't. Not according to those old enough to remember the innocent, engrossing, energetic games played on them before they became yet another part of a vanished town. At the same time as Bolton's cobbled playgrounds were receding into folk memory, another playground was also vanishing. But this one was forty miles away, was much bigger, and for as long as Worktown lasted, it was loved by adults as much as children.

HOLIDAYTOWN

Crowded sands at Blackpool.
Humphrey Spender

In the 1930s, Lancashire was a byword for ugliness; a county synonymous with factories and mills, coal pits and slag heaps, canals, railways, foundries and forges. Worktown had more than its fair share of all of them but it did have one saving grace. In the words of Bolton born author, Allen Clarke, it was surrounded by "sweet, wild moorlands."[1] Unfortunately, the Worktowners rarely saw them because of the pall of smoke produced by the forest of mill chimneys. For seven days each year however, the smoke did clear long enough for the moors to actually be seen but ironically, there was hardly anyone around to appreciate the view because smokeless chimneys could only mean one thing in Worktown – everyone was away on holiday. And to the vast majority of Worktowners, a holiday meant only one place: Blackpool.

At the time of the Worktown investigation an extraordinary sixty-nine per cent of Bolton's population took their one week annual holiday in Blackpool. Equally extraordinary, the vast majority all set off there on the same day – the last Saturday in June, the beginning of Bolton's designated holiday week. In the mid twentieth century, a single holiday week was common to all northern manufacturing towns because they were tied to a Wakes calendar staggered across the spring and summer months. The origins of Wakes weeks are obscure, but it is widely believed they were a legacy of older religious observances which became secularised into traditional factory holiday weeks that came to differentiate each town's holidays, one from another.

Notwithstanding any religious origins, Wakes holidays were in fact a necessity because routine maintenance had to be carried out on factory machines at some point in the year so it suited the mill owners to shut down their operations for a brief spell. Unfortunately this meant somebody had to work on the machines and as they could not take a holiday at another date or enjoy time off in lieu, it was generally carried out by less well off workers who could not afford to go away or those who desperately needed some extra money for one reason or another.

Because Bolton's mill workers were used to decamping to Blackpool all at the same time, when they got there, many Worktowners just whiled their days away counting how many of their neighbours and acquaintances they could spot. Although this may seem strange, it resulted from the dominance of one industry in Bolton and the fact that people were used to living in close proximity to one another. With social interaction between and across generations so normal in the mills and terraced streets, going on holiday all together at the same time, and mostly in the same resort, was just another expression of Worktown's more communal spirit.

For mill and factory workers, their precious week away came at some cost, for until the mid twentieth century holidays with pay were unknown for working class people. Therefore industrial workers could only enjoy a holiday if they put money aside for it throughout the rest of the year. Unsurprisingly, Mass Observation discovered a passion for saving up for holidays amongst people who were determined to enjoy some glorious, carefree spending, even if it only lasted seven days. Poverty as we have seen was no stranger to Worktown so feeling "flush" was an important part of the holiday experience. Consequently, holiday savings were always kept separate from the rest of the household budget, one Boltonian telling an Observer "I save for the holidays, so that one may spend freely without feeling that you cannot really afford it [sic]." To help him and others to "afford it", there were a clutch of savings clubs, "Going off" clubs and "Diddlem" clubs (so called because it was not uncommon for the treasurer to run off with the money) organised and administered by individuals in the churches, workplaces or pubs. Some local corner shops even allowed poorer customers to add sixpence to their bills from April to save for the holiday which was just as well as there was no credit to be had anywhere at all in Blackpool.

Of all the holiday resorts which developed on Britain's coast in the nineteenth century, Blackpool more than any other embraced the culture of working class people and then unashamedly catered for it. Blackpool, like the class it served with such unabashed, vulgar distinction, was a direct product of the industrial revolution. There were two key factors which led to its rapid growth as a holiday resort. The first was Blackpool's close proximity to large towns dominated by the Lancashire cotton industry where "high family incomes, ability to save for unpaid holidays and adapting wakes weeks to seaside purposes put them a generation ahead of other industrial workers."[2] The second was the railways to take them there.

Blackpool's first railway station opened in Talbot Road in 1846 and the resort's subsequent expansion meant it was soon followed by a second station, Blackpool Central, which opened in 1863. By the beginning of the twentieth century, the town's railway termini could muster a total of twenty-nine platforms between them with fourteen at Blackpool Central alone; the same number of platforms as Britain's largest station, London's Paddington station – convincing evidence of the huge numbers of people who were by then visiting the booming resort.

Along with the resort's serendipitous location, Blackpudlians also contributed to their own good fortune with no shortage of ambition, bold entrepreneurship, and aggressive marketing. As early as 1876, Blackpool's hoteliers were adverting in the newspapers of local mill towns, secure in the knowledge that their prospective customers could reach them easily and cheaply.

The resort was blazing a trail in other ways too. In 1879, Blackpool became the first town in the whole world to have electric street lighting and in the same year, in a remarkably innovative strategy, the corporation got a parliamentary sanction to levy a 2d in the pound rate to support municipal advertising. As a result, publicity for Blackpool's attractions began to appear all over Britain and even beyond occasionally with ironic results. One Blackpudlian barber serving on the Western Front in Belgium in the First World War remembered being confronted by a poster exhorting him to "go to bright breezy Blackpool."[3]

Having brought electricity to its street lighting, Blackpool also became home to the first electric tramway in Britain after trams began to ferry passengers along the seafront in 1885. The tram system was further improved in 1905 when the promenade was widened and the tracks were relocated nearer to the shore and away from other road traffic; a factor which goes some way to explaining why Blackpool's trams survived to become one of the resort's attractions long after they disappeared from other towns and cities. Such was the tram system's importance to the resort, for a time it became a barometer for Blackpool's economic prosperity. In 1893, Blackpool's trams carried some 355,512 passengers, within ten years passengers numbered over six million. Just another ten years later, Blackpool's trams carried some 12,542,820 passengers in a single year – a quite astonishing record of growth in such a short period. In 1925, Blackpool Corporation proudly announced that their trams had carried some thirty-three million visitors in one year generating a hugely impressive £250,000 of receipts from passenger tickets.[4]

When Blackpool reflected wider trends in the development of British seaside resorts, it usually dwarfed its rivals in scale and ambition. In the second half of the nineteenth century, there was a frenzy of pier building activity in Britain's coastal resorts. By 1892, Blackpool had three. Its first, the North Pier, opened in 1863, the Central Pier (originally the South) opened five years later which was followed by what became the new South Pier in 1893. In a bid to extend the season and maximise profits, the Winter Gardens were opened in 1878 promising "not a dull moment" for customers sheltering from Blackpool's notoriously bracing climate. It remained unchallenged as the town's premier indoor attraction until 1894, when Blackpool Tower was opened which in true Blackpudlian fashion went one better than its Parisian inspiration by having a massive indoor entertainment complex located beneath it. In the same year, the Grand Theatre, boasting a quite stunning interior designed by celebrated Victorian architect Frank Matcham, was also completed.

Just before the First World War when "the lamps went out all over Europe," they actually came on in Blackpool, the autumn Illuminations lighting up the promenade for the first time in 1912. Six years later, as the end of the Great War brought a blood-drenched curtain down on the Edwardian age, Blackpool was firmly established as Europe's biggest holiday resort and it was primed and ready to become the destination of choice for the industrial working class for much of the rest of the century.

Due to Blackpool's bond with working class people, it was inevitable that it would become an off-shoot of the Worktown Project taking place in Bolton. Just as it was no secret that Worktown was Bolton, Mass Observation openly acknowledged that the place they called "Holidaytown" was in fact Blackpool. Because of the resort's importance to the Worktowners, Mass Observation stationed five permanent Observers in Shetland Road, just 400 yards from the sea front. Starting work in October 1937, they infiltrated the resort for fourteen months, melting into the crowds striving again to meet the project's ambitions that its agents should be "unobserved observers".

Like their counterparts in Bolton, the Observers made counts, secretly recorded the conversations of holidaymakers, and did "follows" of individuals and groups to see what they did whilst away on holiday. Occasionally, the permanent Observers were joined by field workers from Bolton who went for long weekends and at other times, by university students who descended on the resort during the holidays. However, just as in Bolton, the Observers in the resort were not quite as clandestine as Tom Harrisson would lead us to believe for one of them was easily identified by turning up to peer at the working class in his Bentley motor car.[5]

Humphrey Spender also went to Blackpool taking a series of evocative, surreal photographs of holidaymakers on the promenade, gambling on slot machines, crowded together on the sands, and flying through the air on the rides of the Pleasure Beach. In addition, Spender also produced a rich visual record of the Illuminations, the motor coaches and a number of hotels. Like his images of Bolton, Spender's photographs of Blackpool are of immense importance for the type of Holidaytown he recorded then no longer exists – a demise that would have been unthinkable to the Worktowners whose passion for the resort had been ignited by the mesmerising gaudiness and vulgar swagger which characterised Blackpool's glory days.

To cater for the masses wanting to go there, Blackpool's holiday season started in late spring, traditionally with the Oldham Wakes week. However, the rousing of the sleeping giant from its winter slumber was always considered somewhat dull by the resort's raucous standards. According to the oft repeated pun of local comedians, "when Oldham Wakes, Blackpool sleeps!"[6] Fortunately for Blackpool's businesses, the soporific start to the annual holiday season didn't last long for all across Lancashire other workers were frantically saving their money to show they knew how to have a good time when their turn came round.

On Friday 24 June 1938, it was once again the Worktowners' turn. At 5.30 p.m. the machines in the cotton mills stopped abruptly. Within hours the chimneys had ceased belching smoke and an eerie quiet descended on Bolton. Just as the savings clubs had made money disappear during the previous year, it now reappeared ready for the holiday. The first Friday night of the long awaited week was spent preparing for the following day. Mass Observation noted that one paper boy was told not to deliver the newspapers in the following week by all but eight of his ninety-five "usuals". Those doing the cancelling were no doubt looking forward to going away unlike the poor boy and his eight remaining customers who would be left behind in a ghost town.

The first thrill of the holiday week in Blackpool was actually the journey there. Although there were other popular seaside resorts in Lancashire chiefly Morecambe and Southport, and even resorts further away like Rhyll, Scarborough and the Isle of Man, Blackpool's popularity was bolstered by the fact that it was the cheapest to reach. This partly explains why there was a mild disdain for Blackpool amongst people who could afford to travel further expressed in the rather patronising maxim: "Morecambe for the chargehands, Blackpool for the workers."

To get the workers to Blackpool, railways, as we have noted were the dominant form of travel and the train ride to the resort was all part of the holiday experience. On the first Saturday morning of the holiday week, there were enormous queues at Bolton's two train stations on Trinity Street and Great Moor Street with crowds pouring onto the platforms many of them wearing new "Sunday best" clothes, bought a few weeks before from enterprising local shop owners who knew people had saved up money for "going away" clothes.

The *Bolton Evening News* always reported on the Saturday morning getaway with the crowds being duly photographed each year. As well as featuring those going away, photographs of people staying at home – usually frolicking in one of the town's parks – were also printed in the newspaper. With eternal optimism, the holidaymakers hoped for fine weather which was something of an obsession in the local press. The headlines in Saturday's edition of the *Bolton Evening News* in 1938 were typical of the time: "Holiday Breezes Blow away the Clouds!" although the upbeat mood was spoiled somewhat when the report mentioned that a number of the women had already had their holiday "perms" reduced to a state of "saturated straightness" by the earlier rain. On the first evening of the holiday week, another report described the upsurge in sales of roses for buttonholes which were bought each year by the "stay at homes", one flower seller boasting to the reporter that he could "always sell three to four hundred roses in Bolton on a holiday Saturday night" before adding with a somewhat optimistic flourish that "a flower in the coat gives them a holiday feeling."[7]

For those Boltonians fortunate enough to be going away there were specially chartered holiday trains. When they pulled up alongside the platforms, the crowds excitedly swarmed on. The bedlam continued once the hour long ride began, with communal singing in the carriages creating a carnival atmosphere. As well as special trains, a good proportion of Bolton's holidaymakers went to Blackpool by coach, the bus station on Moor Lane again proving an irresistible draw for the photographers of the town's newspaper. At a time when few Boltonians travelled beyond the fringes of the town – indeed Mass Observation noted more Worktowners had been to Blackpool than Manchester – these road journeys were equally exciting with the same communal singing along with frequent stops at cafes on the way, even though it was less than forty miles to the coast.

Whatever way they chose to get to Blackpool, the anticipation and excitement was almost too much to bear especially for children. Just as the factory chimney symbolised what they had left behind, Blackpool Tower was the overwhelming symbol of journey's end and seeing it appear on the horizon was an essential part of the pilgrimage – an excitement which was heightened further because a prize of a "tanner" (6d, just over 2p) was commonly offered to the child on each coach who saw it first. Lancashire mill worker, Winifred Barnes, later recalled the agonising wait saying

"You'd think it was the Eiffel Tower never mind Blackpool Tower" whilst in common with generations of young children, Les Dennis, the Liverpudlian comic and actor, remembered asking his father repeatedly "Are we there yet?" only to be told to look for the tower.[8] The wide-eyed innocence of the young holidaymakers eagerly scanning the horizon contrasts rather starkly with Tom Harrisson's perception of Blackpool's most famous landmark: he thought it was a phallic symbol.

Freudian allusions aside, more than any other feature, Blackpool's tower dominated the resort's image due in no small part to the fact it was replicated on a bewildering array of souvenirs bought in their millions over the years. At an impressive 518 feet nine inches in height, the tower can be seen from miles around and it serves no other purpose than to provide a particularly giddy vantage point from which to view the resort which lies prostrate beneath it. The tower's ironwork has to be continuously painted to prevent corrosion – most of the time in a strangely unappealing dark red, although it was painted silver in 1977 to mark Queen Elizabeth II's Jubilee, and gold in 1994 to celebrate its own centenary. In 1949, in the film *Dick Barton Strikes Back*, the special agent fights his enemy Fouracada to the death at the top of the tower, and in 1984 a gigantic model of King Kong clung to its legs, menacing the people on the promenade below whilst drinking a cup of tea! Apart from the fictional terrors, one Observer recorded that many Worktowners visiting the top of the tower most enjoyed throwing things or spitting from it which he concluded was one of its main attractions.

Shortly after the first tantalising view of the tower, the excited holidaymakers arrived in Blackpool. After pouring out onto the platform, the crowds rapidly thinned out as they began the final part of the journey to their accommodation. The Observers noted that those arriving at the Central Station usually walked to their lodgings rather than taking a taxi presumably to preserve their spending money although local children tried to relieve them of some of it as they often gathered at the station in the hope of carrying the holidaymakers' luggage in return for tips.

Mass Observation categorised the accommodation awaiting the holidaymakers into four main types. Hotels with a license charging 15/– (75p) a day, private hotels that didn't have a license costing over 10/– (50p) a day; boarding houses without licenses charging approximately 7-6/– (37p) a day; and finally family houses known as "kippaxes" offering the cheapest accommodation at 6/– (30p) or less but where rules about overcrowding were often broken.[9]

As might be expected, the hierarchy of accommodation on offer in Blackpool indicated the social class of the visitors. According to Tom Harrisson, the grander licensed hotels had no Worktowners in them as they generally attracted people from further away and the big cities. His observation raises an intriguing point, for despite Blackpool's entrenchment as a working class resort, historian J.K. Walton is keen to stress that it did also cater for middle class visitors. This often forgotten aspect of the resort's history can be discerned in the world famous golf course at Lytham St Anne's along with a further four 18-hole golf courses scattered across the resort. Also appealing to middle class tastes were a number of attractive sunken gardens and squares, the impressive Empress Ballroom, several gargantuan hotels like the magnificently appointed Norbreck Hydro Hotel, the 240 acre Stanley Park which alone had some forty grass and shale tennis courts, two "picturesque" putting greens and a 30 acre boating lake; and the quieter more genteel atmosphere found at the northern and southern ends of the promenade.

Despite catering for more affluent customers, Blackpool's upmarket hotels, with as many as thirty bedrooms, still only had one bathroom for all the guests to share. Two Observers who stayed in one hotel of this type noted: "The hot water was never hot. Next door to the bathroom are two small lavatories, one gents, one ladies, the only ones in the house, but there is a jerry in every room". Those staying in cheaper accommodation would have been thankful even for that because when they needed the lavatory during the night, they had to furtively peep round their bedroom doors before dashing across the landing to use it.

Nevertheless, the "joys" of the accommodation offered in Blackpool were advertised extensively in the northern press. Curiously, many Boltonians after escaping their dismal terraced houses mostly prized a stay in "a home from home" when they went on holiday. They usually got it too, with bedrooms commonly only measuring eight feet by eight feet with oilcloth (linoleum) rather than carpet on the floor. A sizeable proportion of holidaymakers also took their own food from home with them or bought it locally whereupon it was stored in the dining room in a cupboard designated for each families use.[10] Proprietors then cooked the food for them each day – no easy undertaking as each different group of guests might have a range of meals which needed to be cooked and served all at the same time. The cost of preparing the food was included in the tariff but not the seasoning as guests were charged a couple of pennies at the end of the week for the use of salt and pepper, rather grandly called the cruet. However, as the century progressed and competition for customers intensified, hotels advertised the "free use of cruet" as an incentive for holidaymakers to choose a particular establishment.

One aspect of Blackpool's boarding houses more than any other made the Worktowners feel immediately at home: typically, they were run by women. Blackpool's army of landladies had a formidable reputation, the way they conducted their businesses becoming an enduring part of the resort's folklore. In the same way as the rules and regulations of the factory owners imposed order on the working day in Bolton, Blackpool's landladies proved equally harsh taskmasters in ordering the holiday experience. In fact, cards of rules were often the most prominent decorative feature in dining rooms. These charmless documents ordered the guests to rise noiselessly, forbade playing the piano before 8 p.m., insisted on an early departure on the last day and, to ensure that nothing was left to chance, any "extras" had to be paid for on a daily basis. As if these rules weren't strict enough, in some establishments children were banned from using the piano completely, and playing on the stairs or landing was forbidden at all times. There was of course one compensation for the holidaymakers tolerating this rather graceless atmosphere – for seven glorious days at least the lavatory was not down the back yard.

Myriad rules notwithstanding, the Worktowners were at last in Blackpool where the smoky chimneys and grimy red bricks of Bolton could temporarily be forgotten. Tom Harrisson wrote: "here for one week, there are no noticeable policemen, no critical neighbours, no factory whistles. This, as so many people clearly state, is Life, is Paradise, is Dreamland and Heaven…" Spending money freely and "living beyond their station" was all part of this dream. So was eating plenty of food. In terms of holidaymakers' meals there were two tariffs on offer in the hotels and boarding houses: "Bed and Breakfast" or "Full Board". Full Board included supper provided by the landladies in the price whilst holidaymakers staying on a Bed and Breakfast basis, as already noted, had to bring their own food to be cooked for the evening meal.

Whichever tariff guests chose, the times of their meals were rigidly set. Most evening meals were served at the relatively early hour of five o'clock, partly so the guests could get to the evening shows on time, but mainly because it suited the landladies who wanted to get rid of them for the evening. To that end, in most small hotels and boarding houses a gong was a prominent feature in the hall which was struck with due ceremony to announce mealtimes and guests were not expected to be late on being summoned to dine. One typical notice at the Sunnyside Hotel politely advised: "Visitors will add to the general comfort by being punctual to meals"; a directive that rather sums up the atmosphere.

Besides the rigidity of mealtimes and the barely disguised rush to get the guests fed, the experience of dining in a boarding house was made even more joyless by the quite common practice of sharing tables. One Observer described having a meal at one small table with two couples who were strangers to each other and to him. The unavoidable awkwardness was made worse when whispered conversations took place across the table which excluded the other diners even though they were only eighteen inches apart. With so much competition amongst boarding houses in the resort, little wonder some establishments at the cheaper end of the market specifically advertised "separate tables" to attract customers.

Harrisson noted one significant difference between Blackpool's hotels and its boarding houses was the amount of freedom afforded at mealtimes; the more guests paid, the greater the time allotted to eat. But in spite of the relative freedom in more expensive hotels, the minority of middle class Boltonians eating in them didn't have it that much better in terms of food on the table. On witnessing a three-course lunch followed by cheese and biscuits provided in one establishment, one Observer noted "large quantities of badly cooked unwholesome food are served ... coloured junket powders, cheap jelly cream packets, tinned cream, tinned fruit, etc. Potatoes always mashed or boiled, no greens, carrots (served) once." As most British people in the 1930s had yet to discover the pleasures of fine dining, perhaps unsurprisingly the middle class holidaymakers seemed to enjoy the food although quantity was probably as important as quality with the Observer pointedly concluding that "Fat ... people predominate at this hotel."[12]

The holidaymakers' waistlines can hardly have been helped by the fact that once outside their hotels, over half of Blackpool's businesses were food shops with fish and chips shops in particular, found on virtually every street corner. Priced between 6d (just over 2p) and 10d (just under 5p) depending on where it was purchased, Britain's signature supper was a staple on most menus in the resort. Indeed, out of 194 meals recorded by the Observers, thirty-three per cent contained chips and twenty-seven per cent fish.

Mass Observation noted that the Worktowners claimed to like it when it was breezy which is perhaps just as well as the weather was never one of Blackpool's attractions. The resort's publicists as usual made a virtue out of necessity proclaiming that its bracing sea air was a tonic and good for health which was probably just as well considering the landladies could hardly wait to throw their guests out to breathe it. Quite extraordinarily for people supposed to be guests, after breakfast, holidaymakers were not expected to return to their accommodation until the evening meal if they were taking it. Indeed, guests were actively discouraged from spending any time at all in the boarding house during the day. "At no time between nine in the morning and eleven at night from the end of June to October are the streets anything less than packed" one Observer reported which was wholly predictable as most landladies went as far as locking the doors behind their guests to make sure they stayed out all day, even when it was raining.

With so many people virtually forced outside, Blackpool's expansive beach was as packed as its streets with an estimated 150,000 people crammed onto it at peak times. In 1937, the resort's publicists described it as "The Magic Carpet" inviting potential holidaymakers to "Picture a golden carpet seven miles long and at times half a mile wide, not of woven fabrics but of gleaming golden grains of clean, firm sand. Look upon it as a nursery carpet of Brobdingnagian dimensions, for here is the paradise of kiddies, their El Dorado of every happiness."[13] Whether Blackpool's beach deserved such hyperbole is open to question, but surely it is the only time the word Brobdingnagian has ever appeared in any resort's publicity. Naturally, children loved playing on it and also paddling in the sea although the Irish Sea was not too dissimilar in terms of its colour from the dirty grey/browns of industrial Bolton. One little girl obviously did not notice its shortcomings; an Observer overheard her saying with charming naiveté, "Isn't it nice watching the sea come in."[14]

Spender's photographs of the packed beaches bear witness both to the attractions of the sands and also Blackpool's notoriously bracing weather as the way people dressed for a day on the beach appears to be astonishingly conservative. Suits and ties, coats and hats, fur collars and pullovers, were all common beach attire – a phenomenon that says as much about Lancashire's climate as differing notions of respectability. Rather predictably, one Observer reported that of thirty-two conversations he recorded whilst in Blackpool most of them were about the weather. Similarly, another Observer concluded that the holidaymakers talked about the weather most of the time adding that "there were none (conversations) on money or the holiday."[15]

Whatever the weather, the thousands thronging the beach, the promenade, and the streets were well catered for. Ice cream and sweet stalls, oyster carts, hot dog sellers, waffle makers and of course sticks of rock with the name "Blackpool" running through it – all of which could be easily eaten outside – competed to relieve the Worktowners of their holiday spending money. The abundance of affordable treats all added to the indulgence which was so essential to Blackpool's appeal. Just thirty-eight miles to the east, the dark, silent mills awaited the return of Bolton's workers, but while they were away on holiday they enthusiastically embraced Blackpool's other worldliness and surreal atmosphere.

The dislocation from everyday reality was reinforced by a host of attractions which gave Blackpool the air of a permanent gaudy carnival. There were Sharma yogis, an enduring fascination for exotic mysticism, orientalism featuring crude racial caricatures and various games of chance. There were freakshows with animals – most famously the poor five-legged cow – and freakshows with humans featuring reputedly the world's first transsexual on his or her "strange honeymoon". Fortune tellers could be found in abundance, several of whom claimed to be *the* original Gypsy Smith or *the* original Gypsy Rose Lee. On the promenade, there was a Tussaud's waxworks museum featuring several notorious serial killers and a chamber of horrors featuring a graphic display of the ravages of venereal disease on various parts of the human anatomy, the latter a potent warning against indulging too heavily in the sexual activity which supposedly characterised the resort.

More innocently, deckchairs and donkey rides were available on the natural beach whilst thirty yards away on the manmade Pleasure Beach, donkeys as well as every other animal, disappeared two-by-two into Noah's Ark. The Pleasure Beach – one of Blackpool's most enduring attractions –

was originally opened in 1895 by the wondrously named William George Bean and was conceived as a funfair "to make adults feel like children again". A decade later, it was renamed Blackpool Pleasure Beach and it expanded further to eventually occupy a thirty-three acre site. In 1923, following a land reclamation scheme it moved to its current forty-four acre site and unusually for an attraction with a national profile, it has remained in the private ownership of the Thompson family for nearly 100 years. With customary bombast, Blackpool's publicists proclaimed in 1926 that it constituted all "the features of what our American friends call 'Amusement Parks' of which the Pleasure Beach is the greatest and brightest example this side of the Atlantic."[16] When the Holidaytown investigation was underway, this huge playground boasted water chutes, river caves, helter-skelters, rollercoasters and in a particularly ironic twist, a flying machine patented by Hiram Maxim who had invented the machine gun that twenty years previously had scythed down the relatives of those who were now screaming with excitement on his ride.

Right at the heart of the Pleasure Beach was the Funhouse where people could stay as long as they liked for a single admission fee. With a range of "ordeals" that would horrify contemporary Health and Safety officers, holidaymakers crossed parallel planks moving in different directions, were flung off flat discs spinning opposite to each other and were turned topsy-turvy in giant cylinders all the while being knocked repeatedly off their feet and uncontrollably into each other. In the "Mixer" – a giant wooden bowl – men, women, boys and girls were spun until they were dizzy with the quite predictable result that some were often violently sick whilst others skidded around in the vomit. All around the Funhouse, strategically placed gusts of air blew up the skirts of any women brave enough to go in. An Observer noted one eighteen-year-old blonde girl, somewhat knowingly lingering over the gusts which produced tantalising flashes of her knickers while her plainer companion just giggled at her hysterically. As might be expected, groups of lads gathered to cheer and applaud the spectacle but in true seaside fashion, the biggest round of applause was reserved for two plump, older women who lost any remaining shreds of dignity after they fell prey to the gusts of air as well.[17]

In this kind of atmosphere it is little wonder that for all their supposed objectivity, the Observers along with Harrisson were often appalled by what they saw as the grotesque, tacky commercialism of Blackpool.

However, it should be remembered that Blackpool also offered entertainment with broader appeal and genuine star quality. In the 1930s, the resorts of Lancashire vied to get the biggest names in show business and given Blackpool's pre-eminence, it was always able to attract the most popular stars of the day. The greatest demand tended to be for working class heroes with roots in the north. Perhaps the most well-loved of all, Gracie Fields, topped the bill at Blackpool's Grand Theatre regularly. In 1934, holidaymakers on the Pleasure Beach were thrilled to see her making the previously noted feature film *Sing As We Go* although it is a fairly safe bet that the international film star's skirt wasn't blown up by the air nor did she cavort around in any vomit.

The only other serious rival to Rochdale's most famous daughter was ukulele wielding George Formby. Born in Wigan in 1904, Formby's cheeky, light-hearted persona epitomised Blackpool. Tickets for his shows were usually the hottest in town and were priced at 3/6, double what a lesser star might be able to charge. Fittingly for a resort so firmly associated with the working class, both Formby and Fields succeeded as much by wearing their proletarian hearts on their sleeves as by their undoubted talents. With accents and speech patterns that were immediately identifiable to the Lancashire working class – "our Gracie" used the word "lass" frequently, whilst George was happy to be known as "daft" – they were immediately at one with the bulk of their audiences; an appeal neatly summarised by Leslie Halliwell who wrote "it required no effort of imagination for us to be interested in their doings; they were only a slight exaggeration of our everyday life."[18]

Another northerner, Lancastrian comedian Frank Randle also enjoyed extraordinary success topping the bill at the Palace between 1934 and 1939. Although immensely popular at the time, he has not enjoyed the longevity of either Formby or Fields, probably because his routine was considered so risqué, his jokes were subjected to censorship from Blackpool's Chief Constable.

Besides providing some of the country's best audiences and venues, there was a further huge incentive for the stars of the day to appear in Blackpool. The sheer volume of ticket sales across the resort meant many performers were paid enough to rent a house for the duration of the season; a welcome change from the cheap lodgings most variety stars were expected to endure when travelling around the country at other times.

Indeed, viewing George Formby's temporary house in St Anne's was an annual treat for his devoted fans when it became an additional must-see attraction on the schedule of most coach tours.

As well as the household names that appeared live across the resort, there were a further four smaller theatres, five Pierrot halls and, rather more eccentrically for a northern resort, an Indian theatre. All hosted dozens of long-forgotten variety acts aspiring to top the bills one day. After adding the seating at the nineteen cinemas and the Marina Ice Rink, there was an astonishing 70,000 seats available for Blackpool's shows divided between two houses each night. No wonder one of Britain's most fondly remembered comedians, Eric Morecambe, was of the opinion that appearing in Blackpool was the yardstick by which the status and success of any act in Britain could be measured.

Most of the shows in Blackpool in the mid twentieth century stemmed from an earlier music hall tradition with a varied bill of acrobats, novelty acts, magicians, singers and of course comedians. With customary thoroughness, Mass Observation recorded the subjects for jokes told by comics in seven of the most frequented theatres on one night before ranking them in order of popularity. Strangely, in a resort that was supposedly of benefit to one's wellbeing, jokes about "ill health" topped the list of twenty-two subjects intended to raise a laugh which must have been no mean achievement as Mass Observation noted that the jokes referenced "sterilisation, deformity, insanity, stench and suicide." Royalty was the second most popular subject, sex fifth, whilst jokes about war, politics and science were bottom of the list. In addition, there were five jokes involving "lavatory humour" which is hardly surprising given the previously noted charade of using one.[19]

As well as the theatres and cinemas, Blackpool had other entertainments. Swimmers were well catered for both inside and outside. The magnificent art deco style Derby Baths which opened in 1939, welcomed a staggering twelve hundred swimmers on the first day alone. For more hardy souls, the open air lido on the south shore which opened in 1923 came complete with a stunning aquatic amphitheatre that recreated the glory of ancient Rome but unfortunately not the Italian climate. During the 1936 season, no less than 330,000 visitors splashed around in the 214,000,000 gallons of sea water that were pumped into the pool that year.

However, all these attractions were dwarfed in scale by the Winter Gardens which as we have seen, were originally conceived to extend the season. Covering an extraordinary six acres, it remains the largest entertainment complex of its type in the world with a capacity of 16,000 when all its attractions are full. The beautifully appointed Opera House located inside was opened in 1939 and seats an impressive 3000 people alone.

A short distance from the Winter Gardens, Blackpool's other major indoor entertainment complex under the Tower boasted a circus as well as a world famous ballroom, both interiors being redesigned by Frank Matcham in 1900. On completion, the Tower Circus, built between the four legs of the tower, was 110 feet square and accommodated upwards of sixteen hundred patrons. Besides its imposing dimensions, the circus also boasted a stage ring which could be lowered to reveal an enormous water tank for the spectacular finales which were a unique feature of the performances. Its interior, which was meant to represent "a Morroccan Sultan's Palace", was whimsical and fantastic and with some justification it was proclaimed in 1938 to be "the most unique and beautiful circus building in existence."[20] World class circus acts regularly performed there not least the clowns personified by the effervescent Charlie Cairoli whose antics captivated children of all ages for an unprecedented unbroken run of forty years. On one Bank Holiday, an Observer at the circus recorded that "people waited outside at 11 o'clock in the morning, for the afternoon show, bringing their lunch, and in the afternoon from 3 o'clock for the evening show, bringing their teas. Food mostly consisted of meat pies, sandwiches, cakes and fruit."[21] With such enthusiasm, little wonder an Observer reported that two members of a popular trapeze act, the Flying Cadoras, told him "The audiences in Blackpool are the best they know."

Of equal importance to holidaymakers, the Tower Ballroom was – and in truth still is – utterly awe inspiring and could accommodate 1000 dancers at a time while a further 5000 could pack the balconies just to watch the dancers. Those on the balcony could also listen to the mighty Wurlitzer organ which was played between 1930 and 1970 by the hugely popular musician, Reg Dixon "The Wizard of the Tower Wurlitzer", whose uniquely rhythmic playing style set a strict tempo for the dancers massed on the floor below.

Dancing was a huge craze in the 1920s and 1930s and even when male partners were in short supply girls partnered one another. Tom Harrisson was fascinated by the ritual of girls dancing close together which was a common sight on the pier and in the dance halls of Blackpool at the time, partly due to the horrific cull of Britain's young men on the battlefields of the Western Front. One Observer recording his impressions of the Tower Ballroom noted that "dancers are mostly adolescent, going to meet the opposite sex, but quite innocently. Young men wanting to get confidence by dancing with a lot of girls, perhaps wanting love but very vaguely." On the other hand, another rather ungallant customer clearly looking for some kind of romantic liaison, told an Observer that he had "never seen a worse looking set of bitches gathered together in one room" before adding with monumental hypocrisy that "he bloody well wasn't going to go away by himself."[22]

Given the popularity of dance halls amongst working class people, the Tower Ballroom was bound to be an important meeting place where mill girls went to meet lads in the hope of pairing off. They were not short of suitors either as young native Blackpudlians also went hoping to meet gangs of girls enjoying their freedom in the resort's heady atmosphere. For a time, there were even special dance excursion trains which ran to Blackpool from all the industrial towns, including one from Bolton on Saturday nights known as the "Blackpool Belle" or more colloquially the "passion express".

Unfortunately for the panting youths of Bolton, the passion was probably more imagined than real. Although on holiday there was generally more freedom and there were certainly canoodling couples aplenty, their behaviour was still restricted by contemporary notions of respectability. In spite of Blackpool's sleazy reputation – especially in the south of England where it was perceived to be an immoral town – the Observers found that it was mostly undeserved. When couples paired off, they went into the back streets of Blackpool just as they would in Bolton. Observers noted that off Vance Road, a short distance from the Tower Ballroom, there were "seven couples necking against the wall and the corners of doorways" after dark. However, they were also forced to concede there was none of the vigorous activity seen in the backstreets of Bolton at a similar time!

Nevertheless, Mass Observation units in Blackpool did their best to investigate people's sexual habits and went out at night determined to find out what was going on. When they did, they were often disappointed. One team of Observers, buying coffee at 1 a.m., were harangued by a disgusted stallholder who claimed that there were already thousands of young people on the beach ready to spend the night together. In fact, when the Observers headed off to the sands to substantiate his allegation, they found only three couples. Indeed, on most occasions, Observers found little evidence of immorality in Blackpool although it has to be said it was not for the want of trying. Observers combed the beach at all hours and bizarrely "crawled under the piers and hulking pretended to be drunk and fell on couples to feel what they were doing exactly."[23] Mass Observation eventually conceded that any sexual shenanigans in Blackpool were more imagined than real because despite Harrisson's best efforts to uncover Sodom and Gomorrah on the Fylde coast, he was left to conclude: "When we began work in Blackpool, we expected to see copulation everywhere, what we found was petting and feeling". As he also recorded "Whenever a couple get down on the sands in the dark shadows of the Central Pier, they very quickly have a ring of silent, staring individuals around them less than two yards away," it is a wonder any couples bothered at all.[24]

On the surface at least, Holidaytown was saucy rather than sexual, bawdy rather than bacchanalian. When Mr Lockhart, manager of the circus was interviewed by an Observer he was keen to stress that there was no striptease in the show before adding somewhat inconsistently that "there had been once, the only time he could remember, and that was Babette the midget, who took off her garments. (Did this to show that although a midget she had a perfectly formed body)."[25] Mass Observation generally found that when there was a focus on the female form, it tended to come in the guise of "forbidden fruit" – a recurring theme in the smutty, "near the knuckle", comic postcards which were very popular at the time. In the world of Donald McGill – Britain's most famous postcard cartoonist – husbands were henpecked, vicars blushed, wives were overweight and young, shapely girls were oblivious to the impact of their double entendres on the red-cheeked men staring at their pneumatic breasts.

On the other hand, Holidaymakers could if they wished, also ogle real girls in various states of undress in the ubiquitous "What the Butler Saw" slot machines which offered a flickering montage of raunchy photographs for a penny. For his report of 1937, Blackpool's Chief Constable inspected no less than 11,704 pictures displayed in the machines – all in the interests of public decency of course. He might have been better turning his attention to George Formby's show at the Opera House, where for the first time on a Blackpool stage, members of the audience were treated to the sight of a fully exposed female breast in 1939;[26] perhaps Mr Formby wasn't quite as "daft" as he led his audience to believe.

As well as all the formal entertainment, the propensity for drinking amongst Bolton's workers was equally in evidence in Holidaytown. Obviously with no work the following day, restraint where alcohol was concerned was to some extent removed. Just like many contemporary holidaymakers, it seems people were happier to get drunk on holiday. Unsurprisingly, Blackpool's pubs could be notoriously rowdy establishments with huge crowds singing and swaying, and overindulging in drink. The Uncle Tom's Cabin pub was well known for serving Magee Marshall's beer and by 1937 the Bolton based brewery was advertising that its beer was available in nine pubs and hotels in the resort as well as a further three off-licenses.[27] Just as they did in Bolton, men used the pub as a bolthole. One Observer witnessed two women trying to entertain their children while their fathers were happily drinking in one pub. On this occasion they didn't get away with it for long, the wives going in to drag their husbands from the vault insisting they buy them drinks too as well as cursing them for "boozing while we are struggling."[28]

Without the need to get up the day after, with ample money in their pockets for once, and with Bolton's most familiar beer on hand, little wonder that some holidaymakers were seen to "fall into the gutter or vomit in the road." Strangely, the Worktown weekly pattern was carried over to Blackpool with Saturday nights being the rowdiest; an odd quirk that contrasts starkly with the great-grandchildren of the Worktowners who party and get drunk *every* night on holiday in Aya Napa and Magaluf if popular mythology and lurid stories in the media are to be believed.

One Observer's description of four youths urinating against a wall in a backstreet mirrors contemporary concerns about the antisocial behaviour that often accompanies excessive drinking whilst another report about a man being knocked out cold after a fight in the street is also a somewhat depressing echo of modern times. As might be expected, the older generation reacted to the antics of the younger holidaymakers in time-honoured fashion. One woman said to an Observer as a crowd of drunken young men walked past "It's a sin for these young men, what they do these days it is" whilst another elderly woman remarked "It's disgraceful these young girls drunk."[29] In fact, it wasn't only young holidaymakers getting drunk, one Observer recording two older men staggering by drunkenly singing "Nine, ten, fuck me again to the tune of 'The Night is Young'."[30]

Although many holidaymakers enjoyed frequenting the resort's pubs, a lot of others spent relatively little money and whiled away the day doing not much more than they would at home. One report about activities on the beach, states that twenty-one men and seventeen women were simply reading their newspapers whilst others were reading magazines. Perhaps predictably amongst predominantly working class people, only three were seen reading books and even more predictably amongst exhausted workers, eight men and thirteen women were asleep. Even after following two couples around for a whole day an Observer found little worth recording. In fact, he noted that they spent most of the day strolling, reading the newspaper, taking a tram ride, going to the cinema and sitting in deckchairs; strangely enough, all activities with the exception of the latter, which were readily available in Bolton.

This peculiar pattern of indulging in familiar Worktown habits and routines whilst away extended to the preferred newspapers too as many holidaymakers still liked to read the *Bolton Evening News* when holidaying and to satisfy the demand, special editions were sent to the resort. As the newspaper always featured photographs of the holidaymakers living it up in Blackpool during the week, there was of course a further incentive to buy it.

There was however, one notable exception to familiar routines. Cinema did not dominate working class entertainment in Blackpool as much as it did in Bolton. As well as relying on Blackpool's 120,000 strong indigenous population for custom, Blackpool's cinemas were largely dependent on the weather; rainy days obviously being good for cinema owners. As one Observer pointed out, rather than seek entertainment in a cinema whilst away, "the crowds flock to the shows, circuses, reviews with star names which they could not find in their own towns."[31]

Overall, it seems Bolton's holidaymakers of the 1930s wanted to stay in a place that was very much like their own familiar homes, amongst other working class people – some of them, family, friends and acquaintances – in a resort which catered for their preferences. But perhaps most important of all, the precious holiday week in Blackpool offered one thing Worktowners rarely enjoyed: time to rest. Sadly however, all-too-quickly it was over for another year. In much the same way as the queues for flights home in the modern age look and feel very different to the queues for outward bound flights, the journey back to Bolton was more sombre. Bizarrely, the return journey was usually preceded by a mad dash to the station with the holidaymakers panicking in the belief that somehow they might get stuck in Blackpool. As the trains pulled into Bolton's stations, all that remained was a bus ride or a trudge back along the cobbled streets to their terraced houses. All around, the disconcertingly quiet factories and smokeless chimneys reminded them it was all over for another year and it was time to start saving up again. Although it was scant comfort, when the Worktowners returned to the mills on Monday morning, at least their machines had been cleaned and maintained.

The Observers' reports, archived cuttings and printed materials, as well as Humphrey Spender's powerful, plaintive photographs chronicle Blackpool on the cusp of its best years. Indeed in 1938, the year that marked the highpoint of the Worktown investigation, the Holidays with Pay Act became law. This legislation recommending a week's paid holiday for all workers was an important landmark in British social history because it meant holidays were no longer the preserve of the upper and middle class. As might be expected, Blackpool Corporation wholeheartedly supported the legislation confidently predicting that "seaside resorts are in for a good time."

After the Second World War ended, it seemed they were, as record numbers travelled on trains to Britain's holiday resorts, especially Blackpool, partly due to the recent legislation, partly the shared relief that the years of misery caused by the conflict were over. In July 1945, as peace finally returned to Europe if not yet the Far East, a staggering 102,889 people arrived in Blackpool on one Saturday alone – a reassuring curtain raiser to the resort's heyday in the 1950s and early 1960s.[32] In 1949, the Illuminations were at last revived after falling victim to the restrictions of the Second World War. When the famous stage and screen actress, Anna

Neagle, turned them back on again, the lights symbolically illuminated the last autumn of a decade which had seen Britain's "darkest days".

Over the next decade, Blackpool got back to doing what it did best – entertaining the masses. Primed and ready were a new generation of radio performers and typically Blackpool, welcomed the cream of international talent to its theatres. Frank Sinatra performed at the Opera House twice, in 1950 and 1953, and in the same decade, Judy Garland, Sammy Davis Jr and Bob Hope also graced its stage.

There was home-grown talent on offer too. Irish tenor, Josef Locke, played to packed houses in the 1950s as part of a record-breaking nineteen year consecutive run of shows before tax evasion forced him to flee the country leaving the treasury poorer and his legions of female fans pining for his raffish good looks and lachrymose ballads. In keeping with Blackpool's past, the 1950s also witnessed the tail-end of the old northern variety show stars with bills featuring Ken Platt, Ken Dodd, Jewel and Warriss, Morecambe and Wise, and Hylda Baker before they made the transition to television with varying degrees of success.

As the 1960s began, Blackpool remained enduringly popular despite its resolutely old-fashioned appeal. In August 1960, according to figures obtained by Mass Observation, half a million plus visitors came in that month alone. Tom Harrisson recorded that the publicity officer for Blackpool Corporation stated that in the previous twelve months Blackpool had welcomed seven million visitors.[33] Getting them there were 400 trains, and thousands of coaches which were still arriving in the resort each week. Slightly more worrying however, official figures for the pre-war years had been eight million visitors a year.

Nevertheless, in the early part of the decade 36,000 theatre tickets were regularly sold each night for shows that increasingly featured the stars of television rather than radio, reflecting television's growing influence on British society. Overall, family shows remained the most popular as for the time being at least, Blackpool was still able to rely on its chief supporters – working class families from nearby manufacturing districts. In the mid-1960s, Bill Allen, a lorry driver from Bolton, recalled that special deliveries of Magee's beer were still being made to many of Blackpool's working men's clubs to meet the demand from holidaymakers still wanting to drink their local beer whilst away.[34] In 1961, the *Bolton Evening News* was delighted to report that the sun had shone for seven days out of seven during that year's Bolton holidays; an all-to-rare headline for the weather in the resort. Despite a glorious start to the decade however, Blackpool was about to lose its grip on the nation's holidaymakers.

One of the first indications that Blackpool was no longer dominating the holiday preferences of the northern working class was the extraordinary rise in popularity of the Butlins holiday camps. Although Billy Butlin began building his holiday empire before the Second World War, the heyday of his camps came after it, partly because a strong communal spirit – an essential feature of the first holiday camps – still endured when the hostilities ceased. By offering "a week's holiday for a week's wages", Butlins camps were a fresh alternative to traditional resorts. At first they tended to be patronised by "middle management types" and were perceived as being "posh" before they were embraced by the wider British public. Full board was the standard tariff and although guests dined in barrack-like canteens in regimented sittings, at least plentiful wholesome food was served four times a day. Soup, meat pie and vegetables, followed by steamed pudding was typical fare and though the food was mass produced, portions were substantial and well prepared.[35]

Conversely, the accommodation on offer in Butlins camps was more spartan. The rows of chalets where the guests stayed had the appearance of large garden sheds and did not even have running hot water let alone showers or baths, but despite the rudimentary comforts there was one crucial and very welcome difference: the holidaymakers weren't locked out of them for most of the day. In 1963, Butlins camps entertained a million visitors throughout the season for the first time earning a place in *The Guinness Book of Records*; an ominous sign for Blackpool's landladies. It should be remembered, this was not some new demographic of holidaymakers. Although unrecorded, it is fair to assume that a large proportion of those taking part in the "knobbly knees" and "glamorous granny" contests had previously enjoyed holidays in Blackpool. Billy Butlin's empire reached its peak in the mid-sixties with a total of nine British holiday camps and several hotels, including one in Blackpool itself (worryingly for Blackpool's promoters, Butlin's Trojan horse in the heart of their resort was later joined by Butlins main rival, Pontins, which opened a camp on the south shore). More tellingly, Butlins were by then operating a camp in the Bahamas and a hotel in Spain as well. Despite later jibes about "Butlitz" due to their resemblance to prisoner-of-war camps, Butlins success was an indication that the expectations of British holidaymakers were changing.

Different expectations of what holidays might offer were also apparent when motoring became increasingly affordable in the 1950s and 1960s. The widening car ownership discussed in previous chapters meant remote coastlines started to become more accessible. Although cars in the mid-years of the twentieth century were often more unreliable and less comfortable than today, resorts like Bude and Newquay in Cornwall were amongst the country's fastest growing resorts. Other resorts in the south were gaining in popularity too as increasing numbers of holidaymakers started to travel to them by car even though it could be a time-consuming, tortuous journey in the days before motorways bypassed notorious bottlenecks like Launceston in Cornwall. When they eventually got there, these resorts offered a very different kind of seaside experience to Blackpool. Where the Worktowners had largely stood with their backs to the sea looking *inwards* to Blackpool's manmade attractions, in the resorts of Devon, Hampshire, Dorset and Cornwall, the resort was behind them as they looked *outwards* to the natural beauty of sand, surf and deep blue sea – the latter something Blackpool never had.

The peace and quiet offered by secluded beaches was bound to be more appealing to Bolton's aspirant working class who were moving to semi-detached houses in increasing numbers. In their new houses, they only had one set of immediate neighbours, and their gardens and driveways offered more privacy; a distinct contrast to the neighbourliness which had characterised the previous generation used to living on terraced streets in tight-knit communities. When they went away on holiday they tended to seek relative seclusion too. By the end of the decade, Boltonians were simply less inclined to share their holidays with the whole town, especially as the decline in cotton manufacturing meant Bolton was no longer dominated by a single industry anyway. With my own roots in working class Bolton, predictably my first holiday as a two-year-old was in Blackpool in 1962. Before the decade ended however, our family holidays were taken in Weymouth, Teignmouth, Tintagel, Bournemouth and Newquay. More significant still, the holiday in Blackpool over fifty years ago was the one and only time I ever stayed in the resort.

In truth, Boltonians had always aspired to holidays beyond Blackpool. In the late 1930s the local press ran a competition to discover how the people of the town dreamed of spending their holidays. One respondent wanted to go to the Cornish Riviera, even the Italian one, but in the end he went to Blackpool. Another respondent, a single mother, replied that she wanted to go on holiday in Oxford. After the Second World War, with rising prosperity fuelling new trends, what had at first been fanciful dreams started to become a reality.

As more motorways were built and transport networks were improved, there was a boom in caravanning. The manufacturers of the "Sprite", one of a new range of affordable caravans, boasted that it could even be towed by a Mini, a car not exactly endowed with the most powerful engine. Although caravans were resented by some for despoiling the countryside, the increasing popularity of caravanning holidays marked another change in British holiday patterns. Only thirty years previously, Mass Observation had noted how the Worktowners rarely enjoyed nature, not even Bolton's surrounding moorlands. However, the growth of caravan sites in rural areas offered holidaymakers a chance to discover the joys of the countryside for the first time. One worker from a northern mill town later recalled being awestruck by seeing wild rabbits on his first caravan holiday. The conviction that the seaside was the only place to take a holiday was starting to lose its grip on the national psyche.

A further challenge to Britain's seaside resorts was also posed by the explosion in youth culture after Bill Haley and his Comets first rocked around the clock in 1955. Just as a teenage culture distinct from the older generation affected pubs, it also affected the holiday industry. Spender's photographs of Blackpool show people of every generation enjoying holiday activities side by side with adolescents hardly distinguishable from the older generation in terms of their hair and clothes. During the 1960s, teenage fashions, the music they enjoyed, even the way they talked, became more divisive than previously. Not surprisingly, many teenagers preferred to take holidays independently and in doing so usually abandoned the resorts favoured by their parents. Billy Butlin, never one to miss a trick especially when there was a healthy profit to be made, at first welcomed them and his camps became a popular destination for gangs of teenagers. Indeed, for a while, they almost took over the Butlins Camps before they proved more trouble than they were worth and they were eventually discouraged from going.

Blackpool's breezy air was not immune to the scent of teenage rebellion either although whether all teenagers were "delinquent" as a barman told Tom Harrisson in 1960 is more open to question. The Beatles appeared in the resort every Sunday night in the summer of 1963 and a year later The Rolling Stones caused an infamous riot at the Empress Ballroom by their suggestive antics. It *was* only rock n roll but Blackpool council didn't like it, which resulted in an indefinite ban on the band which was only lifted in 2008! In retrospect, the performances in Blackpool of the two bands at the forefront of Britain's cultural and social revolution have a wider significance. As emblems of an emerging youth culture, they symbolised the widening chasm between the tastes of the generation born just after the Second World War and the social patterns of the half century before. As the resort that courted the traditional working class more than any other, Blackpool was becoming increasingly vulnerable.

Its vulnerability was exposed for all to see in 1963 when the film *Summer Holiday* became a huge box office hit. Perhaps the most surprising thing was that it was Cliff Richard – a pop star who by then was nothing if not wholesome – who became the unlikely rebel against the established holiday pattern of the previous generation. The fictional "Bachelor Boy" may well have played a working class mechanic and his mode of transport – a London double-decker bus – may have been reassuringly patriotic, but in rejecting Britain's seaside in favour of a trip to the continent, the film's setting was simply reflecting where many British people were beginning to enjoy their holidays. This truly seismic change in holiday patterns was largely caused by the one factor beyond the control of even the most enthusiastic advocates of Britain's traditional resorts: the country's unpredictable and all too often awful summer weather.

Perhaps more than any other factor, Britain's climate affected resorts like Blackpool. Any cursory glance at photographs of the British seaside including those taken by Humphrey Spender, reveal the Achilles' heel of the nation's resorts. Overcoats, suits, ties, hats and winter coats were a common sight on British beaches at the height of the summer months as were their wearers shivering in deckchairs while clutching umbrellas in the rain. The annual appearance of the hawkers on Blackpool beach selling sunglasses – "Avoid the glare, two shillings a pair!" – was usually a triumph of hope over experience. Unlike popular memory that suggests childhood holidays consist of endless sunny days, on television's *Reel*

Histories – a revealing study of British holiday culture – many of those interviewed for the programme recalled sitting in the rain in the nation's seaside resorts. When there was no alternative people made the best of it but with the advent of the jet aircraft they no longer had to.

Just as the railways were vital in creating Blackpool, the aeroplane helped to destroy it. However, aspiration was one thing, paying for it another, and jet travel in the early 1960s was still prohibitively expensive for most ordinary families. The turning point came when British holidaymakers enthusiastically embraced one of the twentieth century's simplest and most successful marketing strategies: the package holiday. By offering a "package" consisting of flights, transfers and hotel accommodation for an "all in" price, companies like Clarksons according to their advertisements, "opened up a whole new world". In truth, in the early years it was mainly the Spanish Costas, the Balearic islands, Italy and the Greek Islands nevertheless Clarksons grew from handling just 4000 holidays in 1965 to over one million holidays in 1974, a quite extraordinary growth in less than a decade.

The growth in continental summer holidays was soon followed by the growth of winter ones. Amongst others, an advertisement in the *Bolton Evening News* in October 1974 was offering sun-starved Boltonians three days in Majorca from £25, or seven days on the Costa Blanca from just £37-the latter about a week's average wage for a manual worker at the time.[(36)] It was a sign of the changing times and a sharp divergence from the past where an autumn break usually involved eating fish and chips on the promenade whilst viewing the Illuminations.

The growth in winter holidays also marked another important departure from previous British holiday patterns for only a generation before, holidaymakers were not only restricted to the Wakes weeks, but to a largely weather-driven season comprising late spring, summer and early autumn. Indeed, anyone brave enough to go to a British holiday resort in winter would find virtually everything was shut down. Blackpool's hoteliers were being left even further behind as more affluent people were not only embracing the Mediterranean in summer but winter as well. Worse still, after they had enjoyed a taste of Mediterranean sunshine, they rarely returned to Blackpool.

Summer or winter, in much the same way the Worktowners had dressed up to go away, the pioneering holidaymakers going to exotic sounding resorts abroad also dressed up to fly.[37] When they arrived in the (at first) unfamiliar surroundings of the Costas, they discovered umbrellas were provided to shelter from the sun, not the rain. Furthermore, in Mediterranean resorts, holidaymakers were treated to en suite bathrooms as standard, hotels with their own swimming pools, and extravagantly large drinks in bars that were not restricted by licensing laws dating from the First World War. And of course, they enjoyed virtually guaranteed sunshine. Moreover, all this was available at a price that was not that much more expensive than a holiday of the same duration in Blackpool.

As sunshine, suntans and turquoise seas became more affordable with each passing year, Blackpool and other British resorts were increasingly perceived as down-at-heel and second best. In the 1960s, all across British society, attractions and attitudes that still lingered from Victorian times were disappearing except it would seem in traditional holiday resorts. Indeed when the nation was supposedly throwing off the shackles of sexual repression, on Blackpool beach, older holidaymakers still only got as far as taking their shoes and socks off. Meanwhile, younger people in particular were aspiring to modernity in all its forms. In *Dr. No*, the first James Bond film, Ursula Andress stunned audiences when she emerged from the surf in her bikini, an iconic image a new generation of holidaymakers wanted to emulate. At the same time, Brigitte Bardot made Andress look positively overdressed when she went topless in St Tropez. In bright, breezy Blackpool on the other hand, it was still common to see old men in flat caps, suits and ties paddling in the Irish Sea with their trousers rolled up.

Changing social patterns like these are often not immediately apparent and only reveal themselves with hindsight but undoubtedly there was a growing division between different generations of holidaymakers. As a consequence, the British holiday industry lost ground it never recovered to the Mediterranean resorts in the middle years of the twentieth century: a phenomenon which was mirrored in popular culture.

Morecambe and Wise, who had regularly entertained full houses in Blackpool's heyday, "holidayed" on the French coast in the film *That Riviera Touch* released in cinemas in 1966. In the year before the film's release, they had performed at Blackpool's ABC Theatre: tellingly, it was their last ever appearance in the resort. In 1972, the "Carry On" gang went to "Els Bels", a fictional Mediterranean island in the film *Carry On*

Abroad. Only three years previously – in the same series of films – Barbara Windsor had improbably lost her bikini top on a dreary looking British campsite. In the spin-off film of the T.V. series *Are You Being Served*, the staff of the Grace Brothers Department Store went abroad to the "Costa Plonka" while the store was renovated. At about the same time, Les Dawson appeared in a similar comedy sketch in which he arrived at an unfinished hotel on the Costa Packet; hotels that resembled building sites being a familiar news story at the time. Perhaps most telling of all, in 1974, two episodes of *Coronation Street* were filmed in Majorca after six residents of the cobbled street holidayed there.

The changing holiday pattern was equally apparent in songs of the time. In 1974, Swedish chanteuse, Sylvia, lustily sang "Y Viva España" on the iconic television programme, *Top of the Pops*. Her lively song, delivered over an instantly familiar flamenco chord progression and littered with double entendres reminiscent of a McGill postcard, exhorted all and sundry to go and see the attractions of the Iberian Peninsula for themselves. In stark contrast, in 1979, "Day Trip to Bangor" – mercifully Fiddler's Dram's only chart hit – already sounded unashamedly old-fashioned. Moreover, with lyrics about cuddling Jack in the back of a coach whilst drinking cider, the song celebrated the kind of holiday experience that was receding into folk memory. More in tune with the times was Jasper Carrot's parody of it, "Day Trip to Blackpool". With references to blow up dolls, vandalism, drunkenness, chips, bingo and rain, the Birmingham-born comedian hardly did Blackpool's reputation any favours.

Although the numbers holidaying abroad at the expense of the British seaside were increasing year-on-year, it should be noted that the growth was somewhat slower in the north of England than popular perception would lead us to believe. Radio presenter and author Mark Radcliffe, born in Bolton in 1958, later recalled: "The Radcliffe family holidays of my childhood were perfectly normal affairs. We didn't go abroad until I was fourteen, but then, no one did really. Well only rich people and we certainly didn't fall into that category." Indeed, in the late 1960s, only one boy in my primary school class of thirty children had actually holidayed abroad.

There were two crucial factors that eventually made foreign resorts the destinations of choice for most Boltonians. Reginald Dixon when interviewed in 1937 summarised Blackpool's appeal telling an Observer:

"You see it's sentiment ... people come here, and then they get married, and then their children come with them, and grow up with it, and get used to it."[38] That pattern began to fade away as the children of Worktown born in the mid to late 1930s entered middle age in the 1970s. As the first generation of car owners, to some extent they had already broken the kind of loyalty to Blackpool highlighted by Dixon by going to other seaside resorts. Secondly – and more importantly – when their children left home, they could at last afford holidays abroad. Within twenty years many of them, like my parents even bought property there.

In direct contrast, the generation born in the early part of the twentieth century – originally the young adults of Worktown – were mostly living on the state pension by the end of the 1970s. Many had never learned to drive and they stubbornly clung to the familiarity of older resorts like Blackpool. This generation for a time remained the lifeblood of the British seaside, not only returning to the same resort year after year, but often the same boarding house or hotel as well. This papered over the cracks but it came at a price. Colin Crompton, a popular working men's club comedian angered Morecambe's council in the 1970s by telling jokes about the geriatrics of the town watching the bacon slicer for want of any other excitement – an all too common perception of the ailing British seaside. As this generation became too old to travel independently or sadly died, inevitably there were more and more empty rooms in the guest houses and hotels of Blackpool and similar resorts.

Though mass holidaying was disappearing, oddly enough, the old Wakes weeks stubbornly persisted. One woman after moving from the northeast of England in 1966, recalled the impact Wakes weeks still had on Bolton. She was shocked to find "shops closed and what appeared to be an almost total evacuation of people from the streets and houses in the area." She continued: "We wondered if war had been declared and nobody had told us. We thought we were the only people left on the planet at the time."[39] However, despite the entrenched tradition, the old pattern eventually died out due to the emergence of more flexible holiday patterns as more and more people were employed in jobs that were no longer dictated by factory hooters.

As the 1980s dawned – a decade more than any other associated with growing affluence and conspicuous consumption – the rise in the numbers of people taking foreign holidays continued unabated. For the yuppies ("Young Upwardly Mobile") of Margaret Thatcher's Britain, traditional British seaside holidays were becoming an anachronism. In 1983, when Britain's biggest pop stars Wham! released "Club Tropicana", their upbeat homage to Mediterranean club culture, the accompanying video resonated perfectly with the age that spawned it. It wasn't that Wham! were peddling dreams of beaches and swimming pools in Ibiza that were unattainable except for the rich and famous but quite the opposite. By then, continental holiday resorts were totally accessible to any aspiring "young guns" ready to "go for it". Only thirty years before the "Club Tropicana" video was filmed, the Ibiza Rocks Hotel (now in true Thatcherite fashion, cashing in on being the location of the iconic video)[40] would have been the sole preserve of the jet set – a term in itself synonymous with exclusivity. By the time George Michael was sipping cocktails in his white speedos, the jet set included virtually anyone who was prepared to fly.

Like ageing prize fighters who are unwilling to accept their glory days are over, Blackpool's advocates – usually employees of its council with a vested interest in promoting the resort – still defiantly spat statistics to prove it remained the champion of resorts. The reality was rather more depressing. In 1989, the *Arena* television programme made a social documentary film about Blackpool. In it, Barry Morris the town's Director of Tourism, quoted statistics from the previous year's season to show there had been sixteen million individual visits to the resort and £350,000,000 of income generated from tourism. He further boasted that Blackpool still offered 180,000 beds ("more than the population of Portugal") thirty-six discos and nightclubs, three ballrooms, seven cinemas and eight live shows.

But other aspects of the programme simply served to reinforce the town's shabby image. Two teenage girls, Kay Lomax and Collette Charlton, were featured staying for the weekend in a guest house that would not have looked out of a place in a Spender photograph. Worse still, whilst Wham!'s Pepsi and Shirlee sashayed to the Club Tropicana in skimpy bikinis and knitted tops, Kay and Collette, wearing stonewashed jeans, shielded their "mullet" hairstyles from the rain on the way to play bingo. Moreover, unlike the funky air hostesses portrayed by the pop stars, one of the unglamorous northern duo was taking a holiday from her job in a biscuit factory, the other was unemployed.

Unfortunately for Blackpool's promoters, the documentary only piled on the agony. In one scene, shot in Nellie Dean's Bar, a crowd of elderly people bellowed a drunken, tuneless "Land of Hope and Glory", whilst in the lounge of another hotel, the George Formby Society strummed their ukuleles along to a film of the icon singing "With My Little Stick of Blackpool Rock". To complete the marketing disaster, a landlady revealed to the programme makers a typical menu she offered during a week:

Monday: Chicken, Stuffing, Roast Potatoes and Veg
Tuesday: Steak and Onions with Vegetables
Wednesday: Lamb and Mint Sauce
Thursday: Pork Chops
Friday: Fish and Chips
Saturday: Steak and Kidney Pie
Sunday: Roast Beef and Yorkshire pudding

With admirable gusto she continued that all meals were followed by desserts like "homemade rice pudding – no tins." In a tragicomic finale, the forthright landlady told the interviewer that she had tried serving parsley sauce with Friday's Fish and Chips but she eventually stopped because "it doesn't go down." On Bradshawgate in Bolton, the Raj Manzil Indian restaurant and the House of Orchid which served Chinese food were two of Bolton's most popular restaurants. By offering their guests glorified school dinners at a time when middle class tastes were starting to dominate British society, Blackpool's landladies were nailing their colours to the mast of a sinking ship.

In subsequent years, there was little encouragement for the resort's champions. In the late 1990s, a headline in Blackpool's local newspaper read: "Muesli for breakfast puts B and B ahead of the pack."[41] For inadvertently showing how far the resort's accommodation lagged behind contemporary tastes, it is hard to decide who was most culpable: the hotel for displaying the cutting prominently in its window, or the newspaper for printing it in the first place.

As the new millennium dawned, Blackpool's decline appeared ever more unstoppable as the choice of holiday destinations expanded inexorably in a shrinking "global village". Rural holidays and Center Parcs – tellingly at first advertised as "The British holiday the weather can't spoil" – city breaks in Britain, Europe and beyond; and holidays to ever more distant locations like Egypt, India, the Caribbean, Mexico, North Africa, Thailand and Australia all became commonplace – partly fuelled by the use of credit cards, unknown of course until the mid-1960s.

For more adventurous holidaymakers there was backpacking in South East Asia and virtually anywhere else where dust encrusted travellers could find a cheap enough bed for the night, whilst at the other end of the market there was an extraordinary expansion in cruise holidays – once the exclusive preserve of the very wealthy. The growth in the number of holidaymakers choosing to go to Florida, simply rubbed salt into Blackpool's already gaping wounds. After all, why would British holidaymakers continue go to a grotty "14 mile funfair" – as Paul Theroux scathingly described Blackpool – when Florida's more sophisticated theme parks had been an affordable option for many families for two decades?

Consequently, for most people Blackpool became a sideshow, a place to visit for a day not a week let alone a fortnight. The resort's appeal to traditional holidaymakers declined even further, when attractions that once drew people to the coast started to appear in many inland cities and towns. Blackpool's Sandcastle water park – built on the site of the demolished Romanesque Lido – offers nothing more than the chutes, slides and artificial subtropical climates found in Waves Water Park in Blackburn or the Water Place in Bolton (now demolished). The development of Alton Towers, Drayton Manor, Chessington and Legoland amongst dozens of other theme parks of varying sizes, have all challenged the grip of Blackpool's Pleasure Beach on the nation's thrill seekers. There are major ice rinks at Altrincham and Blackburn, both of which boast excellent facilities for aspiring winter Olympians, and Manchester's Chill Factor even offers all year round ski slopes. Although Bolton comic Peter Kay made a breakthrough appearance at Blackpool Tower, and the Stone Roses played a landmark gig in the Tower Ballroom, it was well before either reached anything like the peak of their careers. Any performers with major drawing power now favour the cavernous concert arenas in Manchester and Liverpool. Only the Tower Ballroom maintains its previous appeal partly due to the success of the *Strictly Come Dancing* television show first broadcast in 2004. Poignantly, of all the venues featured in the programme, those taking part most eagerly anticipate dancing in the still wonderful ballroom.

Although it is scant comfort for Blackpool's marketing officials, all British seaside resorts face similar existential challenges. As a result, some have strived to become bases to explore the surrounding countryside and heritage attractions as much as being destinations in their own right. Unfortunately Blackpool has none to offer. As Theroux acidly remarked, most ugly towns have green saving graces around them, "Blackpool doesn't." Even when Blackpool was at its peak, the area surrounding the resort – what the brochures of the 1930s called its "hinterland" – barely merited more than a couple of sentences. Ultimately, Blackpool is hamstrung by a location that was partly responsible for its success. It is too far from the Trough of Bowland, the Lake District or the Yorkshire Dales to provide alternative accommodation for the swarms of visitors attracted by the walking, scenery and rural village "honey pots". Neither is it near enough to be a dormitory town for the cosmopolitan swagger of Liverpool and Manchester with their universities, major concert halls, exhibition centres and industrial heritage museums; the latter ironically preserving the history of working class people who were once the lifeblood of Blackpool.

These challenges have particularly affected Blackpool because unlike some other British resorts, it seems unable to redefine itself for the new millennium. It lacks the "chocolate box" charm of a Polperro, the fish restaurants of a Padstow, the bohemianism of a St Ives, the gentility of a Scarborough, the maritime heritage of a Whitby or the internationally renowned surfing found in a resort like Newquay. Shackled by its location and a brash vulgarity seemingly imprinted in its DNA, even emerging markets like the "pink pound" of Brighton's gay community somehow elude Blackpool. When plans were unveiled to re-energise the resort in the late 1990s, of all places the council might have looked for inspiration, they chose the gaudy casinos of Las Vegas. By striving to become the gambling capital of Europe it simply highlighted further the resort's tacky image. Perhaps fortunately, this particular regeneration plan came to nothing in the end.

By the beginning of the twenty first century, Blackpool's decline as a family resort was so complete that many establishments were all but forced to cater for "Stag" and "Hen" parties – a market that has only made the resort even less appealing. Being notoriously rowdy and difficult to control, most resorts understandably discourage them but Blackpool's hoteliers have to welcome boisterous groups if they are to stay in business at all. In return, alcohol-fuelled parties of lads and girls embrace the fading resort enthusiastically and who can blame them when a double room with breakfast in Blackpool cost just £25 a night in March 2014? Even the mighty Norbreck Hydro Hotel was offering the same tariff for just £39 a night. "Cheap and cheerful" had simply become: "cheap and nasty". Blackpool's denouement was complete; anyone wanting to see for themselves the "Holidaytown" recorded by Mass Observation will find it no longer exists.

Today, most Boltonians speak of Blackpool with no affection whatsoever; even the idea of visiting the resort for any length of time is met with incredulity. Only seventy years ago, generations of Worktowners saved up all year to make the pilgrimage to *their* resort. Mass Observation thought Worktown and Holidaytown were inextricably linked; their simultaneous disappearance proves they were right. On the rare occasions Boltonians can still be bothered to go, the Winter Gardens, the Pleasure Beach, the Illuminations and Blackpool Tower bear witness to the resort's indomitable spirit. On a clear day, looking east from the top of the Tower, the moors above Bolton are just visible on the horizon because the smoke from the factory chimneys that once hid them has vanished. And not just for seven days each year. Permanently. Because Bolton is no longer an industrial town.

KING COTTON

"Lancashire carries England on its back, is the beast of burden for Brittania."

– Allen Clarke 1897

Workers leaving Flash Street Mill.
Humphrey Spender

Cotton was King in Worktown. That it could be otherwise would never have crossed Sir John Holden's mind. Born into poverty in Halliwell in 1862, Holden, through prodigious hard work, became one of Bolton's most powerful cotton mill owners. As he approached his sixtieth birthday – an age when he would have been forgiven for taking life a little easier – he announced plans to build no less than six new mills in Bolton.

In 1921, construction work began on the first of them; a handsome five-storey building with a distinctive copper dome located on the eastern side of Blackburn Road. Tragically, Sir John did not live to see it finished. After falling ill, he died in 1926, a few months before the mill began production. Today Holden's Mill is remembered for far more than just a cameo role at the end of a rags-to-riches story because as things turned out, it was the very last cotton mill to be built in Bolton.

Holden's Mill was also pretty much the last cotton mill to be built in Lancashire: a dubious distinction it shared with the Elk Mill in Oldham which was finished at about the same time. When both mills were proposed, South Lancashire was still the world centre of textile production with the city of Manchester its lynchpin. Such was the city's economic power and influence in the nineteenth century, it became known as "Cottonopolis" leading the political philosopher, Friedrich Engels to write in 1845 that "The Manchester (Cotton) Exchange is the thermometer for all the fluctuations of trade".[1]

Whatever fluctuations there might be, the textile trade utterly dominated the social, economic and political life of a web of manufacturing towns surrounding Manchester. Arguably, Bolton was the most important of them all. Although other Lancashire towns – notably Oldham – might have spun cotton in greater quantities, it was widely acknowledged that none could better the quality of thread produced by the "aristocratic cotton spinners" of Bolton.

For a significant proportion of the twentieth century, six mornings a week in Bolton, a vast army of workers swarmed towards the mills, factories, and workshops of a pulsating, industrial town. Bolton's textile production was once so colossal, its mills consumed virtually all of the raw cotton grown in Egypt. Because the cotton sourced from the Nile Valley was generally acknowledged to be superior to any other, the shirts, vests, underwear, socks, dresses, curtains, towels and bedding produced by Bolton's skilled artisans meant Tillotson's Directory could claim with some justification that the label "Made in Bolton" was synonymous with quality not just in Britain, but all over the world.[2] Indeed, over sixty per cent of the textiles produced in Bolton were exported to the vast markets of the British Empire and beyond.

Bolton's cotton industry reached its productive peak in 1919. In that pivotal year, there were a total of 112 spinning concerns which between them operated 120 mills. There were well over nine million mule, and two million ring spindles spinning cotton all year round in mills of intimidating scale and dimensions. Swan Lane Mill in Daubhill, to the south west of Bolton, alone boasted 210,000 spindles under one roof and was said to be the largest mill of its kind in the world. When it was operating at maximum capacity, the Swan Lane Spinning Company could muster a staggering 330,000 spindles across the three mills that formed the concern.[3]

Alongside the mills dedicated to spinning, a further seventy firms were involved in weaving. These concerns employed a further 14,000 workers in large weaving sheds characterised by north facing, "saw toothed" roofs. Here, amidst cacophonous noise, Worktowners oversaw the shuttles of 40,000 looms flying in an endless dance of "warp" and "weft". Weaving was so important to the town that by 1914, as well as its foremost position in spinning, Bolton also became the premier weaving centre of South Lancashire even surpassing Manchester in the number of its looms.[4]

The sheer scale of Bolton's textile industry meant it supported a number of other related manufacturing processes carried out in workshops and factories of all shapes and sizes spread across the town. There were over 8000 people actively engaged in the finishing trade: the bleaching and dying of textiles. In addition, steam engines of titanic dimensions were necessary to power the spinning and weaving machines, many of the machines actually manufactured in Bolton. To that end, firms like Dobson and Barlow, Mather and Platt, and Hick Hargreaves employed some 12,000 engineers in massive workshops to build new engines as well as providing the skilled workers to constantly repair and maintain existing ones.

In turn, the steam engines devoured coal at a frightening rate. At Swan Lane Mills alone, 450 tons of coal disappeared into the incendiary mouths each week. The mills' boiler houses therefore provided a further 10,000 jobs for Bolton's miners who toiled in filthy and often dangerous conditions to hack it from Lancashire's seams. All the while, to build new mills, factories, foundries and forges, as well as extending already established businesses in a seemingly ever expanding industry, another 5000 people were employed in the construction trades. Quite extraordinarily, in 1919, it was estimated that Bolton's textile industry provided jobs for some 58,000 people.

Without the textile industry and those who worked in it, it is unlikely Tom Harrisson and his Observers would have chosen Bolton to be their representative Worktown. When Harrisson arrived in Bolton for a second time in the spring of 1937, he could hardly have picked a better street for his headquarters. Whatever its domestic deficiencies, the house on Davenport Street skulked in the shadows of the mills so important to the lives of the people its occupants had come to study. The Union Mill was the closest mill, less than 100 yards from Harrisson's front door. At the other end of the adjacent Vernon Street, the gigantic Mossfield Mill leered over the rows of terraced houses surrounding it on all sides. Looking west from Davenport Street, the perspective suggested by the houses on Snowden Street and John Brown Street ended abruptly in the fearsome facade of Park Mill which completely blocked the view to the moorlands beyond. Just a quarter of a mile to the east, the Egyptian Mill proclaimed the quality of the cotton made there by enshrining the source of its raw material in its name.

Inevitably, with their "dark satanic" appearance and proximity to Davenport Street, all the aforementioned mills feature in Humphrey Spender's photographs. He also took several pictures of the exteriors and interiors of other less easily identified mills. In addition, Spender took photographs of Worktowners toiling at their machines and in a particularly memorable sequence of images, a shift of workers as they were leaving Flash Street Mill *en masse* at the end of a working day. In truth, the textile industry was so omnipotent at the time of the Worktown project we can safely assume that most Boltonians who appear in *any* of Spender's photographs were directly or indirectly involved in it. Even though the cotton industry was in fact declining by the 1930s, Spender's photographs still chronicle a town where 35,500 of its inhabitants were employed in textile manufacture; an astounding fifty per cent of the overall workforce at the time.

The distinctive industrial townscape Spender photographed was forged in the furnace of an industrial revolution which had been propelled from the beginning by the growth of textile manufacture. Bolton only became an important cotton spinning town because of its serendipitous location married with a damp climate peculiar to the area. The weather in South Lancashire is often grey and wet as anyone who has ever lived there will testify, but it is an ideal climate for cotton spinning. Consequently, spinning and weaving was undertaken in the farms, folds and hamlets that once surrounded medieval Bolton with many households producing small quantities of cloth by hand.

In 1779, Samuel Crompton, a cotton spinner born in Bolton, invented the Spinning Mule. At a stroke, his new machine accelerated the quantity and quality of cotton which could be produced by one spinner. Seeing the potential benefits, the most forward-thinking cotton spinners embraced mechanisation and consequently, the cottage textile industry went into terminal decline after the space and power needed for machines led to ever bigger factories. This brought another set of challenges as installing several of the cumbersome mules in larger premises required a concentration of power to drive them all. At first, the power was provided by water and in turn coal following the development of steam locomotion; fortunately, both sources of power were readily available in Bolton due to the proximity of the River Croal and the Lancashire coalfields.

Bolton's first cotton enterprise, Thweate's Mill, began production in 1780. Although the mill was tiny by later standards, its history and the development of the surrounding area exemplify the way the textile industry gained an unstoppable momentum. When cotton spinning first started in Thweate's Mill, the River Croal which meanders through Bolton provided power for the machines. In 1820, the mill was rebuilt and renamed the St Helena Mill – most likely because the vanquished Napoleon Bonaparte died on the island of St Helena in 1821. At about the same time, the mill was converted to steam power. The area soon became a nucleus for textile production with other related businesses drawn towards it and ultimately, it was this unprepossessing, tiny nexus that was responsible for the complete transformation in Bolton's visual appearance.

With the advent of mechanisation, a tidal wave of industrialisation soon engulfed the small market town. As mills and factories expanded both in size and numbers, workers were needed and as a result Bolton experienced an unprecedented growth in its population. In 1801, the town's population numbered just under 30,000, within fifty years it had more than doubled. By the beginning of the twentieth century the population numbered 180,000; an astounding growth in a single century. In fact, between 1775 and 1911, apart from Salford and Oldham, Bolton was Lancashire's fastest growing town.

In common with Britain's other manufacturing towns, Bolton's extraordinary growth was accompanied by appalling social consequences. Squalid jerry built housing, poor sanitation and inadequate health care was the everyday reality for most of Bolton's impoverished workers. In 1845, Engels travelling through the north to see for himself the effects of the industrial revolution gave a damning verdict on Bolton:

> Among the worst of these towns after Preston and Oldham is Bolton, eleven miles north-west of Manchester ... the older part of the town is especially ruinous and miserable. A dark-coloured body of water, which leaves the beholder in doubt whether it is a brook or a long string of stagnant puddles, flows through the town and contributes its share to the total pollution of the air, by no means pure without it.[5]

The century which followed saw scant improvement in living conditions. Worktown was a product of Victorian times: the age when Britain's industrial towns became synonymous with grime, pollution and ugliness. When the Worktown investigation was conducted, Bolton still had more than its fair share of all three. Indeed the scars inflicted by rapid industrialisation were still deeply scored into its back though Tom Harrisson it seems was less puzzled by the appearance of the River Croal than Engels. After seeing the culvert that now took it through the depressing urban sprawl, Harrisson dryly commented that the Croal was "the only paved river in England."[6]

Industrialisation however did more than transform Bolton's physical appearance; it exerted a vice-like grip on the people who lived there. It was the cotton industry that largely defined their day-to-day experience whether it was the prices of yarns at the Manchester Exchange reported dutifully in the evening newspaper each day, or the filthy soot belched from the chimneys which covered everything and everybody. Perhaps most importantly of all, the cotton mills determined what life had to offer for the majority of Bolton's sons and daughters most of whom were resigned to spending their lives anchored to clattering machines on the hot floors of gigantic mills. Tom Harrisson summed up their lot in life: "All year through, 65,000 Worktowners spend their days in these new tropics, and in winter, when moor enriched Worktown is bitterly cold, they go there each day (the mills) before the sun, if any, comes up, and come home each day after the sun has gone down. From age 14 this is the life available to most Worktowners."[7]

And for most of them living this life, a typical day began at dawn. At a time when alarm clocks were relatively expensive, knocker-ups went round tapping on the bedroom windows of sleeping workers to wake them up. Although an assumption persisted that knocker-ups were always men, it was in fact an occupation open to both sexes and all ages; indeed one well remembered knocker-up, Sally Hardman, was still working at some seventy years old.[8] Mystery surrounds the types of poles they used to knock on the upstairs windows, some believing that bamboo poles were used so the glass didn't break, others, that old umbrella wires were tied to the ends of their wooden sticks.

Like window cleaners, knocker-ups had to wait for an available round and when they got one, worked hard to build a reputation for reliability. This meant "good uns" returned to check that the lights had come on in the houses they had visited despite often being viciously sworn at by their bleary eyed occupants. Almost by definition, knocker-ups were shadowy, faceless people as most people were in bed when he (or she) called. Furthermore, as it was traditionally the head of any given family who hired and then paid the knocker-up their weekly wages, there was only one person from each household who ever spoke to them.[9]

As the knocker-ups finished their rounds, Worktown came alive. In Bolton's working class communities, thousands of doors opened, the occupants stepped out and the early morning "March" to work began. Wearing their characteristic shawls, clogs, flat caps, and mufflers, Lowryesque figures tramped through narrow streets regimentally laid out so workers were as near as possible to the mills that employed them. Besides getting to the mill itself, the March was considered a social event as it was a valuable opportunity to gossip and catch up with neighbours each day. As well as the greetings and chatter from dozens of voices, the March was accompanied by the noise made by the wooden-soled clogs worn by mill workers. The way they drummed on the pavements and cobbles made a vivid impression on Tom Harrisson who commented on "the innumerable clogs clatter before daylight": a unique sound that was almost unavoidable in Worktown.

When Tom Harrisson heard it for the first time, the March took place on six mornings of a forty-seven hour working week. Although it was a long working week by contemporary norms, it was in fact an improvement because workers had toiled for fifty-five hours a week in the years just after the First World War. Pitifully, many of them at that time were just thirteen years of age. Supplementing young teenage full time operatives, certified "half timers" – children aged just twelve years old – also worked in the mills in the morning before attending school in the afternoon; a book signed by the mill foreman providing proof for the school authorities that they had actually been at work.[10] Most of these wretched creatures came from the poorest homes where the wages they earned were a vital supplement to household budgets. Whether working "half-time" or "full-time", all of them were expected to be hard at it on their machines from six in the morning. With such an exhausting daily regime, it is hardly surprising that many of the "half-timers" regularly fell asleep at school during their afternoon classes.

Almost without exception, working days in Bolton's cotton mills followed the same pattern. After the first two hours of work, there was half an hour's break for breakfast at 8 a.m. This was followed at midday by an hour's break for lunch, a meal industrial workers always called "dinner". Given the benefits of a calorie-laden midday meal for those engaged in manual work, rather unsympathetically, the provision of kitchens and canteens was considered unnecessary in mills or factories before the middle years of the twentieth century.

For those workers who for one reason or another couldn't go home for dinner, food was taken to the mill by school children in return for pocket money. In the 1920s, my grandfather considered himself fortunate to earn 6d (two and a half pence) a week for delivering a dinner to a worker each day. According to his recollections, it was an "honour" for children to run these errands as they were allowed to leave school early to collect the meal from the worker's home. Pocket money however was not always given for this errand neither in some cases was there much gratitude. One Boltonian schoolgirl, Isobel Tattersall, recalled that she was expected to deliver her brother's midday meal unpaid, and if she was ever late all she got from her disgruntled sibling was a slap.[11]

In transit, workers' dinners – often a homemade hot potato pie in a bowl – were kept warm with large handkerchiefs that for some mysterious reason were always either spotted or red. This rudimentary insulation was essential as in my grandfather's case, his daily errand including a lengthy walk before running up six flights of steps to deliver the food. After handing the meal over, my grandfather and other children like him could at least escape the oppressive atmosphere leaving the workers to eat their "dinners" sitting on the machinery or even the oily floor.

At the time of the Worktown project, most young people entering the mills began their working lives at fourteen years of age, a consequence of the same government legislation that had brought a reduction of working hours in 1919. Notwithstanding being a little older when they began work, many young Boltonians still recall the visceral shock of starting work for their first impressions of mill life were rarely if ever, positive. Some ex-mill workers in later life remembered just the sheer trepidation they felt upon entering a mill for the first time; a sensation that brought an initial gut reaction of wanting to escape by any means. "The first day the noise in the mill drove me nuts … the first thing that hits you is the noise and secondly the heat," Mavis Wilson, a Bolton mill girl, recalled. [12] Indeed, almost universally amongst mill workers' accounts, it was the combination of noise and heat that tended to overpower any other first impressions they may have had. However, perhaps the most shocking thing to young new-to-the-mill workers was simply the abrupt change in their circumstances. After leaving school on a Friday afternoon, barely adolescent Boltonians were in the mill the following Monday, one Observer's report concluding that their "life changes overnight and this is at a time when his won [sic] development of body and mind is at a crucial stage."[13]

Weaving sheds were particularly frightful when first encountered. They were stupendously noisy and such was the jolt to the senses that a queasiness known as "weaving sickness" was quite common in the uninitiated. In the era before regulations forced employers to consider the health and safety of their workers, the unceasing cacophony was something weavers just had to get used to. Amidst the din, speaking normally was totally impossible so mill workers quickly learned to communicate by lip reading and watching the exaggerated mouth, arm and hand gestures of their fellow workers – known colloquially as "mee-mawing" – a form of communication that has all but died out apart from a humorous reminder of it in Peter Kay's famous "Do you wanna brew" routine. Unsurprisingly, mee-mawing was mostly used by mill workers for asking the time with one Observer noting that "50 people are constantly asking the time."[14]

Although mee-mawing helped workers to communicate over the clatter of hundreds of machines, industrial deafness developed unchecked in an age when widespread compensation for industrial injuries simply did not exist. One of the most shocking aspects of Spender's photographs of Bolton's mill workers as well as contemporary films and photographs of other Lancashire textile workers is the complete absence of any kind of ear protection – a callous disregard for workers' welfare that would quite rightly be considered totally unacceptable in any modern, regulated factory.

Although mill workers did share similar experiences, working conditions in Bolton's mills varied considerably. By nature, all mills were dirty, oily and unpleasant, but some developed a reputation for being worse than others. The previously noted Park Mill was considered by workers to be a particularly horrible environment, its unwelcome reputation a result of a peculiar species of cockroach infesting the mill widely believed to have been imported in the bales of cotton. According to the memoirs of Boltonian, Albert Williams, the pests made a visit to the lavatory especially repulsive, although Mr Williams with laudable stoicism recalled that at least a stick was provided in the filthy cubicle to deal with them.[15]

Fortunately for mill workers who wanted a cockroach-free lavatory or who disliked their current employment for any other reason, moving between a job in one mill to an identical job in another was relatively easy; the happy corollary of a single mass industry in a town. Indeed, when economic conditions were favourable, workers could leave one mill in the morning and start working at another in the afternoon doing precisely the same work they had left behind. This movement of workers was quite common in Worktown because skills were so easily transferable; after all, one spinning mule or weaving loom was much the same as another. Moreover, dozens of mills were in sight of each other and a skilled operative would usually find a choice of mills to work in within a short walk, tram or bus ride from their home.

Whatever stage of their working life, workers entering any particular mill would find an entrenched, collectively acknowledged hierarchy. Obviously this would affect the youngest and least experienced most as they would start at the bottom of it. From the first day, they were invariably treated as "dogsbodies" by more established workers who often gave them the most menial of tasks. Most new-to-the-mill workers began as "setters on" which involved putting bobbins on the machine and "little piecers", whose principle task was to piece the ends of the cotton together when they broke. Interestingly, it was the spinner rather than the mill owner who was responsible for paying the wages of his assistants whilst they learned their trade which perhaps explains why mule spinners were often thought to be somewhat mean, harsh taskmasters.

Given the arduousness of mill work, it would be reasonable to suppose young people entering this frightening world might be treated with some compassion or at least empathy however, this was not always the case. Benign paternalism, or equally likely maternalism considering the number of women employed in the cotton industry, was often in short supply when the wages of the spinner depended directly on their own productivity. Bolton mill girl, Barbara Shucker, born in 1938, did not forget the humiliation of being shouted at when she got something wrong on her first day at work and even more appallingly, another mill girl, Winnie Crompton, recalled actually being slapped by an older woman who she was working for. Little wonder, Mrs Crompton went home crying begging her mother not to force her to return the next day however, as she subsequently became a lifelong mill worker, her pleas clearly fell on deaf ears.[16]

One of the worst tasks demanded of young mill workers was going under the mules several times a day in order to clean them. If the back breaking work wasn't bad enough, cleaning the mules often led to accidents with fingers proving particularly vulnerable to the hazards of unforgiving machines. Safety precautions were almost unknown before the Second World War and as such, workers' hair could get caught in the looms' rapidly spinning straps and fatalities could and did occur. My grandmother, a lifelong mill worker, recalled with considerable horror witnessing the "scalping" of a young colleague after her hair got caught in the straps of a machine although whether the unfortunate girl survived the grisly ordeal remains unrecorded. Because of the dangers, many female workers wore turbans and hairnets to protect themselves whilst at work.

On the other hand, minor injuries were virtually a daily occurrence but the response to them was typically unfussy; one mill girl later recalled "They would send you to first aid and that were it."[17] However, there was an even more insidious danger in the mills. Without any form of air conditioning, minute specks of cotton got everywhere and it was so invasive that it found its way onto sandwiches and pies, and could even be seen floating on the surface of cups of tea. Compared with some more obvious dangers, cotton dust might appear to have been a mere irritation but it was breathed in daily and it could lead to lung diseases and fatal respiratory problems in later life.

After the initial period as "dogsbodies" had been served, younger mill workers soon took on other roles as loom sweepers, bobbins carriers, weavers, tacklers and in some cases over time, they might became managers. It is worth remembering that although there was a general uniformity in pay for most jobs in the mills and weaving sheds, the hierarchy amongst workers was reinforced by the fact some roles were paid at higher rates than others depending on the skills and experience required. Foreman ring spinners for example were considerably better paid than other shop floor workers in spinning mills just as power loom overlookers known as "tacklers", were some of the highest paid employees in the weaving sheds. Understandably, many weavers were determined to join the ranks of the latter.[18]

As well as personal ambition and familial encouragement, Bolton Education Committee also played their part in getting young people to aspire to the ranks of these better paid jobs. In April 1938, they wrote to the parents of imminent school leavers informing them: "Your boy is nearing the age when he will be leaving school to enter employment … If he intends to follow one of the undermentioned occupations we strongly advise you to give him training which will enable him to qualify in later years, for one of the more highly paid responsible positions, such as foreman, tester, assistant manager etc."[19] To achieve the necessary qualifications however, apprentices would be expected to attend evening classes for between five and seven years; this on top of a long working day.

Despite the opportunities for advancement, many workers it seemed simply aspired to operating a machine for which they were solely responsible known as "having a side of your own". Reaching this milestone in the lifecycle of a mill worker was of huge significance because not only had they successfully negotiated the rites of passage of early apprenticeship but more importantly, they were now fully assimilated into the cotton industry's social culture and way of life.

Despite the apparent inevitability of a life spent working in a mill, it is worth pointing out that young people often did harbour other ambitions for themselves. One Boltonian recalled that she wanted to be a confectioner but knew her mother couldn't afford to support her and like so many of her generation, she "just went into the mill where my other sister had gone."[20] Girls who aspired to be nurses – an attractive alternative to mill work especially after the National Health Service was founded in 1948 – might still end up spinning or weaving for a living because nursing required qualifications and an investment in books and uniforms; often unaffordable for working class families at the time. In the mid twentieth century, even those who wanted to be shop assistants – generally thought of as a better occupation – would need qualifications that could only be acquired at a grammar school.

Sadly, in the rare circumstances when better educational opportunities arose, they could not always be taken. Winnie Crompton recalled that her sister passed the exam to go to the grammar school but her mother had no money to support her beyond the age of fourteen, so she reluctantly joined her elder sister in the mill.[21] Indeed, one of the most poignant aspects of the recollections of some of the town's mill workers is the sense of unfulfilled ambitions because undoubtedly many people were denied the opportunity to do the job they would have really liked to do. Although there was occasionally some bitterness, it seems most people just accepted it and got on with life anyway. There were rare occasions when Worktowners broke free of the expected route to the mills but Tom Harrisson noted that when this happened there was a "tendency for people who are economically or intellectually successful to leave the town and the district."

To a large extent, the lack of alternative employment for young working class people in the mid twentieth century was the result of more rigid social patterns. A child's gender and the kind of school they attended – grammar, technical or secondary modern – ruthlessly reinforced expectations which meant mill or factory work of one type or another for the vast majority. If education is supposed to be an engine for social change, in reality there was not much evidence of it in Worktown. Mass Observation archived some documents from one school for boys whose literature uncompromisingly stated that there were three streams for the students: "A is for bright boys; B for average; C for dull boys." For the latter, lessons in basket-making and more bizarrely bookbinding shows what was expected of them in later life.[22]

On the other hand, students of all streams could look forward to field trips in geography lessons but rather than widening horizons, the proposed visits were to spinning mills, weaving sheds, paper works, a bleachworks and a quarry. Expectations of girls were made just as obvious. Mass Observation's reports on the curriculum of a girl's school records needlecraft, handicrafts and housecraft had only marginally less time on the timetable than maths and English.[(23)]

Strangely enough, despite the spectre of mills and factories on the horizon, Tom Harrisson thought most children did not fully appreciate that mill work was likely to be their lives noting:

> Few realise it. Less than one per cent think they will go through the mill. Living near to the ground finding beetles in crevices, having long holidays and time to roam, they can see the seasons differently. Thus a typical Elementary School of 36 twelve year olds wrote, without notice or help … poems about spring. 30 wrote about flowers, 22 trees, 16 weather and 14 animals. Eight mentioned fields. Only two mentioned the town or its mills.[(24)]

But in the end, the social and economic realities of Worktown life drove young people into the mills with Mass Observation finding that most millworkers were recruited directly from local schools or through family connections.

Inevitably, the sacrifice of personal ambition on the altar of the mules and looms was mostly if not exclusively confined to working class families. Despite the long hours and the grim, oppressive environments, working in a mill did at least provide a regular income although it should be stressed that up to the Second World War especially, periods of unemployment, hardship and insecurity were accepted as just part and parcel of daily life.

Given the precarious nature of economic cycles, the wages of younger family members were a vital addition to household budgets where to all intents and purposes their earnings were given to their parents who gave them spending money in return; a practice known as "tipping up". Indeed, in some poorer households, young wage earners actually did more than just "tip up". Irene McVittie, a Bolton mill girl, recalled that being the eldest daughter, her family actually looked on her as the main wage earner; a far from unusual occurrence. Viewed from the perspective of a more affluent society, it may seem quite strange that young adults "tipped up" *all* their wages and received only a tiny proportion back as spending money but the notion of "paying for your keep" was accepted as perfectly normal in virtually all of Worktown's households. Indeed, in the feature films, *The Family Way* (1965) and *Spring and Port Wine (*1970) – both filmed in and around Bolton at a time when it was still predominantly a mill town – patriarchal figures demanding obedience from family members even when they are wage earning young adults is the source of much of the dramatic tension.

Mass Observation noted the unusually high percentage of working women in Bolton and Spender's photographs confirm mills were as much a woman's world as a man's. In the mid twentieth century, this was an important distinction between working class women and their middle class counterparts who were far less likely to work, and certainly not in a manual semi-skilled occupation. In fact "the housewives shift" starting around 6 p.m. was one of the most enduring features of Lancashire's textile industry. Bolton's mills offered married women, especially those with young children, an opportunity to supplement the household income by working in the evening. This gave them time for childcare and domestic routines during the day especially making sure their husbands "tea" was "on't table" when he came home from work as was expected of women at the time. After their own exhausting day, many women then rushed out to do an evening's work in the mill leaving their husband's to look after the children and put them to bed; interestingly, one of the rare times in Worktown when men played any kind of domestic role.

Besides the regular wages they provided, Bolton's mills and factories also played an important socialising role, especially in the lives of young girls many of whom were experienced workers before their adolescence had ended. As we have seen, older women mill workers often treated young girls harshly but whatever their initial relationship might be, a sense of solidarity usually developed amongst them with new-to-the-mill girls being taught about life in the widest sense by their older workmates. This enduring female comradeship can be discerned in the shared moral values that governed the behaviour of the town's young women. This surrogate maternal influence often extended to the learning of more practical skills as well, with older women sometimes giving up part of their breaks to teach younger mill girls how to crochet and on other occasions how to dance; the latter, a particularly useful skill as up until the late 1960s, most of the local mills still held their own exclusive "invitation only" dance evenings at the Palais de Danse, one of Bolton's most fondly remembered dance halls.

These kinds of experiences undoubtedly contributed to Worktown's more communal social spirit. Mills often had their own football teams, rounders teams and bowling teams competing in leagues with matches played on pitches and greens provided by the employers. Many concerns like Dobson and Barlow had their own social clubs as well with bars, concert rooms, snooker tables and gambling machines bringing workers together in the evening and at weekends (at the time of writing Dobbies Social Club on Radcliffe Moor Road is a rare surviving example of a traditional working man's club though the engineering firm has long disappeared).

More informally, there were regular picnics and outings organised by the workers themselves which usually involved drinking lots of beer. In addition, mill workers put money into savings clubs run by colleagues; a habit which helped them save for the annual Wakes holidays and Christmas festivities. Charles Madge on a rare excursion from Blackheath to Bolton witnessed one Christmas footing; the parties held in mills so named because the workers footed the bills. Describing it Madge wrote:

> I have just found out about "Footings" which happen in all the mills on Christmas Eve – terrific unofficial beanfests with pies, cakes and a great deal of rum, whisky, gin, vermouth and Pink Petal cocktails. They are organised and paid for by the mill girls and the men expect to be treated. Foremen are bribed with drink, and if the manager walks through, everyone rushes back to their loom. As soon as he goes out, the signal is given and the fun starts again. It happens in every mill and they save up for twelve weeks to pay for it.[25]

In truth, they were probably not as secret as Madge believed. The *Bolton Evening News* Christmas Eve edition in 1939 had a picture of one headlined: "A Christmas Eve Festivity at a Bolton Mill Today" with an accompanying caption recording that "the girls had plenty of cakes and even champagne for their footing" which suggests it was more of a case of those in authority "turning a blind eye" to the fun and shenanigans taking place during working hours.

Contrary to some of the benign sepia-tinged representations of working class life common in popular culture, Britain's industrial towns were grubby and frankly, downright ugly, however the sense of community that clearly existed amongst Worktown's millworkers is one aspect of life that is usually recalled with great affection by those who experienced it. Beyond the shared purpose, the dignity of useful work and regular wages, the kind of supportive friendships forged amongst mill workers were cherished. My grandmother told me how when she was a young mill worker, she regularly used to beg for a loan of 6d (just over 2p) from a stern older colleague – the price of admission to a night dancing at the aforementioned Palais. According to her, on each occasion there was disapproval followed by a lecture about profligacy before a drawn out wait for a final decision. But before the working day had ended, my grandmother recalled that the 6d was always thrust into her hand.

Another mill worker Dorothy Thornley, born in 1933, when recalling a life spent working in the mills thought mill girls were "great girls in spite of all the muck." Similarly Brenda McKay born in 1926, recalled that mills "were really happy places to work 'cos you used to have fun with one another." Dorothy Sharples, when describing mill life said "Y' found mates easily 'cos people were genuine … unlike today."[26] This important social aspect of mill life did not go unrecorded by Mass Observation either. Penelope Barlow, a member of Edgworth's wealthy Barlow family and notable supporters of Tom Harrisson's project, worked in Cobden mill as an Observer. She noted how during breaks, the mill girls enjoyed talking about George Formby, food, Keep-fit, the Government's programme for gas masks, dancing and cinema, and a particularly important topic of conversation, each other's families. The bonds of friendship amongst those who in many instances spent their entire working lives in mills, are affectionately recalled time and again in oral and written accounts suggesting such sentiments are rooted in much more than nostalgia.

Like other aspects of the town chronicled by Mass Observation, the mills and the way of life they fostered seemed unchanging and steadfast. It proved not to be so because "King Cotton" fell spectacularly from grace. Quite unbelievably, less than fifty years after the Mass Observation project chronicled a mill town on the cusp of some of its best years, there were just two working mills left. By the end of the twentieth century, there were none.

In reality, the decline of Lancashire's cotton industry had started in the century before. As early as 1899, Bolton born author Allen Clarke had forecast with remarkable prescience "We cannot keep the world's cotton trade forever. Already there are ominous signs that it is gradually leaving us; other nations are rapidly competing with us."[27] With chilling foresight Clarke predicted:

> More facts and figures ... show that the Lancashire cotton trade is doomed. Not that it will die quickly: the actual end may be years in coming; the process will be more of a slow shrinkage rather than a galloping consumption. But the fatal symptoms are already unmistakeable, and the end, speedy or delayed is sure.[28]

It might appear that Clarke was being unduly pessimistic given the scale of Lancashire's cotton industry at the time he was writing, but his bleak vision was shaped by uncomfortable realities because before the nineteenth century ended, the USA had already surpassed Britain in the total volume of its cotton production.

As Clarke predicted, the decline of the cotton industry turned out to be slow. Indeed in 1913, Bolton actually recorded its highest output of cotton in a single year which suggested that all was well in the cradle of the cotton industry.[29] Moreover, it should be noted that between 1900 and 1914, twenty-five new cotton mills and weaving sheds were built in Bolton along with a further 216 warehouses, workshops, foundries and iron works.[30] Seemingly, there was little cause for concern. However, in August 1914, Britain entered the First World War and although the carnage mainly occurred on European soil, the war was to have far-reaching effects for the town's textile workers.

When peace returned to Europe in November 1918, old certainties seemed to disappear. Most significantly, Britain's position as the world's foremost industrial nation could no longer be taken for granted. The four years of war had disrupted trading routes to the empire and beyond and as a result China, India and Japan – some of the biggest markets for British textiles – started to develop their own textile industries; a development recorded by the Observers who preserved several documents relating to the rise of Indian and Japanese competition and its potential effect on Worktown. When Lancashire's cotton trade started to be adversely affected by growing foreign competition, a painful irony began to emerge: the expanding factories on the other side of the world had been largely equipped with new and second-hand British textile machinery.

Despite more sluggish exports, textile production still remained extremely important to the British economy. Indeed in 1926, the British cotton industry all together reached its maximum productive capacity. Notwithstanding the overall slowdown across Lancashire, there were still over half a million people employed as operatives overlooking a jaw dropping 57,300,000 spindles. At that time, eighty per cent of the textiles manufactured in Britain were still being exported. However, this of course meant that eight out of ten jobs in the British textile industry were dependent on the increasingly precarious international markets. Nevertheless in 1926, Bolton remained home to 102 spinning mills with nearly seven million spindles and the town could still muster over thirteen per cent of all of Lancashire's spindles. Unfortunately, these impressive statistics masked a more disturbing trend for eight years previously there had been 120 mills with over eleven million spindles. The wider picture for those involved in the textile industry was even more alarming still because in 1929, the USA surpassed Britain in the number of looms its cotton manufacturers had at their disposal for the first time in history.

By the beginning of the 1930s, the disruption of trade caused by the First World War, the loss of the Chinese market to Japan, and the growth of an indigenous Indian textile industry began to seriously affect the textile towns of Lancashire. In Japan especially, the productivity of their fledgling textile industry was increased markedly by the introduction of a 24-hour shift pattern. As a result, Japanese mules were spinning cotton around the clock unlike the machines in Bolton, which were unused for at least half the day. Furthermore, Japanese engineers made improvements to imported British machinery which in turn reduced labour costs making their textiles cheaper to buy as less people were now being paid to operate each loom. In a further twist of the knife, Japanese workers were often paid less than their British counterparts which presented a huge challenge to the competitiveness of the Lancashire cotton industry. As a result, by the end of the 1920s, Japan had emerged as a major centre of textile production. An even more crushing blow to British pride followed in 1933, when Japan could claim for the first time to be the world's leading producer of cotton in terms of output.

Although the decline of Lancashire's cotton industry was becoming plain to see, the publishers of Bolton's Trade Directory in 1932 weren't having any of it. Against mounting evidence to the contrary it boasted "The town indisputably holds the premier place as the fine cotton spinning centre of the world," continuing "there are over 200 firms with more than 300 mills engaged in the cotton spinning and manufacturing trades in the aggregate 9,397, 985 spindles and 38,500 looms." Although there may have been some truth in these assertions, by then Lancashire's cotton manufacturers were finding it increasingly difficult to compete on price in its traditional markets, a situation made worse by the worldwide depression caused by the Wall Street Crash in 1929.

The manufacturers of coarse cotton were at first the most vulnerable to cheaper prices so for a while at least, the elite fine cotton spinners of Bolton were sheltered from the problems affecting neighbouring textile towns. Soon however, the whole of the British textile industry started to struggle, a plight mirrored in the previously discussed film, *Sing As We Go*. The film's plot is woven around the closure of a mill that forces Gracie Platt – played by Gracie Fields – to go to Blackpool in search of work. In spite of its upbeat and improbable ending when the factory is reopened (a scene filmed near Union Road, just half a mile from Bolton town centre) unemployment and recession were spectres that haunted the industrial north throughout the 1930s. The title song's optimistic lyric "I see a better day coming in sight" proved to be nothing more than a silver screen fantasy as the textile industry's fortunes remained perilously vulnerable throughout a decade which became synonymous with unemployment and depression.

From late 1937 to early 1938 alone, unemployment in the Lancashire cotton trade rose from 39,153 to 88,164 prompting a demand for government assistance.[31] Alarmingly, at the height of the Worktown project, the number of spindles and looms in Lancashire had already fallen by one-third of their number in 1912. More ominous still, Lancashire's output of cotton had dropped to half of what it had been before the First World War.[32]

Inevitably Mass Observation registered the concerns. In a report from the Daily Worker preserved by Observers one correspondent recorded a conversation with a businessman on a train from London: "It's 20 years since I was in Lancashire last," said the businessman "but in the meantime it's degenerated from a county of prosperity to a position where its main industry is finished." Discussing the prospects for the future he somewhat depressingly concluded that "there was no future for the industry in view of the cotton competition from Japan…" Another article in *The Listener* picked up the same theme: "many of the countries which used to buy our goods are making their own; some of them like Japan compete with us in other markets. By the help of tariffs and low wages – in some cases by direct government assistance – they have brought our export trade down to less than one-third of what it was before the war."[33] It may have pained those reading it but it was nevertheless a concise summary of the challenges facing Bolton's mills.

In September 1939, Hitler unleashed his armies across Europe and the world was engulfed by war again. When peace finally returned to the shattered continent, the cotton industry enjoyed a welcome boom as world demand for textiles at first increased after six years of encouraging people to "make do and mend" rather than buy new. The importance of the cotton industry to the recovering national economy after clothes came "off the ration" in 1949, was recognised by the British government who revived the old adage "Britain's bread hangs by Lancashire's thread" to encourage the recruitment of workers for the mills. But despite the government's best efforts, Lancashire's thread was about to break.

Whilst at first there was a welcome investment in electric power, air conditioning, canteens and in some mills such as Swan Lane, even crèches to provide childcare – all innovative incentives to get people back to work in mills – there was not nearly enough investment in new machinery.[34] This lack of foresight was a longstanding problem in the cotton industry. As we have seen, after British companies had exported machinery to other countries with embryonic textile industries, the machines abroad were increasingly improved by technical innovations. Sadly, this didn't happen to the same extent in Britain with most factories – partly due to economic factors, partly inertia – continuing to be equipped with outdated machinery the factory owners appeared reluctant to modify or modernise.

Furthermore, ring spinning machines – much faster and more efficient than the old mules – had been developed rapidly in other countries. By the mid twentieth century, spinning mules had almost disappeared in the USA but tellingly, in Britain they still provided about seventy per cent of the machines. To underline just how disastrous this anachronism was, as Yuri Gagarin was orbiting the Earth in 1961 thanks to the development of space age technology, the vast majority of Bolton's textile workers were still using a machine invented when George III had been King. Although new canteens and air conditioning proved popular amongst workers making mills more attractive places to work, they disguised the overall failure to invest in newer, more profitable machinery.

To address concerns that the British textile industry was lagging behind its chief competitors, attempts were made to rationalise and support the industry. The 1948 Cotton Spinning (re-equipment subsidy) Act gave grants of twenty five per cent to firms re-equipping and modernising certain mills, subject to closing others. It was almost certainly too little, too late. Indeed, just ten years after Mass Observation was abandoned in Bolton, jobs in the town's cotton industry had fallen to 24,600: less than half the 1919 figure and already some 10,000 less than a decade before.

Faced with declining fortunes, there were some attempts to modernise working practices leading to the introduction of new shift patterns in the mills of Bolton. Unfortunately, twenty years had already passed since the Japanese had "stolen a march" on Britain in this respect but perhaps it was better late than never. As a result, immigrants from across the commonwealth were encouraged to come to Britain to do the less popular night time shifts. As well as bringing new working patterns, the introduction of night shifts in the 1950s had far-reaching consequences for the town's social composition with the arrival of the first Pakistani and Indian immigrants. Perhaps a less well known aspect of this important change is that contrary to the belief that unskilled immigrants were taking jobs from British workers, many were in fact themselves already skilled textile workers used to working in mills in Asia.

It is significant that the social composition of Bolton was one of the few noticeably different things according to Tom Harrisson when he came back to Bolton to observe the town again in 1959. On returning to 85 Davenport Street, Harrisson found that the house next door now housed a black family which led him to write "None of us could remember seeing a coloured man in Worktown before."[35] For younger Boltonians who have grown up knowing only a multiracial town, it is remarkable that Harrisson felt it worthy of note at all.

In truth, it was the influx of skilled immigrant workers that was prolonging the cotton industry's agony by disguising its terminal decline. Their specialist skills at first plugged the gaps in the workforce of what was increasingly perceived to be an outdated and declining industry by Boltonians with different aspirations. Indeed, twenty years earlier Penelope Barlow had already noted "no one wanting to go into weaving-weaving is very noisy, dirty and the shed is inclined to smell of oils, a weaver must stand practically the whole day."[36] When she wrote those words, it would be fair to say Boltonians had far less choice in such matters, but as Britain's employment sector diversified with new light engineering, technical, service and public sector occupations, many Boltonians were no longer willing to follow their parents into jobs which had an unwelcome reputation for dirty, unhealthy conditions and poor rates of pay.

In the meantime, whether from exhaustion after fighting a major war, lack of vision, poor management, outdated machines or simply the inevitable progress of other countries which developed their own industrial capacity in Britain's wake, Lancashire's cotton industry was losing markets to other textile manufacturing countries which initially played catch up, and then overtook the world's first industrial nation. By then most of Britain's traditional heavy industries were also suffering a similar decline. However, nowhere was this more evident than in the industry which had been in the vanguard of Britain's industrial transformation. Put simply, by the middle of the twentieth century, Lancashire's cotton industry could no longer compete.

Just as statistics had once proclaimed the industry's triumphant, unstoppable procession to world dominance, they now bore witness to a long slow funeral march. Between 1909 and 1913, Britain had exported 2669 million yards of textiles to India; by 1938 this figure had dropped catastrophically by ninety per cent. To add insult to injury, India was by then importing 441 million yards of textiles from Japan each year. The wider picture was equally depressing. In 1910, Britain exported over 5000 million yards of cloth in total; by 1959 it was just over 500 million. In a "coals to Newcastle" twist, India and China – once the two biggest markets for Lancashire's cotton industry – now produced their own cotton goods and exported them to Britain. Most painfully of all, in 1960, Britain became a net importer of cotton manufactures. In the same pivotal year, Tom Harrisson noted that the proportion of working people dependent on the textile trade in Bolton had declined from seventy per cent at its peak to a mere twenty-five per cent.

The decline was there for all to see. Alderman H. Chorlton at a gathering of the Cardroom Workers Amalgamation in May 1960 concluded his speech by saying that Bolton's cotton industry was "a very sick patient."[37] In truth, the decline was only to be expected. Seventy years before, Allen Clarke had warned: "For many years now Lancashire men have been hard at it building mills abroad, and teaching the foreigners how to spin and weave. Today the great machine works of Lancashire are almost entirely engaged in fitting up mills abroad." It was this British support for the development of indigenous textile industries in India, Japan and later China which so disastrously sowed the seeds of the destruction of Lancashire's textile industry. One Bolton millworker, if not as eloquent as Clarke, was equally forthright about foreign competition being helped by British ingenuity. When she experienced unemployment for the first time in the 1950s she recalled being warned by her father some years before that when the Dobson and Barlow Company had first started sending fitters to Russia and India that "it would be the end of cotton… and it were."[38]

Faced with so many adverse economic pressures, Bolton's cotton mills closed with monotonous regularity in the years after the Second World War. The depressing list of mill closures grew bigger after the 1959 Cotton Industry Act made provision for the payment of compensation for scrapping old machinery in an attempt to reduce the number of outdated mills. For many of the original Worktowners the well-meaning legislation offered too little too late. One letter in the *Bolton Evening News* submitted by a "redundant spinner" amply illustrates the bleak mood:

> I wish to express my disappointment at the Cotton Compensation Scheme announced this week. I see no mention of the already redundant cotton workers who have become redundant during the past 12 months and are unable to find work owing to age. I have been in the cotton industry for 45 years and have worked as a mule spinner for the past 34 and I find it difficult to find any kind of work. Surely men such as me ought to receive a little consideration after giving a lifetime of service to the industry. We feel that we are a forgotten legion.[39]

Along with all the other redundant cotton spinners, he would remain "forgotten" because there was to be no miraculous revival, only continued decline. Although other grants were made available to equip mills with modern machinery, the number of mills fell overall and between 1957 and 1965 alone, Bolton lost seventy of its mills. As the 1960s drew to a close, there were only thirty-seven spinning mills left in Bolton and by then, Britain had become a net importer of all textiles

It was however, not all doom and gloom. Ironically, the old mills were at first a lifeline for towns where the cotton industry was in decline. Mills provided a ready source of cheap industrial space as they could be easily converted and re-used by a wide range of emerging light industries at the forefront of an economic revival requiring a different kind of skilled worker. Tillotson's Directory of 1967 noted that Bolton's empty cotton mills were being advertised nationally as "readymade factories." Even though they were no longer being used for manufacturing, the floors that had once housed mules and looms were often taken over by mail-order firms like Littlewoods selling goods from catalogues creating new jobs in mills whose acres of floor space were ideal for conversion into distribution warehouses. In 1960, when Tom Harrisson took a "romantic pilgrimage" back to the mill he had worked in less than twenty-five years before, he found: "The great red cotton mill was now fragmented into a furniture maker, carpentry for boat hulls, an estate agency, engineering pattern makers, export packers, and floor space to let-and no trace anywhere of old Ma Cotton." He also recorded that one of the largest mills in Bolton had become a battery chicken factory![40]

My family history illustrates only too well this rupture between the original Worktowners employed in textile-related jobs and their children who were employed in more specialised occupations as the town's reliance on one mass industry disappeared. In the 1970s, Ron Cain, my uncle, followed my grandmother into a mill but tellingly not to spin cotton. He was the managing director of Ronco Precision Engineering which operated from a tiny corner of Peel Mill surrounded by other similar businesses which had by then taken over the whole mill.

In the dwindling number of mills that were still producing textiles, Harrisson noted that there was a growth of new shift systems and also specialised textile work in ring spinning and carpet making. This change gathered pace through the 1960s with an increasing concentration in the town's remaining mills on synthetic textiles manufactured by amalgamated companies like Courtauld's and Viyella. Such was the sheer scale of textile manufacturing, even though the cotton industry was entering its twilight years in the 1960s, job vacancies in textile mills were still a dominant feature on the "situations vacant" pages of the *Bolton Evening News*. Amongst numerous examples, in July 1961, Barlow and Jones (Spinners) operating from Prospect and Falcon Mills, were still posting blanket advertisements stating "Vacancies in all departments for Boys and Girls leaving school." It couldn't last however, and by the time the next generation of school leavers were leaving in the 1970s, there were no longer any mass employment opportunities in a single industry.

Of course this brought huge challenges, especially for young people. In August, 1976, the *Bolton Evening News* reported on the growing "job crisis" facing the town's school leavers. Richard O'Brien, in charge of the government's job finding services, while visiting Manchester, warned that "This year's job crisis may well be repeated in future years, irrespective of the state of the economy."[41] He was to be proved right because when he made his statement, even when jobs were on offer in Bolton's remaining textile mills, the vast majority were only available to "skilled workers". The Worktown pattern of young people leaving school on a Friday in spring, starting work in a local mill the following Monday, being trained to do a semi-skilled job relatively quickly, and then working in one particular industry until retirement was vanishing. And fast.

As the end of the twentieth century approached, Bolton's last few mills were closing down: depressing events which were always chronicled by the local press. At the beginning of the 1980s, the *Bolton Evening News* had highlighted the industry's prospects reporting that from mid-May to mid-November "there had been an even greater decline in the trade than had been anticipated earlier in the year." The accompanying headline "Gloomy Months for Mills" said it all.[42] By 1985, only five of them – Brownlow Fold Mill, Falcon Mill, Halliwell Mill, New Stone Mill and Swan Lane Mill – still spun cotton. As the 1990s dawned, just two were left and the once all-conquering textile industry provided jobs for just 1000 people.

In December 1999, the Dorma weaving plant at Bradley Fold was earmarked for closure with the loss of 153 jobs. By then, Dorma was the only factory left that was still involved in traditional textile production. The newspaper article in the *Bolton Evening News* announcing its imminent closure didn't even make the front page. The headline simply stated: "Job Losses Will Hit Community Hard."[43] Rarely can an event of such significance in the story of any town have been registered with so little moment. Unbelievably, with that desultory, bland headline, Bolton's iconic cotton industry slipped quietly into history.

Unlike the empty mills which at least afforded useful space, Bolton's disused mill chimneys had over time became superfluous and in some cases downright dangerous. Unceremoniously, the physical totems of Worktown started to come crashing down in a swathe of demolition. By 1985, of the 200 chimneys which dominated Worktown's skyline, only forty remained. Ironically, Bolton born steeplejack, Fred Dibnah, the man largely responsible for demolishing them became an unlikely celebrity. Due in no small measure to his hail-fellow-well-met, northern bluster, he was one of the first "reality" television stars when he was featured in a BAFTA winning documentary in 1979. His fame led to celebrity status, two honorary doctorates, an MBE and a statue in Bolton town centre but for a man with a burning passion for Britain's industrial heritage, his success was bittersweet. In later life, Dibnah ruefully commented "I started my career wanting to preserve the things, but have ended up knocking them all down."[44]

With their chimneys demolished and those mills spared the wrecking balls disembowelled and completely divorced from their original function, Bolton's post-industrial townscape was a whole world away from Worktown. Where the "aristocratic cotton spinners of Egyptian cotton" had once met at the Spinner's Hall, their grandchildren ate chow mein and sweet and sour pork in the Noble House Chinese restaurant located in its basement (at the time of writing the Spice Valley Indian Restaurant). Just to the right of the entrance to Flash Street Mills so memorably captured in Spender's photographs, many Boltonians enjoyed their first ever taste of curry in the red flock wallpapered splendour of the Bombay Indian Restaurant located in the mill's basement before the restaurant was in turn buried under the Grosvenor Casino and Bingo club along with the rest of the mill.

Three hundred yards to the South, the gargantuan Hick Hargreaves engineering factory finally succumbed to the changed times and it too was demolished, its grave marked ignominiously by a huge supermarket and a nondescript retail park. On Kay Street, yet another soulless retail park eradicates all traces of the formidable Globe Iron Works which dominated the southern end of Halliwell just beyond the fringes of the town centre. Even the splendid mansions of Bolton's industrialists have not survived unscathed. The Watermillock, a handsome Victorian mansion on Crompton Way, once the home of the bleach works owning Thwaites family, is today part of a "carvery" chain offering self-service roast dinners in what was once its magnificent billiards room.

With such fundamental changes in the town's visual appearance, anyone coming to Bolton to see the industrial world of the Worktowners will find only its forlorn, ghostly reminders. While some mills have survived demolition by being converted for other uses, others remain part of the townscape only because their architectural significance has deservedly led to listed building status and the protection that goes with it. A couple add to the preservation of the region's manufacturing heritage with displays of working steam engines; part of the wider "museumification" of Britain's industrial history.

Because several mills have survived, just like the Worktowners of the 1930s, most contemporary Boltonians are usually never far from one. Their names – Atlas, Mossfield, Union, Clyde, Egyptian, Falcon, Sunnyside, Swan, Dove and Gilnow – still resonate in area boundaries, and the names of shops and fast food takeaways. Names of eminent mill owning families like Ashworth, Holden, Musgrave and Heaton also linger in the collective consciousness; faint reminders of a not too distant past. On St Georges Road, the grand facade of the Spinner's Hall remains unchanged and one of Hick Hargreaves' magnificent steam engines is housed somewhat incongruously in a glass case across the road from a McDonald's fast food restaurant. Pubs like the Weavers Arms, the Finisher's Arms, the Collier's Arms, and the Founders Arms are reminders of some of the jobs Worktowners once did whilst in a remarkably ironic twist, some people even live in the mills where their grandparents worked; a consequence of the twenty-first century trend for converting the old power houses of industry into luxury apartments.

One of them is Sir John Holden's. Where its floors once rattled with the clatter of thousands of spindles, coffee percolators now hum gently in space age kitchens. Just 600 yards away, Hall-i-th-Wood, the Tudor house where Samuel Crompton perfected the first mule, has nearly been swallowed up by a housing estate. Barely 150 years ago, Crompton's grandson claimed: "the hammer that rung in the old hall set millions of hammers to work to the end of time." He was wrong for the mighty industry that was the heart and soul of Worktown, came and went. Purely by chance, Hall–i–th-Wood where it all started, and Holden's mill where it ended, are within sight of each other. On rare fine evenings, the rays of the setting sun fade over the birthplace of King Cotton a split second before its resting place. It is somehow both touching and fitting, for the years when Bolton was a proud, industrial, never-to-be-forgotten Worktown, also seemed to have come and gone in little more than the blink of an eye.

POSTSCRIPT

Bolton, 2017.

Drab, cheerless, characterless. Two hundred and eighty thousand people. Grey skies, most days. Clean air, every day. Still damp. Un-industrial. Chimney-less. Red bricks, blue slates; here and there. Cars, everywhere. Cobbles covered by tarmac. Flyovers, dual carriageways, motorways, supermarkets. Terraced houses upgraded, semi-detached houses desirable, detached houses aspired to. Bathrooms, normal. Retail parks, proliferating. Pubs, a few. Churches, even fewer.

Televisions: universal. Multiplex Cinemas: pre-fabricated. Football stadium: demolished. Newspaper: online. Wash days: a memory. Blackpool: anachronistic. Industry: gone. Way of life: transformed.

Worktown: vanished.

ACKNOWLEDGEMENTS

Much of this book reflects my own family history so first and foremost I must thank all of them for their support, help, and encouragement during the writing of it. I especially want to thank my cousin, Matthew Cain, for editing, amending and making suggestions for the first tentative draft; my brother, Graham, for reading each chapter and encouraging me so much by insisting the first drafts of the chapters were better than they really were; and my uncle, Gordon Cain – his recollections of Bolton Wanderers, shops and Blackpool proved invaluable in completing those chapters.

I would especially like to pay tribute to another uncle, Ron Cain, who sadly died a couple of months before the book was due to be published. Fortunately for me, long before he fell ill, he read through the chapter on pubs correcting several mistakes and suggesting a number of additions. Ron's encyclopaedic knowledge of Bolton's pubs resulted from the fact that he claimed to have enjoyed at least one pint in each and every one of them.

Beyond family, I would particularly like to thank Jason Tyler for reading and then discussing each chapter-usually over a pint of beer in the Brewery Tap. Thankfully, his unnatural, almost photographic memory of Bolton remained unaffected by the beer and it has ensured the book is more accurate than it would have been. I would also like to thank Malcolm Cummings for suggesting important additions and making improvements to the chapter on the mills of Bolton where he spent all of his working life.

I am immensely grateful to the staff at Bolton Central Library, especially those in the History Centre for all their assistance as well as their unending patience as I wrestled with the technological challenges of the microfilm machine. I would also like to thank the staff at the Keep at the University of Sussex where the original Worktown documents are stored. They were equally helpful and equally patient too as the online document ordering system proved as usual, beyond my limited ICT skills. I would also like to thank Bolton Council for permission to reproduce Humphrey Spender's photographs on the cover and throughout the book.

And of course last, but certainly not least, I would like to acknowledge the extraordinary foresight, endeavour and fortitude of Tom Harrisson, Humphrey Spender and all the other people who eighty years ago lived in a grubby house on Davenport Street. Without their pioneering efforts to chronicle life in Worktown this book could not have been written.

SELECT BIBLIOGRAPHY

Barnie John *Tales of the Shopocracy* Gomer 2009

Blythman Joanna *Shopped: the Shocking Power of British Supermarkets* Fourth Estate 2004

Brodie, Sargent and Winter *Seaside Holidays in the Past* English Heritage 2000

Clarke Allen *The Effects of the Factory System* Nabu Press 2010

Cross Gary *Worktowners at Blackpool: Mass Observation and Popular Leisure in the 1930s* Taylor and Francis Ltd. 1990

Engels Friedrich *The Condition of the Working Class in England* Penguin 1987

Fletcher Paul *The Clatter of Clogs* Clog Lamp Press 1972

Foley Alice *A Bolton Childhood* Bolton Libraries and Arts 1990

Freethy Ron *Those were the days in Lancashire in the 40's, 50's and 60's* Countryside Books 2001

Gardiner Juliet *From the Bomb to the Beatles* Collins and Brown 1999

Kingsmill Hugh *The English Genius* London 1939

Hall David *Worktown* Wiedenfield and Nicholson 2015

Halliwell Leslie *Seats in all Parts: Half a lifetime at the Movies* Granada Publishing 1985

Harrisson Tom *Britain Revisited* Victor Gollancz 1961

Haydon Peter *Beer and Britannia: An inebriated History of Britain* Sutton Publishing 2001

Hayes Dean *Bolton Wanderers* A-Z Palatine 1994

Hudson John *Wakes Week: Memories of Mill Town Holidays* Alan Sutton Publishing 1992

Jennings Paul *The Local: A history of the English Pub* Tempus Publishing 2007

Kenny Christine *Cotton Everywhere: Recollections of Northern Women Millworkers* Aurora Publishing 1994

Kynaston David *Austerity Britain 1945-51* Bloomsbury Publishing 2008

Lewis Peter *The 50s* Book Club Associates 1978

Longworth James H *The Cotton Mills of Bolton 1780-1985 A Historical Directory* Bolton Museum and Art Gallery 1987

Madge and Harrisson *Britain by Mass Observation* Penguin Books 1939

Mass Observation *The Pub and the People: A Worktown Study* London Gollancz 1943

Opie Robert *Remember when* Mitchell and Beazley 1999

Ponting and Hugman *The Trotters: The Concise Post war History of Bolton Wanderers* Repvern Publishing

Readyhough Gordon *Bolton Pubs 1800-2000* Neil Richardson 2000

Richards Jeffrey and Sheridan Dorothy *Mass Observation at the Movies* Routledge and Kegan Paul 1987

Secombe Harry *On the Move: Bygone Britain 1900-1970* HMSO 1995

Sedgwick John *Popular Filmgoing in 1930s Britain* University of Exeter Press 2000

Simms Andrew *Tescopoly* Constable and Robinson 2007

Spender Humphrey *Worktown People: Photographs from Northern England 1937-38* Falling Wall Press 1982

Todd Selina *The People The Rise and Fall of the Working Class* John Murray 2015

Trevelyan Julian *Indigo Days* MacGibbon and Key 1957

Viner Brian *Cream teas, traffic jams and sunburn* Simon and Schuster 2011

Walton John K *The British Seaside: Holidays and Resorts in the Twentieth Century* Manchester University Press 2000

Williams Albert *36 Stewart Street: An Exercise in Nostalgia* Neil Richardson 1983

Williams and Farnie *Cotton Mills in Greater Manchester* Carnegie Publishing 1992

Wilkinson Philip *The High Street* Quercus

FOOTNOTES

Guidance on the footnotes

In writing this book, I used a number of original documents stored in the Mass Observation Archive at the Keep at the University of Sussex. The same documents are also stored electronically on film at the History Centre in Bolton Central Library. To differentiate between them, footnotes that state for example, W26 / G, refer to the box number and file letter as they appear in the Worktown Archive stored at the University of Sussex. Footnotes that state for example, MO Reel 33, refer to the microfilm stored in Bolton Central Library.

Introduction: The "Savages" of Bolton

(1)   Tom Harrisson *Britain Revisited* (Victor Gollancz Ltd, 1961) p.26
(2)   Summarised in the documentary film *Return Journey* British Film Institute www. bfi.org.uk
(3)   *Worktown People: Photographs from Northern England 1937-38* Falling Wall Press, 1982
(4)   Tom Harrisson W26/ G
(5)   Tom Harrisson "Britain Revisited" P.26
(6)   Humphrey Spender interview *Return Journey*: www.bfi.org.uk
(7)   Julian Trevalyan *Indigo Days* (MacGibbon and Key London 1957) p.81
(8)   www.archiveadventure.wordpress.com
(9)   MO Reel 33
(10)   *Return Journey* www.bfi.org.uk

The Bolton Odeon

(1)   Reproduced in Avril Aston *The Odeon Cinema Bolton A study of a Bolton Cinema* Bolton History Centre
(2)   Leslie Halliwell *Seats in all Parts: Half a lifetime at the Movies* (Granada Publishing 1985) p.59
(3)   Ibid.
(4)   David Hall *Worktown* (Wiedenfield and Nicholson) 2015 p.227
(5)   Selina Todd *The People The Rise and Fall of the Working Class* (John Murray 2015) p.43
(6)   Hall op.cit. p.225

(7)   www.cinematreasures.org
(8)   Halliwell op.cit. p.27
(9)   Halliwell op.cit. p.4
(10)   W 35/ A
(11)   Richards Jeffrey and Sheridan Dorothy *Mass Observation at the Movies* (Routledge and Kegan Paul) 1987 p.1
(12)   Richards and Sheridan Op. Cit. p.29
(13)   Halliwell Op.cit. p.72
(14)   Halliwell Op.cit. p.71
(15)   Richards Jeffrey and Sheridan Dorothy Op.Cit. p.80
(16)   Richards Jeffrey and Sheridan Dorothy Op.Cit. p.33
(17)   Richards Jeffrey and Sheridan Dorothy Op.Cit. p.49
(18)   W35/ A
(19)   W35/ B
(20)   W35/ B
(21)   Richards Jeffrey and Sheridan Dorothy Op.Cit.p.85
(22)   John Sedgwick *Popular Filmgoing in 1930s Britain* (University of Exeter Press 2000) p.140
(23)   W35 / A
(24)   Reproduced in Aston
(25)   Hall op.cit.p.226
(26)   Bolton Evening News Sept.2, 1938
(27)   Halliwell op.cit. p.48
(28)   Bolton Evening News Jan. 10, 1941
(29)   David Kynaston *Austerity Britain 1945-51* (Bloomsbury Publishing 2008) p.95
(30)   Kynaston op.cit. p.305
(31)   Peter Lewis *The 50s* (Book Club Associates 1978) p.208
(32)   Lewis op.cit. p.211
(33)   Quoted in Lewis op.cit. P.216
(34)   Lewis op.cit. p.219
(35)   Harrisson Tom *Britain Revisited* (Victor Gollancz 1961) p.41
(36)   Todd op.cit. p.245
(37)   Bolton Evening News Aug.19, 1958
(38)   www.jimihendrix.com
(39)   Author's conversation with Christopher Whittam
(40)   Bolton Evening News Aug.10,1972
(41)   Bolton Evening News June 1, 1972

Wash days, bath nights

(1)   William Gerhardi *The English Genius* (London 1939) p.7
(2)   MO Reel 23
(3)   Bolton Evening News Sept.9, 1937
(4)   W26/ G
(5)   Brian Ferris in www.boltonrevisited.org.uk
(6)   W44/ F
(7)   From Manchester Metropolitan University "Donkey Stone" film on Youtube
(8)   W26/ G
(9)   Ron Freethy *Those were the days in Lancashire in the 40's, 50's and 60's* (Countryside Books 2001)

(10)   www.1900s.org.uk
(11)   Bolton Evening News Nov.1937
(12)   Bolton Evening News advertisements between September and November 1937
(13)   Conversation with author 2016
(14)   Cited in Freethy op.cit. p.73
(15)   Philip Wilkinson *The High Street* (Quercus) p.210
(16)   Bolton Evening News Sept.21, 1937
(17)   Robert Opie *Remember when* Mitchell and Beazley 1999 pp.102-146
(18)   Green Park DVD "Living Memories"
(19)   Figures from University of Warwick quoted in Daily Express Jan. 24, 2017
(20)   www.servis.co.uk
(21)   Bolton Evening News Nov.23, 1962
(22)   Bolton Evening News Aug.1, 1974
(23)   www.servis.co.uk
(24)   Bolton Evening News Nov.2, 1962
(25)   Ibid.
(26)   Selina Todd *The People The Rise and Fall of the Working Class* (John Murray 2015) p.179
(27)   Brian Ferris in www.boltonrevisited.org.uk
(28)   Todd op.cit. p.179
(29)   Roger Bingham *Lost Resort* (Cicerone Press 1990) p.275
(30)   W35/ C
(31)   Tony Visconti *Bowie, Bolan and the Brooklyn Boy* (Harper Collins 2007) p.20 and 83

Burnden Park

(1)   Mass Observation *The Pub and the People: A Worktown Study* (London Gollancz 1943) p.19
(2)   W4/ A
(3)   www.guardian.com
(4)   Cited in Gary Cross *Worktowners at Blackpool: Mass Observation and Popular Leisure in the 1930s* Taylor and Francis Ltd. 1990 p.30
(5)   Bolton Evening News, Dec.1,1999
(6)   Dean Hayes *Bolton Wanderers* A-Z (Palatine 1994) p.26
(7)   W4/ A
(8)   Ibid.
(9)   quoted in Matthew Bazell *Theatre of silence: the lost soul of football* (Pegasus 2011)
(10)   Bolton Evening News, March 8, 1946
(11)   Bolton Evening News, March 11, 1946
(12)   Bolton Evening News, March 12, 1946
(13)   Bolton Evening News, March 11, 1946
(14)   Nat Lofthouse *Goals Galore* Stanley Paul and Co. p.106
(15)   Dominic Sandbrook *State of Emergency* (Penguin 2011) Ch.14
(16)   Doug Mitchell *Walking Down the Manny Road; Inside Bolton's football hooligan gangs* Fort Publishing Ltd. 2011
(17)   Bolton Evening News Aug.26, 1974
(18)   Ibid.
(19)   Anthony King *The End of the Terraces: The Transformation of English Football* (Leicester University Press 2002) pp.38-39

(20)   Quoted in Adrian Tempany *And the Sun Shines Now: How Hillsborough and the Premier League Changed Britain* (Faber & Faber 2016)
(21)   Simon Marland *Burnden Park: The Final Years 1987-1997* (Bolton: the Club 1997)
(22)   Ex-steward Jason Tyler's conversation with author
(23)   www.11v11.com

Are you being served?

(1)   W29/ C
(2)   W29/ C
(3)   www.prestonsdiamonds.co.uk/ourheritage.asp
(4)   Tillotson's Trade Directory 1932
(5)   Brian Feriss writing in in www.boltonrevisited.org
(6)   W29/ C
(7)   W29/ B
(8)   Oliver Miller writing in www.boltonrevisited.org
(9)   W29/ C
(10)   W29/ B
(11)   W29/ B
(12)   Cited in David Hall *Worktown* (Wiedenfield and Nicholson) 2015 p.271
(13)   Mass Observation Archive Adam Matthew Publication p.14
(14)   W29/ B
(15)   W29/ B
(16)   John Barnie *Tales of the Shopocracy* (Gomer 2009) p.18
(17)   Tom Harrisson *Britain Revisited* Victor Gollancz 1961 pp.35-36
(18)   Ibid.
(19)   www.telegraph.co.uk
(20)   www.co-operative.coop/
(21)   Robert Opie *Remember when* (Mitchell and Beazley 1999) pp.128-129
(22)   Ibid.
(23)   Philip Wilkinson *The High Street* (Quercus) p.225
(24)   Bolton Evening News Oct.1, 1983
(25)   Andrew Simms *Tescopoly* Constable and Robinson 2007 p.74
(26)   Bolton Evening News Dec.4, 1981
(27)   Simms op.cit. p.26
(28)   Wilkinson op.cit. p.254
(29)   Bolton Evening News Dec.1, 1999
(30)   Bolton Evening News Nov.2, 1999
(31)   Bolton Evening News July 17, 2012
(32)   Simms op.cit. p.149

Spit and sawdust

(1)   Gordon Readyhough *Bolton Pubs 1800-2000* (Neil Richardson 2000)
(2)   Mass Observation *The Pub and the People: A Worktown Study* (London Gollancz 1943) p.17
(3)   Ibid.
(4)   Ibid. p.105
(5)   Ibid. p.105

(6) Peter Haydon *Beer and Britannia: An inebriated History of Britain* (Sutton Publishing 2001) p.255

(7) W3/ A

(8) W3/ A

(9) MO Reel 8

(10) *The Pub and the People* p.107

(11) MO Reel 8

(12) W3/ B

(13) MO Reel 8

(14) W3/ A

(15) MO Reel 8

(16) W3/ A

(17) W3/ B

(18) W3/ A

(19) W3/ A

(20) MO Reel 8 and W3/ A

(21) W3/ B

(22) Paul Jennings Paul *The Local: A history of the English Pub* (Tempus Publishing 2007) p.203

(23) W3/ A

(24) W3/ A

(25) MO Reel 8

(26) MO Reel 8

(27) Bolton Evening News advertisements 1937

(28) *The Pub and the People*

(29) Bolton Evening News Nov. 25, 1937

(30) Bolton Evening News March 9, 1946

(31) Selina Todd *The People The Rise and Fall of the Working Class* (John Murray 2015) p.175

(32) Robert Opie *Remember when* (Mitchell and Beazley 1999) p.125

(33) *The Pub and the People* p.17

(34) Tom Harrisson *Britain Revisited* (Victor Gollancz 1961) p.178

(35) Ibid. p.180

(36) http://lostpubsofbolton.blogspot.co.uk/

(37) Readyhough op.cit. p.32

(38) Sir Harry Secombe Harry On the Move: Bygone Britain (1900-1970 HMSO 1995) p.139

(39) Ibid p.147 and MO Reel 8

(40) Jennings op.cit. p.201

(41) Bolton Local Economic Assessment 2015

Cobbles to Carpet

(1) www/boltonworktown.co.uk/

(2) W49/ A

(3) Robert Opie *Remember when* (Mitchell and Beazley 1999) p.84

(4) W49/ A

(5) W44/ F

(6) Alice Foley *A Bolton Childhood* Bolton Libraries and Arts 1990 pp.18-19

(7)   W49/ D
(8)   W49/ D
(9)   W49/ D
(10)   W49/ D
(11)   W49/ D
(12)   MO Reel 23
(13)   Jeffrey Richards and Dorothy Sheridan Dorothy *Mass Observation at the Movies* (Routledge and Kegan Paul 1987) p.92
(14)   Ibid. p.110
(15)   Tillotson's Directory 1932
(16)   W26/ A
(17)   W26/ B
(18)   W26/ F
(19)   W26/ F
(20)   www.boltonrevisited.org.uk
(21)   W29/ B
(22)   W49/ E
(23)   Bolton Evening News Dec.16, 1937
(24)   Bolton Evening News Dec.2, 1937
(25)   Tillotson's Directory 1932
(26)   W49/ G)
(27)   Bolton Evening News Nov.24, 1937
(28)   www.telegraph.co.uk
(29)   Bolton Evening News March 11, 1946
(30)   Bolton Evening News, April 2, 1959
(31)   Tom Harrisson *Britain Revisited* (Victor Gollancz 1961) p.38
(32)   Leslie Halliwell *Seats in all Parts: Half a lifetime at the Movies* (Granada Publishing 1985) p.65
(33)   David Smith interview www.youtube.com
(34)   W35/ C
(35)   Juliet Gardiner *From the Bomb to the Beatles* (Collins and Brown 1999) p.102
(36)   Harrisson op.cit. p.39

Holidaytown

(1)   Allen Clarke *Moorlands and Memories* (Tillotson's Ltd.) P.1
(2)   John K Walton *The British Seaside: Holidays and Resorts in the Twentieth Century* (Manchester University Press 2000) p.15
(3)   Gary Cross *Worktowners at Blackpool: Mass Observation and Popular Leisure in the 1930s* Taylor and Francis Ltd. 1990 p.209
(4)   W53/ A
(5)   Cross op.cit. p.2
(6)   Arena *Blackpool Wakes* BBC 1989 Youtube
(7)   Bolton Evening News June 28, 1937
(8)   Les Dennis interviewed on *Reel History of Britain: Sun Sea and Sangria* BBC Manchester, Youtube
(9)   Cross op.cit. p.65
(10)   John Hudson *Wakes Week: Memories of Mill Town Holidays* (Alan Sutton Publishing 1992) p.28
(11)   Cross op.cit. pp.68-69

(12) Ibid.
(13) W35/ A
(14) W57/ A
(15) W57/ C
(16) W53/ D
(17) Cross op.cit. p.189
(18) Leslie Halliwell *Seats in all Parts: Half a lifetime at the Movies* Granada Publishing 1985 p.18
(19) W57/ E
(20) www.arthurlloyd.co.uk
(21) W57/ D
(22) W57/ C
(23) Cross op.cit. p.189
(24) Ibid. p.188
(25) W57/ C
(26) Cross op.cit. p.182
(27) Bolton Evening News Sept.2, 1937
(28) W57/ E
(29) Cross op.cit.pp.162-166
(30) W57/ C
(31) W57/ C
(32) Walton op.cit. p.86
(33) Tom Harrisson *Britain Revisited* (Victor Gollancz 1961) p.143
(34) Bill Allen conversation with author December 2016
(35) Hudson op.cit. p.77
(36) Bolton Evening News Aug.1,1974
(37) Noted in *Reel Histories* op.cit.
(38) W57/ F
(39) www.theboltonnews.co.uk
(40) http://www.dailymail.co.uk/ Wham Hotel
(41) Brian Viner *Cream teas, traffic jams and sunburn* (Simon and Schuster 2011) pp.34-35

King Cotton

(1) Friedrich Engels *The Condition of the Working Class in England* (Penguin 1987) p.82
(2) W44/ E
(3) James Longworth *The Cotton Mills of Bolton 1780-1985 A Historical Directory* (Bolton Museum and Art Gallery 1987) p.94-95
(4) Williams and Farnie *Cotton Mills in Greater Manchester* (Carnegie Publishing 1992) p.31
(5) Engels op.cit. p.83
(6) Mass Observation *The Pub and the People: A Worktown Study* (London Gollancz 1943) p.18
(7) Reel 23 MO microfilm
(8) Recollections of Joe Hulton www.boltonrevisited.org.uk
(9) Christine Kenny *Cotton Everywhere: Recollections of Northern Women Millworkers* Aurora Publishing 1994
(10) Recollections of Catherine Walton www.boltonrevisited.org.uk

(11) Malcolm Cummings in conversation with author- recollections of his mother
(12) National Lottery funded project, Voices from the Mills: http:// voicesfromthemills.org.uk/ and DVD
(13) W49/ G
(14) W40/ D
(15) Williams Albert *36 Stewart Street: An Exercise in Nostalgia* (Neil Richardson 1983)
(16) Voices from the Mills op.cit.
(17) Ibid.
(18) Malcolm Cummings lifelong fitter in mills in conversation with author
(19) W49/ G
(20) Voices from the Mills op.cit.
(21) Ibid.
(22) W49/ G
(23) W49/ G
(24) W40/ D
(25) Quoted in David Hall *Worktown* (Wiedenfield and Nicholson 2015) p.280
(26) Voices from the Mills op.cit.
(27) Allen Clarke *The Effects of the Factory System* (Nabu Press 2010) p.159
(28) Ibid. p.172
(29) Longworth op.cit. p.96
(30) Ibid. p.78
(31) Hall op.cit. p.125
(32) Longworth op.cit. p.113
(33) W40/ D
(34) Boltonian Julie Gregory in conversation with author- recollections of her mother's experiences at Swan Mill
(35) Tom Harrisson *Britain Revisited* (Victor Gollancz 1961) p.29
(36) W40/ D
(37) Bolton Evening News May 5, 1960
(38) Voices from the Mills op.cit.
(39) Bolton Evening News May 22, 1959
(40) Harrisson op.cit. p.34
(41) Bolton Evening News Aug.1, 1976
(42) Bolton Evening News Dec.1, 1981
(43) Bolton Evening News Dec.1, 1999
(44) Alan McEwen Fred Dibnah's Chimney Drops (Sledgehammer Engineering Press Limited 2008) p.128